CW00456382

Heartbreak Hotel

The life and music of
Elvis Presley

Cover Photograph: Pictorial Press Ltd.
Photographs: Official Elvis Presley Fan Club, Pictorial Press Ltd.

Printed by: Staples of Rochester, Kent.

Published by Castle Communications plc, A29 Barwell Business
Park, Leatherhead Road, Chessington, Surrey KT9 2NY.

ISBN: 1 860 740 553

Heartbreak Hotel

The life and music of
Elvis Presley

by
Robert Matthew-Walker

Contents

Introduction

The original edition of this study was begun in 1978, a few months after Elvis Presley's death in August 1977. It was published the following year, and was soon reprinted several times, appearing in a number of editions. It caused something of a stir, as it was the first attempt to explain Presley's genius through his artistry, without sensationalism or accusations of drug addiction or sex scandals – the usual subjects which seem to make up the public's knowledge of just about every famous performer, and which, as time went by, came to be levied posthumously against Presley. In large part I believe I succeeded in my determination to concentrate on the only thing that mattered – Presley's inherent musicianship, concentrated in his singing, as left to us in hundreds of his recordings.

I was equally determined that the book's comments on Presley's recordings would not be consistently 'analytical', in the generally accepted sense of the word, but in the nature of a guide, a starting point, from which the reader could be encouraged to explore the material personally and should not, therefore, just take my word for it. Among the factors which led me to believe that I succeeded in my aim was the quite extraordinary number of letters I received from a wide variety of members of the public, every one of whom wrote in appreciative terms. I have kept all the letters, and even now – many years after I received it – I am moved by one from an unmarried mother in Glasgow, whose education was clearly not the best she could have received, but whose message was unmistakable: I had put into words what she had felt for many years about Presley's singing.

When the idea that I might write a book on Presley was first mooted, I did not respond very favourably. But I knew that, having worked for RCA – his only record company – I might be able to obtain material without too much difficulty. Eventually, I agreed to write the book although I was by no means a Presley admirer. But as I began to listen critically to hundreds of his recordings I had never heard before, I soon became an avid admirer. When I had heard them all, I knew that I had been privileged to hear the complete life's work of a truly great artist – a genuinely original and supremely gifted creative musician.

However, the original edition of the book – subtitled 'A Study In Music' – was not published as first written. Much of what I considered important was removed and I only agreed that it should be published in truncated form after a great deal of discussion. After all, what was published was written by me, but I felt that my discoveries on listening to Presley's recordings were such that they ought to form part of the book – no matter if this kind of thing had not been attempted before.

It remained in print for over fifteen years, during which time I wrote a number of other books on rock musicians, and during which time also the kind of approach I wanted to see carried through completely in my original Presley manuscript became less of a publisher's risk. With the approach of the anniversary of Elvis Presley's sixtieth birthday in 1995, I decided to update the book and write a new edition. In this way I resurrected much of my original manuscript and revised the entire book with new chapters on other aspects of Presley's life and work, as well as expanding and rewriting the first published manuscript in the light of new developments. This book – 'Heartbreak Hotel' – is the result.

Like most people of my generation, I was totally unprepared for the impact of early rock music on the world, especially Bill Haley's 'Rock Around The Clock' but more importantly, Elvis Presley's astounding 'Heartbreak Hotel'. It was unlike any other music I had ever heard, and for virtually forty years Elvis Presley's performances have moved, excited, exasperated or disappointed me – but the fascination has remained.

Although many books have been published on Elvis Presley, I felt that his essential importance – his life's work as a singer – remained largely untouched. This book is not therefore a standard biography, although I make no apology for tracing the historical background to the society into which Presley was born in chapter one, nor for continuing with a biographical outline further in the first part of this book, as I believe it is only when the background to an artist's life is grasped that his life's work falls into place.

The second part traces Presley's recording career in chronological order of recording sessions, and within each session the titles are usually dealt with in alphabetical order, unless the published order seems more suitable. I have refrained from using music examples or detailed technical language although on the rare occasions when technical terms are used the meaning is clear. Part two is not intended, therefore, to be read straight through; the idea behind it is essentially that of a reference guide.

The third part comprises three chapters which are concerned with aspects of Presley's work, and which attempt to define his genius. Finally, the fourth part of the book is a documentary schedule.

This book does not claim to discuss every known Presley recording, made at every session, for in recent years many outtakes and alternate versions have become available. These are of interest, and occasionally of much fascination, to the enthusiast and collector, but in terms of charting Presley's development and importance as an artist they add little, if anything to our understanding. Rather than clutter up this book with discussions of, in some instances, up to 15 different released takes of the same song, I have confined myself mainly to the songs first issued from the sessions, or to the first issued master take. In the latter case, this remains, after all, the one that Elvis himself chose best to reflect his performance and the one by which he wished to be judged. Occasionally, however, I have noted alternative takes where they add to the point in question.

This book could not have been written without the help and encouragement of a number of people. Todd Slaughter, president of the Official Elvis Presley Fan Club of Great Britain, supplied much material in the first instance, and his own book – 'Elvis Presley' – remains the best short biography. The full-hearted co-operation I received from my ex-colleagues at RCA deserves special mention. In particular, Peter Bailey and Dave Machray, Shaun Greenfield and especially Paul Rustad, whose complete collection of Elvis Presley recordings was placed unhesitatingly at my disposal. Paul also discussed various aspects of the original book with me at several stages, and took part in stimulating conversations on Presley's performances.

My thanks are also due to Barbara Kettle-Williams and Dr Tim Dowley, Brian Adams, Bill Williams, Ray Jenks, Chris Giles, John Henderson and Paul Robinson, and to those people who wrote with comments and suggestions after the publication of the original book. They have been personally thankted and acknowledged.

Although there have been many books published on Elvis Presley, I have refrained from including a bibliography. I have also refrained from including a list of recommended videos. All Presley films are now available on video; the interested reader will find no difficulty in locating the better of these books or films, but the books mentioned in paragraph six of Chapter Eight are especially recommended to those readers keen to pursue the documentary aspects of Elvis Presley's recordings.

It has been a heart-warming experience to see how much Presley's artistry has come to be so widely recognised in the years since his death; I now believe – even more strongly than in 1977 – that as time goes by he will come to be recognised as one of the two or three most important singers of the twentieth century, with implications for the performance of popular music that will run well into the twenty-first century. If this study is able to make some further contribution to the greater understanding of these implications, then it will have more than served its purpose.

Finally, without my wife's loving forbearance and continual encouragement, the following study would have remained unwritten, and it is to her that this book is dedicated.

Robert Matthew-Walker
London, SE12
June 1995

Part I

The Man

Chapter One

War and peace

At the time of the birth of Vernon Presley in 1916, a Great War raged in Europe. Since the sinking by a German U-boat of the Cunard passenger liner *Lusitania* in 1915 with the loss of 1,198 lives, including those of 124 Americans, it had been only a matter of time before the United States entered the fray on the side of the Allies. Such powerful events had little bearing initially on the poor farming community of Clay Community, west of Fulton, where the Presley family then lived. They, like their neighbours, knew of the war, of course, but only as some far-off event, away from the homespun and humdrum daily lives of the township of the seat of Itawamba Country, which lies near the East Fork of the Tombigbee River, north of Columbus in north-east Mississippi.

Woodrow Wilson, twenty-eighth president of the United States, who had been narrowly re-elected in 1916, found himself in a dilemma over the *Lusitania* outrage. He had little desire to permit America to become involved in the war in Europe, and hoped the conflict could be resolved without the United States intervening. But early in 1917 the Germans resumed unrestricted submarine warfare, six weeks after Wilson's Peace Note had been published. The following day the USA began to arm American merchant ships, and on 6 April, 1917 the United States declared war on Germany.

For some American troops sent to Europe, it meant a return after only a few years. Unlike the European armies, war-weary after nearly four years of incessant fighting, the Americans were fresh and backed with a virtually limitless supply of men and matériel. It was not entirely a one-sided affair: a German submarine, the heavily camouflaged U-155, shelled shipping off the shore of Cape Cod,

Massachusetts, early in July 1918. But this was little more than a token, if futile, gesture, as it became likely during the summer of 1918 that the Germans were eventually going to be defeated.

The realities of war had struck home, and, following an initiative by President Wilson, Germany approached the United States to negotiate an armistice. All German submarines were recalled from the Atlantic; it was merely a matter of time before the apparatus of war would be dismantled. On 9 November, Kaiser Wilhelm II of Germany abdicated and fled to Holland. The following day, in the morning, the Armistice was signed in Marshal Foch's railway carriage near Compiegne in France, and at 11 am the bugles sounded 'cease-fire'. The Great War, begun over four years previously by Tsar Nicholas II of Russia to defend Serbia against Austrian domination, was over, yet it was Russia which paid the heaviest price: with over nine million dead or injured out of a mobilised force of twelve million – over forty per cent of all Allied casualties. In human terms, Russia suffered most of all.

The United States into which Vernon Presley had been born in war was a vastly different place from that in which his son lived his mature life in peacetime. In 1917, the population of the United States just topped the hundred million mark, and more than one in ten of all American citizens had actually been born in Europe. This massive migration, on a scale never before seen in world history, and certainly never since, was concentrated on several areas of America.

The new population, however, hardly touched the Deep South, the states of Mississippi, Tennessee, Louisiana, Alabama and Georgia particularly, although, like many white Americans, the Presley's (or 'Pressley' as an earlier spelling of the name has it) were descended from immigrants from the British Isles. They could eventually trace their ancestry back two hundred years to an Irishman, David Pressley, who landed at New Bern, now the seat of Craven County in east North Carolina, in the 1740s, and they were therefore strongly descended from much earlier British, indeed Celtic, stock than the then-recent refugees from war-torn Europe. The Great War had changed the world in other ways than personal ones. During those four years American loans to the Allies meant that a shift, a deep and irreversible one in world power, had occurred. The fact was largely political, but events were not to allow the country to call the tune to the degree that was possibly desirable.

To the exhausted Europeans, when President Wilson arrived to preside over the peace negotiations in France, he came as a conquering hero. During these negotiations, Wilson was obliged to compromise on many things, but he obtained several concessions, including self-determination for Poland, Yugoslavia and Czechoslovakia, and above all the agreement for the Covenant of the League of Nations, which formed part of the Treaty signed by all the combatant nations in the Palace of Versailles on 28 June, 1919.

But back in the United States, Wilson's absence of many months, together with the concessions he was forced to make, angered his detractors and dismayed several of his supporters in the Democratic Party. Many Americans had not wanted to become involved in the war in the first place, and they had seen over 125,000 of their soldiers die in battle. Many had originally left Europe for the New World precisely to get away from internal strife and warfare. The mid-term elections in 1918 gave the Republicans a majority in the Senate, and Wilson made a serious error of judgement by not including any prominent Republicans in his peace delegation to Europe.

On his return, he faced mounting opposition, but was unwilling to compromise. Against doctor's orders he decided to appeal directly to the people, but in the days before radio, television, talking pictures and regular air travel, this meant a gruelling speaking tour. It virtually killed him. The President collapsed after twenty-three days, suffering a stroke, and for the rest of his second term Wilson was manifestly incapable of fulfilling his duties. His illness meant the end of the Treaty for the Senate. It was rejected twice, and as a result the United States failed to join the League of Nations, fatally weakening Wilson's dream of a world forum for peaceful debate, and dooming the League to eventual failure. The United States, especially after a highly-publicised communist scare in 1919 (the Russian Revolution had occurred eighteen months before), withdrew into a long period of detachment from Europe.

Yet again, world events mattered little to the folk of Clay Community, and even less to Vernon's father, Jessie, although just after the end of the war the owner of the farm on which Jessie had worked to support his growing dependents (he had married in 1913 at the age of seventeen) sold it, and the family moved to East Tupelo. Jessie, by all accounts, was a remarkable man, but he would frequently travel far afield to look for work, with the result that his wife Minnie often had no financial support from him for months on end. Their story was very common, and a further consequence was the lack of formal education for Jessie and Minnie's children. They were educationally disadvantaged, and therefore economically so in their own lives, for they were unable to participate in America's economic boom during the 'Roaring Twenties'.

The economic growth of the USA during the 1920s was unprecedented, and not only for legitimate businesses. The Abolition amendment to the Constitution, which became Law on 16 January, 1920 opened up a massive trade in illicit alcohol-trafficking which, allied to gangsterism and corruption, led to increasing demands for the Amendment to be repealed. The motion-picture industry in Hollywood, a suburb of Los Angeles to which Vernon Presley's son would eventually make an individual and extensive contribution thirty to forty years later, exploded across the western world, becoming a further example of the success of the American dream.

15

It might appear at first sight that the United States in the 1920s was a particularly prosperous place and time for Vernon Presley, his brother Vester and their three sisters, in which to grow up. But while this was true for many American children, one must remember that Mississippi had never been part of the industrial heart of America, and, as a largely agricultural state, was particularly vulnerable to the vicissitudes of economic change, as we have seen in Jessie's case.

By 1929, the economy of the United States had grown at an enormous rate. The automobile industry, the thermometer of any capitalist economy, produced 4.6 million cars that year – the highest figure then achieved, and one which remained an all-time high until 1940. In 1929 there were 24,000 banks in the USA, as businesses boomed. It was clear the 'return to normalcy' of President Warren Harding (Wilson's Republican successor in 1920), the 'keeping cool with Coolidge' (Calvin Coolidge, Harding's second-term vice-president and successor on Harding's death soon after the latter's re-election in 1924) and the *laissez-faire* attitude of the then president, Herbert Hoover (elected in 1928, the third Republican president in a row), demonstrated the success of the isolationism of unbroken Republican administrations. The booming of the United States economy in the 1920s gave Americans and the world a false image of its real strength, and no one questioned the security of the foundations upon which its success was based, or could foretell in the summer of 1929 this success was soon to come to a catastrophic end.

The causes of the disaster were many and interacting: the wealth that was being created, leading to immense personal fortunes for some, was not re-circulated through sufficient people to sustain a national purchasing power, which the increase in output demanded. By 1929, some factories were producing more goods than they could sell. This gradually led to lay-offs, precipitating a drop in demand, for people out of work have no money to spend, and in the 'self-sufficient' society there was no national system of unemployment welfare. Furthermore, the trading balance of the United States was precarious: in order for the European countries which had borrowed money from the United States during the war to repay their loans, the American government should have stimulated world trade but the Republican administrations, from Harding to Hoover, had erected tariff barriers, preventing foreign imports. The result was to bolster internal trade, but it forced these other countries to erect tariff barriers in return which, far more dangerously for the American economy, acted as a brake to United States exports.

To these troubles must be added another basic flaw – a labrynthine national debt system had evolved, whereby legitimate profits were deposited within the complex banking system to be lent to finance further industry or to purchase shares in a system which itself was flawed: stocks and shares on Wall Street could be bought for ten per cent of the total price, 'on the margin', creating illusionary paper fortunes.

Millions of Americans, flushed with prosperity – or rather the trappings of it – became debtors to loan companies and finance houses, buying goods on the hire-purchase system. The goods were bought with money loaned by small banks to small industries whose profits were literally figures on pieces of paper. It was an unreal system which could not last, but the world had never seen anything like it before, and it appeared to work, so no one bothered to learn the lessons of an over-heated economy, or inflationary growth – apart from one country, Germany, in 1923, but that had largely been ignored by outsiders (although not by all Germans) as many felt it was a just retribution for the misery caused by that country's arrogant militarism.

In America, with small factories laying off workers, the workers in turn went to the banks to withdraw their savings. There was a run on the smaller banks, who began calling in loans from their debtors. The debtors could not pay, for their goods had been sold on very favourable credit terms. One or two small banks closed, which caused larger runs on the bigger banks, which ultimately led to demands for payment of the remaining balances, and began selling their shares: immediately, prices and confidence fell and the whole fiscal house of cards collapsed.

Not all areas of American society prospered in the 1920s. Farmers, because of the increase in mechanisation – mainly through tractors – found they were producing more food than they could sell, and the trade barriers made it impossible for the surpluses to be exported. The over-production led to falling prices, which in turn devalued the land, itself mortgaged to the banks to buy the tractors to produce more. It was a crazy, inhuman situation, highlighted in John Steinbeck's masterly novel *The Grapes Of Wrath*, but even if the banks foreclosed – and they did – few could afford to buy the land now up for sale.

In Mississippi – indeed throughout the rural communities of the Deep South – the American Dream had become as bad a nightmare as it had in the industrial centres of the country. When Vernon Presley was born, his father Jessie, a farm-worker, would average $40 a month in pay. By the beginning of 1933, when Vernon first met his future wife Gladys Smith, Jessie would earn less than $25 a month on the land. The grain farmers received less than half for their produce in 1933 than they did in 1910. Millions of Americans were disenchanted and dispossessed by a system that had utterly failed them, and in the presidential election at the end of 1932, while Herbert Hoover retained a reasonably respectable 15.7 million votes, he was swept from office by the Democratic candidate Franklin Delano Roosevelt, who polled 22.8 million votes. Roosevelt took forty-two of the then forty-eight states, and with them the vast majority of the votes in the electoral college. With Roosevelt's election on his promise of a 'New Deal', the die was cast for the gradual rebirth – by no means painlessly achieved – in which Vernon's and Gladys's famous son played an important character-forming and reflecting role.

But when Vernon first met Gladys their families, like those of most working-class America, whether industrial or agricultural, were suffering from the effects of the Depression. The 1929 crash affected all America, as we have seen, but of all the states of the Union none was more severely affected than Mississippi.

In 1933, East Tupelo, the little township where Vernon and Gladys grew up, had a tiny population; combined with that of the small city of Tupelo, in whose environs it was situated, it stood at around seven thousand. Tupelo boasted two claims to a kind of fame: it was a stop on the Chicago–New Orleans railroad, and the court house of Lee County was situated there. Not so long afterwards, it added a third: as a mixed-economy town with agricultural and industry cheek-by-jowl, it became a model town of what was termed the 'New South', the kind of community admired by Roosevelt's New Deal.

But life in Mississippi remained basic and hard. The state population numbered almost two million, half of which was black. Mississippi had the highest proportion of blacks of any state. It also led in other, more disturbing statistics: more lynchings had taken place in Mississippi than in any other state, almost six hundred in seventy years, with fewer than fifty of the victims being white men. Integration was virtually unknown, and was indeed positively discouraged, with much active discrimination. Blacks and whites kept themselves to themselves, and rarely met together, even in such areas as music and religion.

The marriage rate in Mississippi in the early 1930s was more than double the national average, but the divorce rate was just fractionally higher. During times of economic stress, it is not unusual for family ties to become stronger, and the highest birth-rates are almost always found among the lowest-income families, tending to reinforce family bonds.

Moreover, the white population was greatly influenced by fundamentalist religion, which preached a strict moral code and which was widespread throughout the South. Strict it may have been, but it was not so widely observed, even in the Presley family, although Gladys – in the early months of 1933 soon to become the family's newest member – at least was a regular church-goer. Last, and perhaps most importantly, the age of consent for marriage was then the lowest in the USA. Boys could marry at fourteen, and girls at twelve.

Nevertheless, it was by no means common in those days for a young man to marry an older girl. Vernon was four years younger than Gladys, but they altered their ages when they upped and went twenty miles west of Tupelo, to Pontotoc, to marry in the region from whence Gladys had come. Although Gladys was then twenty-one, she claimed to be only nineteen; Vernon – then merely seventeen –

said he was twenty-two when they entered details of their ages for the licence, issued when they were married on 17 June, 1933 prior to moving back to Tupelo almost immediately. It had not been a long courtship, but given the state laws it was not therefore surprising that Vernon was in fact only seventeen when he married Gladys, the same age his father had been when he had married exactly twenty years earlier.

A year went by before Gladys became pregnant, at which time she was obliged to give up her job as a sewing-machine operator. Vernon attempted to find work on the land, and he succeeded, if only sporadically, but the current economic conditions made life extremely hard. Wages had fallen, and the average standard of living in such communities as Tupelo was desperately low. The possession of a radio was a great luxury for the poorer sections of the community, and that of a car was merely a dream.

In the course of looking for fresh work Vernon was forced to consider other than farming jobs. In the changing circumstances he eventually secured a post as a milk delivery man – not unrelated to farming, it is true, but certainly not land-work. However, this proved to be a valuable position, for at least Vernon now was sure of steady pay, and his new employer helped finance a home for the young couple, apart from the in-laws with whom they had been living until a short time before, affording them the privacy which a marriage, especially a new one, demands. But it was not quite as it may seem: Vernon had to build the house himself, which he did in collaboration with his brother and father, largely out of wood, on land owned by his father. This tiny two-roomed dwelling was built next to his father's home, and it still stands, now transformed for today's important tourist industry from the basic dwelling it must originally have been into a somewhat picturesque cottage.

In many ways, the possession of their own home – however humble and basic and lacking some amenities compared with low-grade housing today – was a notable turn for the better for Vernon and Gladys. As a result of his father Jessie's uncertain earnings and habitat during the 1920s Vernon, together with his brothers and sisters, was virtually illiterate, being unable to read or write with any proficiency. But for all his lack of education, Vernon was not stupid. He knew the necessity of hard work and of trying to improve, however marginally and always with great difficulty against the prevailing harsh economic climate, the lot of his wife and their soon-to-be-born offspring. Vernon was no saint, and did not always succeed as he would have wished, but given the circumstances, it is remarkable that he did as well as he did during the first few years of his marriage.

During her pregnancy, as Gladys later claimed, she instinctively knew all along that she was expecting twins, and she indeed gave birth to twin boys on the afternoon of 8 January 8, 1935. But one, Jesse Garon, did not survive. He was buried the following day in an unmarked grave in Priceville Cemetery, Tupelo. The surviving boy was christened Elvis Aron.

Chapter Two

'A nice kid'

It is common for parents who lose a baby to idolise their surviving children, and understandably more so if a twin dies. Vernon and Gladys were no exception, but such idolisation often turns to a quite extraordinary desire on the part of the parents to succeed in whatever way they can, in order to provide their surviving child with a degree of material comfort, and occasionally moral and spiritual guidance, which the child would otherwise not have had.

Elvis remained Vernon and Gladys's only child, and Gladys doted on him to a degree that undoubtedly brought some psycho-sexual problems for him in adult life. Vernon, too, contributed to these problems, or rather exacerbated them, perhaps as a result of trying too hard to provide his wife and son with a little more.

But at first they were sustained by the love showered on Elvis and by the mores of small-town life in the southern states of the USA. These qualities were those of an honest, hard-working, God-fearing neighbourliness – qualities that are not so universally admired as they once were, nor were they ever universally adopted. It cannot be denied that Vernon himself, while possibly doing all he could to live up to Gladys's sense of propriety and his own natural desire to provide the best he could for his dependents, was not as invariably honest, hard-working or God-fearing as he might have been, but he was not a rogue. He always had a reputation of being something of a ladies' man, and was not always frank with Gladys. Occasionally, also, he took up with bad company – later, as we shall see, with disastrous results – but given the very difficult circumstances in which he, like many others, found himself, few men today could honestly claim that they might have behaved very differently.

Nevertheless, the first years of Elvis's life were marked both by his parents' devotion to him and his induction into fundamentalist religion, the latter having almost as big an impact on his life as did the former. The regular church-going of Elvis's parents – even if it was not every Sunday, and even if Vernon did not always accompany his wife and son – to the Pentecostal Church of the First Assembly of God, which was a small wooden building on Adams Street, not only taught Elvis standards of behaviour that are apparent in early recorded interviews with him, but also led to his first musical awakening.

It is fascinating to consider the influences and events that lead to the initial musical expressions of a later musical genius. In Elvis's case, there is no doubt that the impact on him of the singing he heard as a child in church was a prime factor in his development. However, it may be that an event which, as well as having a longer-term traumatic effect, led immediately to a drastic reversal of the family's fortunes, contributed to the dependence on religious comfort and a greater association with the music of the church.

Towards the end of 1937, while working for the dairy owned by Orville S. Bean, Vernon and two other men altered the amount of a cheque drawn by Mr Bean by $10, increasing an amount of $18 to $28. It was a crude forgery, and was soon discovered, as were the culprits. In November of that year, Vernon and the two others were charged with forgery: six months later, after the trial in which they were clearly guilty, Vernon and his accomplices were sentenced. Considering the amount – $10, presumably split three ways – was quite small (although in purchasing terms the dollar was worth substantially more then than it is today) the sentence seems out of all proportion to the crime. For this first offence, Vernon was sentenced to three years imprisonment, and began serving his term in May 1938.

Elvis was then almost three-and-a-half, and the sudden removal of his father must have come as something of a shock. The jail sentence meant Gladys had no income (there being minimum welfare and virtually no social security payments in those days) and, unable to keep up the payments on their home, mortgaged to the Mr Bean against whom the fraud had been perpetrated, they were obliged to leave it and move in to Vernon's parents' house next door. The lingering death of Gladys's mother in 1937 from tuberculosis must have exacerbated Gladys's misery in losing her home, her husband and, presumably, her self-respect in the following year.

Whatever cumulative effects these troubles had on Gladys, the long-term effects of such a separation from his father on a boy of that age cannot be overestimated: although Vernon's father was in their new home, and was then only forty-five years old, quite capable of providing a daily father figure for his grandson, Elvis did not have his own bed and shared with his mother. The result was inadvertently to run the greatest risk of a classic Oedipus complex in later life, which undoubtedly occurred. There is equally no doubt that, with her husband in jail, Gladys would have gone out of her way to impress upon her surviving son the virtues of honesty to perhaps an almost unbearable degree. With Vernon absent, Elvis had no choice but to be a willing listener to his mother's homilies, which included for her the attraction, and possibly also the social rehabilitation, of strictly regular church-going.

In later life Elvis recalled: 'We were a religious family, going round together to sing at camp meetings and revivals. Since I was two years old, all I knew was gospel music.' Gladys later told Elvis that when he was about two years of age he would stand by her in church, wriggling from her lap on to the floor, to join in with the choir. He added: 'I could carry the tune, even though I didn't know the words. That music became such a part of my life, it was as natural as dancing.'

These are significant words, and they seem to have the ring of truth about them in spite of recent attempts to disprove such early manifestations of Elvis's musicality. The fact is that he was musical: that simply cannot be denied. It is also true that when we come to consider his initial world-wide success, the extraordinary thing is that he had virtually no contact with any other musician before he started singing in public and making records: therefore, whatever musicianship was in him had to have been there from the beginning, and nurtured by something. We know he accompanied his mother to church, and both he and she claimed his first attraction to music on hearing the choir sing – surely, in the light of his later development, his recollections, as well as those of his mother, are accurate. Quite apart from anything else, he made a number of albums of hymns and religious songs, which are undoubtedly genuinely sung and felt. There was no obligation on his part to have undertaken these recordings had he not wanted to, and in some ways, placed as they are a little apart from his rock singing, they appear puzzling choices – but not so puzzling if one accepts his claims to an early love of fundamentalist church music.

Therefore, for a musical boy, the fascination of the church choir must have been considerable, and unwittingly his hymn-singing proved the best possible musical education he could have had. Singing is the most natural of all musical expressions and the harmonies of the church choir must have entered his subconscious. Nor are we talking about particularly sophisticated music-making in this small wooden building, certainly not Anglican church music: merely a gospel song orientated type of singing, in musical terms perhaps not so far removed from barbershop quartets. We must remember that the congregation could only be numbered in dozens, rather than hundreds. The singer would not be 'trained' in the classic sense, and might only number four to eight of the community's best voices, accompanied by a run-down piano. The result was basic, but pure, simple and direct.

Before his jail sentence, Vernon occasionally joined Elvis and Gladys at campside hymn-singing services, during which Vernon and his father would feature as solo singers once in a while, Vernon by some accounts possessing a fine baritone voice. Another family member of Vernon's father's generation, Luther Presley, also enjoyed a local reputation as a musician, and had arranged several well-known hymns. Later in life, Elvis would record one of Luther's arrangements on one of his albums of religious songs.

Other musical influences at the campside meetings were recalled by Elvis: 'During the singing, the preachers would cut up all over the place, jumping on the piano, moving every which way... I guess I learned a lot from them.' This is another comment that has brought counter-claims, but they can be dismissed. The period in Elvis's life we are discussing is from about 1938 to 1944, six years during which his father was away from the home for half of the time, and at the end of which Elvis was approaching his tenth birthday. The only counter-evidence comes from a preacher of the actual branch of the church the Presleys attended, who denies that services were conducted in this manner. But this man was appointed to the post in Tupelo in 1944, after all these events occurred, and is therefore someone who can not be regarded as a witness to anything prior to his arrival. In any event, Elvis was not recalling a service in the church building, but open-air meetings. Elvis's comments, borne out by his contemporaries, were made in the late 1950s – between a dozen and twenty years or so after they were supposed to have occurred. If he had been lying then, it is curious that no one came forward to challenge him, especially as at that time he did not enjoy the universal admiration he did later; the short answer is that there is nothing to cause us to disbelieve Elvis's recollections here, or at any other time.

We should regard his recollection as a penetrating remark because when Elvis burst upon the world popular music scene in the mid-1950s, many people felt that his stage movements were done merely for vulgar effect. Such a view is quite wrong. Elvis moved naturally, responding physically to the heart of the music – the beat – as did those open-air preachers of his youth. In any event, his claims are by no means unique.

But the singing was the main attraction for him. Elvis also recalled: 'When I was four or five [*actually, he probably means five or six, in view of Vernon's prison sentence and his later comments*] all I looked forward to was Sundays, when we could all go to church. I loved the old church, filled with sunlight and the security of my mother and father beside me. [*This tends to pinpoint the recollection to summer 1941, after Vernon's release.*] This was the only singing training I had – I never had lessons. I'd just try to sing as loud and in tune as I could. I was always singing. People living on the same housing project as me [*this refers to later life in Memphis*] would stop and listen.'

As a toddler the boy had few friends outside the family; but it was a large family. At the age of five, Elvis began school, and came into daily contact with other children of his own age. Gladys, however, continuing to dote on him, would never let him out of her sight. 'I couldn't go down to the creek with the other kids,' he later said (but as his father was in prison at the time Elvis started school, this could equally have been the desire of the parents of the other children not to have him mix with them). He was not an outstanding pupil, and surprisingly few of his contemporaries remember much about him, but his love of music was clear for all to see.

In September 1939, Germany invaded Poland, an event which marked the outbreak of World War II. As with the hostilities in Europe when Vernon had been born, the war had little immediate effect on America's Deep South. But sociologically, times had changed in the intervening quarter-century, even in reactionary Mississippi townships. The two most significant developments had been the growth of the automobile industry and the rise of radio.

Vernon was released from prison, after serving his full term, on 4 June, 1941. Almost exactly six months later, on 7 December, Japan attacked the United States 7th Fleet at Pearl Harbor, Hawaii, inflicting massive losses; immediately, the United States became a fighting part of the Allied cause. Soon afterwards, national conscription was introduced in the USA, but as an ex-convict Vernon was automatically exempted. In addition, he had a diabetic problem, so even without his prison record it is likely he would have been rejected for Army service on medical grounds.

In spite of their continuing comparative poverty, Vernon and his family were able to take advantage of the growth of the motor car and radio broadcasting. Vernon learned to drive, and obtained an old car; they also had a radio, and – along with all other civilians – the family was drawn to following the war news from broadcast bulletins (for Vernon remained a poor reader throughout his life, and would not have followed events from newspapers). Vernon, Gladys and, most importantly, Elvis soon became avid radio listeners, which in turn led to another formative musical influence on the boy. 'I used to listen quite a lot,' he recalled in the 1950s, 'and I loved records by Sister Rosetta Thorpe, and country singers like Roy Acuff, Ernest Tubbs, Ted Daffan, Jimmie Rodgers, Jimmy Davies and Bob Wills.'

Another singer he could have mentioned was Red Foley, who recorded the song 'Old Shep', which became very popular through radio exposure and must have made a deep impression on the young listener. One day at school when he was in the fifth grade he sang the song for his teacher, Mrs Grimes. She was impressed, and arranged for Elvis to sing it for the school's principal. He was also moved by Elvis's singing, and entered him for a local talent show, which was part of the annual Mississippi–Alabama States Fair. Although Elvis's voice had not yet broken, the years of singing must have moulded it into an expressive instrument. 'Old Shep' is not that easy a song to sing, and Elvis performed without accompaniment at the contest. He came second and won $5 and free rides on all the sideshows and amusements, but when he came home late his mother was certain he had been delayed by some mischief or another, and beat him, unimpressed by his success. However, his singing must have had some effect on his parents, for by the time he was thirteen they had managed to buy him his own guitar. This certainly would have entailed a major sacrifice for them; he had asked for a bicycle, but eagerly accepted the $12 musical instrument instead. His interest in the guitar quickly grew; as a keen singer, he soon learned to accompany himself.

Much later in life, when Elvis was asked about his mother, his reply was revealing:

'I used to get bad at Mama once in a while. But I guess a growing boy always does. I was the only child and Mama was always right with me. Maybe she was too good. I could wake her up in the middle of the night if I was worried about something. She'd get up, fix me a sandwich and a glass of milk, and talk to me; help me figure things out... I suppose because I was an only child I was a little closer. I mean, everyone loves their mother but I was an only child and my mother was always with me, all my life, and it wasn't like losing a mother, it was like losing a friend, a companion, someone to talk to. I would wake her up any hour of the night and if I was worried or troubled about something she'd get up and try to help me. I used to get very angry at her when I was growing up, it's a natural thing isn't it? A young person wants to go somewhere, do something and your mother won't let you and you think, well, what's wrong with you? But later on in years you find out that she was right, that she was only doing it to protect you and keep you from getting into trouble and getting hurt. And I'm very happy that she was kind of strict.'

Mrs Faye Harris, a neighbour and friend of the Presley family in Tupelo, recalled:

26

'Gladys thought Elvis was the greatest thing that ever happened. And she treated him that way. She worshipped that child from the day he was born until the day she died. She would always keep him at home and when she let him go out to play, she was always out looking to see that he was all right. And wherever she went, whether it was out visiting or down to the grocery store, she always had her little boy along...'

The end of World War II, in August 1945, brought no improvement in the rural townships of the Deep South. It was more difficult for Vernon to find continuous work in Tupelo, possibly made worse by his prison record and the return to civilian life of that large number of able-bodied young men who had been called-up into the Army, and had returned home more experienced than those who remained. By September 1948, the Presley family decided to move to Memphis, Tennessee. Vernon, Gladys and Elvis packed their belongings into their old green Plymouth car, and drove to the largest city of the neighbouring state.

On arrival in Memphis, they lived for several months in one room on Poplar Avenue in the downtown area of the city, about a mile from the Mississippi River. Vernon was now able to get a regular job, and with Elvis approaching fourteen, Gladys was also able to work part-time in a succession of various jobs – in a sewing shop, a restaurant and a local hospital. Elvis enrolled in L.C. Humes High School, a forbidding three-storey brown-brick building on Manassas Street. It was a whites-only school, with 1,700 pupils. Only six subjects were taught there.

The Presleys' living accommodation remained comparatively primitive, nonetheless. They shared a bath with three other families. In these cramped conditions Elvis began sleep-walking. Red West, a later friend and confidant, wrote: 'Like most transplanted kids in a new town, Elvis withdrew into a shell of timidity and shyness. Whatever he lacked in friends on the street, Gladys Presley more than made up for with attention and affection.'

In the summer of 1949, they were able to improve their circumstances by moving into a three-roomed ground-floor apartment in a concrete federal-funded housing project called Lauderdale Courts, on Winchester Street. This complex was constructed exclusively for families with an income of less than $200 a month, who were charged $35 a month rent.

Although they were poor, Vernon and Gladys did all they could to give their son what he wanted. We have seen how much they must have sacrificed to give Elvis his guitar, and this was clearly not a misplaced gesture. In the eleventh grade at L.C. Humes, he performed a song 'Cold, Cold Icy Fingers' at a school concert which was so successful that Miss Scrivener, a history teacher, urged him to sing an encore. He went on to give a public performance at the Memphis Veterans' Hospital in early 1950, just after his fifteenth birthday. This was his first public appearance outside of school.

By November 1950 Elvis, then almost sixteen, obtained a job at Loew's State Theater in Memphis for $12.60 a week, working from 5 pm until 10 pm each night. He enjoyed his evening work, and gave all the money he earned to Gladys. The drawback was that he tended to keep very late hours and as a result regularly fell asleep in class the following day. When Gladys heard of this she insisted he quit the job, but the family's finances were such that early in 1951 Elvis was obliged to return to Loew's. He left their employment a second time when the manager, Arthur Groom, fired him following a fight over a candy-seller.

Elvis's next job was with the Marl Metal Products Company – but this was a full night-shift. Inevitably, Elvis again fell asleep in class, and Gladys once more told him to give up evening work, exclaiming, 'We're not that poor!' – although one wonders what led to her agreeing he should take the job in the first place. In spite of their low income, like all families they managed to get by.

Although Elvis was a quiet and reserved child, he had matured early, his adult voice developing sooner than that of most other boys. His strong interest in music and singing gave him an outlet for self-expression, but this was not the only way in which the adolescent asserted his individuality, as Red West recalled:

> '...seventeen year old Presley [ie, 1952] was a nice kid, even if he looked a little out of place in the sea of kids with their crew cuts and pink scalps. Pasty-faced with... long brown hair, in ducktail fashion, the handfuls of Vaseline he put on it made it look much darker than it was... He had a preference for leather jackets and would often tie a red bandanna around his neck, in the fashion popular with inter-state truck drivers of the era... When he wasn't wearing a leather jacket and jeans, it was some outrageously coloured pair of pegged pants. In the sea of over 1,600 pink-scalped kids at school, Elvis stood out like a camel in the Arctic. Intentionally or not, his appearance expressed a defiance which his demeanour did not match...'

Elvis's individuality in clothes attracted unwelcome attention from his contemporaries. Red West continued:

> '...someone was always picking on him, don't know why. He was easy going enough, well mannered, was always respectful of his elders, and he

28

never wised off anyone. In many ways, he was a very good kid, a lot nicer than some of the others around...'

Red was also able to help Elvis out of a few scrapes, and their long friendship began at this time. Red recalled another, more significant school variety concert at Christmas 1952:

> *'...one of the big events of the year was the school variety concert. It consisted of about thirty acts... the person who ran the show was a history teacher [Miss Scrivener]... I put an act in the show. I payed the trumpet and I got together a guitar and a bass. It was a heck of a big day and we were all very nervous...'*

Red had finished his act when he got the shock of his life, seeing Elvis come out on to the stage with his guitar:

> *'To be honest, I never thought he would have the guts to go out there in front of all those people... Then it happened. Elvis put one foot up on a chair to act as a prop, and he started to plunk away at the tune 'Old Shep'. Then he whipped into a fast song, then a ballad... Hell, do you know while Elvis was singing the love songs, there was one old lady [Miss Scrivener?] crying? When he finished his show, the kids went crazy; they applauded and applauded. They just went mad... He seemed to be amazed that for the first time in his life someone other than his family really liked him. I'll never really know when Elvis got bitten by the bug of loving the applause of the audience, but my guess is that it happened right there in Humes High School. At last, it seemed, he had found a way to make outsiders love him... As shy as he was, he had a definite magic on stage...'*

This concert took place a few months before Elvis graduated; the success made his last months at school more pleasant and much more bearable. He became popular and greatly in demand, no longer 'the outsider'.

Elvis graduated in the summer of 1953: he was now eighteen. At first he got a job with the Precision Tool Company. He had no clear ambition and whatever ideas he may have harboured about becoming a singer he kept to himself. He clearly realised that he had to have regular employment to help with the family's finances. Later, he became a truck driver with the Crown Electric Company, earning about $35 a week. Crown was situated on Poplar Avenue where the

Presleys had first lived on their arrival in Memphis. With Elvis now working, the family could afford to move to a bigger and better apartment on Lamar Avenue. To better himself, Elvis studied in the evenings to become an electrician. But his day-time delivery route as a truck driver took him along Union Avenue, where a small building had caught his interest.

Chapter Three

The young singer

The small building stood a little way back from the road at 706 Union Avenue, Memphis, at the time Elvis began driving the truck for Crown Electric. A single-storeyed construction, it housed Sun Records and the Sun Recording Studios, which was owned by a former radio announcer, Sam Phillips, who had opened it several years before, in 1950. During the few years he had been in business, Phillips had achieved a fair measure of success, for by 1953, he had already recorded such significant local singers as Howlin' Wolf, Junior Parker and B.B. King, as well as Johnny Cash, Jerry Lee Lewis, Roy Orbison and Charlie Rich – all of whom, without exception, went on to make enormously important international careers for themselves for larger and more famous record companies.

Two years after starting out, Phillips had launched his own record label, Sun (his previous recordings were either licensed or sold directly to other companies), but a lucrative sideline for the studios was the Memphis Recording Service, a facility for budding artists who wanted to make records. By paying $4, anybody could go in to the studios and record two songs. Apart from bringing in a reasonably regular supply of small change, this facility was also an excellent way for Phillips to discover local talent at no cost to himself. One Saturday afternoon in 1953, after finishing work at lunchtime, and a few days before his mother's birthday, Elvis dropped by the Memphis Recordings Service office. As he recalled:

'I went to Sun, paid my four bucks to the lady, because I had a notion to find out what I really sounded like. I had been singing all my life, and I was kind of curious. But when I heard the recording it was terrible – I was terrible – I sounded like someone banging a trash-can lid.'

Apart from what must by then have become a powerful natural curiosity – as he says, that of wanting to know what his voice sounded like – another reason for making the recording was that Elvis decided to give it to his mother as a birthday present. Gladys was ecstatic about it, so much so that 'she played it over and over until it was plumb near worn out.' The recording was an acetate (a direct-cut on to disc, either from tape or through the cutter), so its playing life was considerably shorter than that of normal commercially issued shellac (78 rpm) or vinyl (45 or 33.3 rpm) discs. In usual circumstances, an acetate will have deteriorated markedly after fifty or sixty playings at most. It is entirely possible that Gladys would have played the record many more times than that, so Elvis's comment about the disc becoming 'near worn out' would have been the literal truth.

But Gladys was not the only person to disagree with Elvis over the quality of his singing. The young woman who worked for Sam Phillips, Miss Marion Keisker, was immediately attracted by the unique quality of Elvis's voice. When he was only half-way through his first song, 'My Happiness', she managed to get a spare tape machine switched on, and caught the second part as well as the whole of the second song, 'That's When Your Heartaches Begin'. She was compelled to tape Elvis's voice because she had not forgotten Sam Phillips's oft-repeated comment to her: 'If you can find a white singer with a black man's voice, we could make a fortune.' She clearly thought that Elvis was just such a singer, and, after he had left with the acetate, she played the tape to Phillips. However, Sam was unimpressed with what he heard, although Marion Keisker kept badgering him to reconsider.

After several months of continuing to drive trucks for Crown, as well as pursuing his electrical studies at night, Elvis returned to Sun on 4 January, 1954 to invest another $4. Perhaps by this time, with his own birthday approaching (on 8 January) and his mother likely to have literally 'worn out' the first record, the family needed another record of Elvis to play at home. This time the songs were 'Casual Love' and 'I'll Never Stand In Your Way'. But Marion Keisker was not in the office, although on this occasion Sam Phillips himself was present. He heard Elvis's singing, but remained unconvinced, advising that Elvis had a great deal more to do before he could be considered for commercial recording, although he now admitted that the singer had 'something'. Whatever this 'something' was, Sam Phillips noted Elvis's name, address and telephone number in case he should ever need him.

A month or two later, eight months after Elvis's original visit to Sun, Phillips came across a demonstration disc of an unknown black singer's performance of the song 'Without You'. The song attracted Phillips, who decided to get the black singer in to record it under studio conditions. But he was unable to locate him, and Marion Keisker suggested Elvis instead. Sam Phillips agreed, perhaps because of what she later claimed was her persistence in putting Elvis's name forward, and she called Elvis at home. Presley remembered: 'It was twelve o'clock on a Saturday, and they said "Can you be here by three?". I ran all the way. I was there by the time they hung up the phone.'

All afternoon Presley sang 'Without You', and another song, 'Rag Mop', but the results were by all accounts disappointing. Phillips was on the point of calling the whole thing off and sending the singer home when he asked Elvis if he would like to choose something himself to record. Elvis needed no second bidding, and all the musical influences of his life poured out in a succession of gospel songs, country and western numbers, blues, current chart hits, songs from films, urban songs and black songs that dominated the old rhythm and blues charts, but hardly ever broke into the national ones. It could only have been an amazingly varied performance and it convinced Phillips that maybe he should stick with Presley. He called a local musician, the twenty-one year old guitarist Scotty Moore, to see if he and Elvis could team up for a recording session. Moore asked Elvis to come to his home that evening to try and work something out, but when he arrived at Moore's house, Elvis astonished Mrs Moore by his flamboyant clothes, seemingly at odds with his polite and reserved personality. A neighbour, Bill Black, who was a bass-playing friend of the Moores, heard the music coming from their home and dropped by, but neither he nor Scotty were much taken with Elvis. Perhaps, in view of the fact that this might have been only the first or second time that Elvis had actually made music with professional musicians in his life, Elvis was too reserved in his singing; perhaps, also, he found it difficult to communicate with them verbally at first; but in any event they agreed to call Sam Phillips and arrange a recording session for the three of them at the Sun studios on the following Monday evening.

And so Elvis Presley's professional recording career began, at the age of nineteen, that Monday night, 6 July, 1954, at the Sun studios in Memphis. The first song recorded was 'I Love You Because'; four performances of it were taped, and the first version that was released was spliced from takes two and four. The first take, complete with *parlando* talking, remained unissued for over twenty years. After the four takes had been successfully completed, the boys took a break, presumably to hear all that they had taped so far, and during this break Presley picked up his guitar and started to play and sing 'That's All Right, Mama'. This was a very different number; in fact, a crucial song in the upwardly mobile forces that were soon to burst through the consciousness of music to form rock 'n' roll. Scotty and Bill found themselves joining in freely and, without anyone realising what was happening, the music came together with a freshness and vitality that had not happened before. Now Phillips was truly impressed: he immediately sent the boys back into the studio to repeat on tape what they had just created in the engineering room.

They did not need telling twice, for they must have know that this was it – this was what they had instinctively been striving towards for so long. It was a fusion of separate musical elements, joined by a steady, unvaried yet syncopated beat, but sung in an original manner by a singer whose voice had a naturally distinctive quality. It was unsophisticated and direct, like the best of country music. It was sincere, like the best of folk music. It seemed to be reaching out for some

33

unattainable goal, like the best of blues music. It was rhythmically solid and firm, like the best of dance music. It was all of these things, yet above everything, dominating and leading the resultant mixture, was Elvis Presley's unique and compelling voice – and his manner with the very words of the song, infusing each one, at times, like the best 'art' singer, with underlying meanings and subtleties. Yet it was all essentially so unsubtle, artless and spontaneous: it was the way in which all these elements blended that proved to be utterly and forever fascinatingly original. No music like this had ever before been heard.

Sam Phillips was well pleased with the results of this session. He took an acetate of the intended single to Dewey Phillips – no relation to Sam – who was a white disc jockey on station WHBQ in Memphis. It is important to mention the colour of the DJ; racial discrimination was a fact of life throughout large areas of the Deep South at that time (and for many years afterwards) and, as an example of such discrimination, white DJs did not customarily play records by white and black singers side by side. Almost invariably, they would play entire programmes devoted to singers of one race or the other, but only exceptionally rarely of both. Dewey Phillips's radio programme was devoted to black artists, and the disc jockey had obviously never heard of a truck driver called Elvis Presley, but he must have been as immediately impressed with the record as Sam Phillips was, for he agreed to play the acetate of 'That's All Right, Mama' over the air on his programme the following evening. Sam Phillips had had the recordings edited, and the reference acetate cut, on the day following the evening when the recordings had been made (this day was a Tuesday), and had seen Dewey that same afternoon. With this important airplay promotion guarantee, Sam again lost no time in putting the record into production; he was clearly excited by what he had captured on tape.

We should remember also that the record was first played over the air within forty-eight hours of its actually being taped; this is an aspect of popular record-making in the early 1950s that has not lasted until the present day, but one that some may feel should have. It also indicates how fast the small independent record label can react when it genuinely believes it has a hit on its hands. Like his namesake Sam, Dewey Phillips was taking a risk, but his ears told him the record was well worth the shot. The result was extraordinary, for following the broadcast of the acetate, WHBQ was besieged with calls enquiring about the singer. Knowing the record was to be played over the air, Elvis's reticence finally got the better of him. He decided not to listen to the broadcast, but went to see a movie. As he recalled, 'I was too nervous to sit with Mom to hear the transmission... my parents came looking for me because the radio station received lots of calls.'

Many listeners, so excited by the broadcast that they called the station to demand a replay, were astonished when they discovered that the singer was a white youth; most of them, hearing Elvis's voice for the first time, especially on Dewey Phillips's *Red, Hot And Blue* programme, imagined he was a black singer.

By the time the evening was over, Elvis had been brought from the cinema to be interviewed by Dewey Phillips over the air, and every listener knew he was white.

Sam Phillips continued to move quickly. Ten days after the record had been played on Dewey Phillips's radio show, it was on sale in the stores. At first, some disc jockeys objected to playing what was regarded as a black song by a white singer – and we ought not to forget that it was the unknown black singer's demonstration record that had first led Sam Phillips to call Elvis – and moreover a white singer who sounded as though he was black. But by the end of the month, on 31 July, Elvis's first single stood at number three in the Memphis Country Music chart, and not for the first time the commercial success of a record had caused such reservations by the few doubting disc jockeys to be swept aside.

As we can imagine, Elvis and particularly Gladys and Vernon, together with Sam Phillips and Scotty, Bill and Marion Keisker – all of those who had played their part in the making of the hit record – were thrilled at the success of 'That's All Right, Mama'. The demand for the single led to calls for Elvis and the boys to appear in public. It was comparatively easy for them to get bookings, and they were engaged to appear at both Nashville's famous Grand Ole Opry and Shreveport's Louisiana Hayride – both of which were broadcast. Perhaps because of his comparative unfamiliarity with appearing in public, and also doubtless because of his distinctive stage movements, which were unlike those of any other country singer, Elvis's appearance at the Opry was disastrous. As he left the stage, to desultory applause, the MC Jim Denny told Elvis that he should quit singing and go back to driving a truck. The singer was deeply upset by this remark, although at the time he was still truck driving for Crown, and he never forgot it, but the Louisiana Hayride engagement was quite another matter. By all accounts, Elvis hit it off with the large and enthusiastic audience (although presumably his show was virtually the same as it had been in Nashville) and also with the show's director, Horace Logan, so much so that Elvis and the boys were immediately offered a return booking for a few weeks later. On this second occasion they scored an even bigger success, with the result that Logan lost no time in offering Elvis a year's contract to appear at Shreveport.

To anyone following the early months of Elvis's career, such portents as these – the immediate realisation of the quality and distinctive originality of the first single, the single's success, and the Shreveport contract – would have certainly created the impression that here was someone to be watched. But we should remember that the music business in those days was a very different one form that which it has become today. At this stage of Elvis's career, he was still on an upward learning curve, and it did not take long for him to pick up the essentials of microphone technique even though he never really lost his inherent shyness. Recordings of his last shows, although visually flamboyant, reveal that underneath the trappings he was still a nervous public speaker.

However, the increased number of engagements the boys now commanded meant that they were earning enough money for Elvis to give up his truck-driving

35

job with Crown, although Vernon apparently harboured some misgivings. But his experience of the Depression years of the 1920s and 30s had little impact on the natural ambition of his son, and it is unlikely that Gladys would have done anything to stand in Elvis's way. From then on, therefore, Elvis Presley became a full-time professional singer.

Within the next few months, Bob Neal – a local disc jockey – managed the affairs of the 'Hillbilly Cat', as Elvis had come to be known, as well as those of the band's members, which had now risen to three with the addition of the drummer D.J. Fontana. The success of the first single and the growing number of concerts in southern Tennessee and neighbouring states, led to more sessions with Sam Phillips. Strangely, from our position of hindsight, Phillips did not keep a detailed log of Elvis's recording sessions. This was by no means unusual for popular recordings in those days, although the need for accurate data had certainly arisen with the advent of tape recording (as it brought with it the ability to splice from one take to another) and became essential later on with mixing from various stereophonic channels.

In 1954, popular songs were largely issued on recordings which were straightforward tapings of complete performances. However, as a consequence of the lack of proper documentation, much valuable detailed information is now lost (more correctly, it was never collated) and a certain amount of conjecture is necessary. Nevertheless, it is a fact that in August or September 1954, Elvis recorded at least three more titles, 'I Don't Care If The Sun Don't Shine', 'Good Rockin' Tonight' and 'Just Because'. It is also highly probable that 'Harbour Lights' was recorded at this time, although it was not released until 1976, when it appeared on the album *A Legendary Performer* (Volume 2). Of these songs, 'Good Rockin' Tonight', repeated the success of the first single, reaching number three in the same Memphis charts. This single was released in January 1955, by which time Elvis had recorded (very likely during the previous December), four more titles, 'Milkcow Blues Boogie', 'You're A Heartbreaker', 'I'm Left, You're Right, She's Gone', and 'I'll Never Let You Go' – although it is also possible that this last song was recorded in January 1955.

It may seem puzzling that so many months elapsed between Elvis's first Sun recording session and his second, but again we should not forget that this was common practice in the early and mid-1950s, when the album was by no means the dominant force in recording marketing it later became, and when communication in the world moved at a less technologically instantaneous manner than it does now, in spite of the speed with which Sam Phillips had got Elvis's first single played over the air.

'Milkcow Blues Boogie' was Elvis's third single, but it did not equal the chart success of his first two. However, his public appearances were continuing to grow, and proved crucial both in building up a fan club and providing him with priceless experience in performing before a live audience. Bob Neal was able to use his influence to get Elvis an engagement on 'The Hank Snow Jamboree', a Southern tour which began on 1 May. This was a major step forward in his career, but in more ways than perhaps anyone at that time could have realised, for the person who was employed in promoting the tour was Hank Snow's manager, Colonel Tom Parker.

Colonel Parker was born in Holland in 1909; his original name had been André (nicknamed Dries) van Kuijk and he travelled to the USA first in 1927 and secondly in 1929, before adopting the name Thomas Andrew Parker a few years later. The title 'Colonel' is a valid, although honorary, one, having been granted to him after World War II by a governor of the state of Tennessee. Colonel Parker has always relished the fact that very little is known about certain aspects of his early career, taking the not unreasonable view that the public might feel justified in being interested in the private lives of famous stars, but they ought not to feel the same about those of their staff and managers, and he has often laid a number of false trails concerning himself. He has never hidden his Dutch origins, however. These are largely irrelevant, certainly to a discussion of Elvis Presley's genius, but what is not irrelevant is Colonel Parker's own genius as a promotion man and artist's manager. Whatever his early life in the United States taught him, he evidently was drawn to show business almost from the beginning, and in the 1940s had become the personal manager of the famous country singer Eddy Arnold. Colonel Parker was instrumental in getting Arnold signed to RCA Records at that time, but the singer and his manager parted company in 1951 – amicably, by all accounts – during which year Colonel Parker became Hank Snow's manager.

Within a few days of the start of 'The Hank Snow Jamboree' tour, Colonel Parker saw for himself the tremendous impact Elvis was beginning to have on the youthful element of the audiences, and although he apparently had been aware of Elvis for some time before the tour (which was likely, as he probably had had a say in the support acts for his star, and would not have approved Snow appearing with too inferior, or too major, a talent) he saw at first hand what the 'Hillbilly Cat' could achieve.

In a move that left no ill feeling on the part of anyone involved, Colonel Parker eventually took over the sole management of Elvis's affairs. First, he won the confidence of Vernon and Gladys, and then of the singer himself. Once he had become Elvis's manager, he made steps to get Elvis signed to a major record company, for it was very clear that Sam Phillips did not possess the resources to capitalise on his 'find' as a national record company could, nor could he give the kind of financial support usual for the tour, which Elvis had undertaken with Hank Snow.

Atlantic Records, at the time a comparatively new but nevertheless nationally-established record company, run by a great record man, Ahmet Ertegun, offered $25,000 for the Presley contract. This was indeed a tempting offer, certainly for the time, but Atlantic then lacked the corporate strength of the older established companies. Both CBS (in the United States, then known as Columbia Records) and RCA Records possessed the kind of resources the Colonel evidently had in mind for his singer, and in the event, it was the Colonel's previous association, persistence and negotiating skills that led to his clinching the deal with RCA. In addition, RCA had a growing roster of country and western artists and had an office in Nashville: in those early days, Elvis was still regarded as a Southern country singer. CBS (Columbia) Records, which was then run by the legendary Goddard Lieberson, whose judgement was almost infallible, if in the final analysis a shade too elegant to embrace the rawness of Presley, might have posed some problems for the Colonel. Significantly, in the early years of rock 'n' roll, from about 1956 to 1961, CBS Records had virtually no rock stars of any real note on their label.

And so Steve Sholes of RCA signed Elvis Presley to that company. In addition, RCA bought all the Sun material, both released and unreleased tapes (a move which enabled Sam Phillips to recoup immediately not just his investment but a significant profit for it, typical of Colonel Parker's fairness in his negotiations, and a part of the deal, which Sam Phillips never complained about either at the time or since). In this way, RCA bought everything concerning Elvis Presley on record, and the price was a high one for the times – $35,000 – on top of which has to be added a non-recoverable advance of $5,000 to Elvis himself, who had, of course, never seen so much money in his life before. It seems likely that Elvis started the fashion that was later to be adopted by so many young pop stars when with his $5,000 he 'went out and bought Momma a pink Cadillac'.

Elvis Presley had clearly come a long way in a short time. Circumstances, over which in retrospect we can see he had virtually no control at all, had conspired to place him in the ideal position from which his music-making could reach the world – if indeed the world wanted it. He had been signed to a major record company, and the size of the company's investment was such that it was in their strongest interests to see it recouped. Elvis had also acquired one of the shrewdest, ablest and best-connected managers and publicists in show business, and RCA's international connections were world-wide. There wasn't a market not covered extensively and thoroughly by the RCA Corporation, either directly or through licensing. This was often, as is the case of Great Britain for example, through EMI companies at the time – for both RCA and EMI had the rights to use the trademark His Master's Voice with the famous dog and trumpet; RCA in the USA, and EMI for the rest of the world, a fact that signifies the close ties existing then between the companies.

RCA's financial resources were considerable, and were able to be placed at the disposal of any artist under contract to them. All Elvis Presley had to do was deliver the goods. In spite of all these positive aspects, nobody could have surely foreseen how soon or in what magnitude these goods were triumphantly to be delivered.

Chapter Four

Superstar

E lvis Presley's first recording sessions for RCA had been fixed to take place in Nashville. This was the home of RCA's large and important Country Music organisation, into which part of RCA Record Division Elvis was considered to belong for A&R purposes: there was, of course, no such thing as a separate musical identity for 'rock 'n' roll' in the general public's and record company's perceptions at the end of 1955. No sooner had the release date for his first single for the company been tentatively made, than Colonel Parker arranged for Elvis's first television appearance, on the *Tommy And Jimmy Dorsey Stage Show*, which was networked by CBS. In some ways, this was in the nature of a coup for the Colonel, for the Dorsey ratings appeared to be fighting a losing battle against the *Perry Como Show*, shown at the same time on the NBC network. Interestingly enough, NBC (the National Broadcasting Corporation) was a division within the RCA Corporation.

The classic recordings that emanated from the first RCA sessions in January 1956, including the great and incomparable performance of 'Heartbreak Hotel', led immediately to the release date at the end of the month being confirmed, and the realisation within a significant section of RCA Records that they had a remarkable property on their hands. Television was then – as it is now – the most potent medium for the widest possible exposure, and Elvis's appearance on the *...Stage Show* gave a significant boost to its ratings. He was immediately re-booked, and made such an impact that within weeks he was the talk of America.

Show business moguls could not grasp the massive impact that Elvis's appearances seemed to be having on the youth of America, or the unprecedented demand for his record which followed. Parents tended to be shocked at his apparently explicit sexual movements during these performances, to say nothing of being alarmed by the radically new type of music he seemed to personify.

Within weeks, 'Heartbreak Hotel' had become the biggest selling record on sale in the USA, reaching number 1 in three charts at the same time – the first time in popular music history that this had been achieved. Nor was this all, for with such immediate success within the USA, RCA's world-wide affiliates lost no time in releasing the record in all countries and territories outside America. A few months later, Elvis Presley's impact had become world-wide, for 'Heartbreak Hotel' reached number 1 in the charts of no less than fourteen countries. The demand was remarkable, although many felt that Presley was probably a nine-day wonder. There was therefore much pressure on RCA to issue an album quickly, to capitalise on this sudden demand in case it should suddenly evaporate. As Presley had only recorded a handful of songs for RCA there was not enough material to fill an album. RCA therefore turned to the Sun recordings that had been purchased, and the album was topped-up by the inclusion of several of Sam Phillips's original tapes. This decision was later criticised by some people, who felt that RCA should have waited to get fresh Presley material, and that the inclusion of Sun recordings was an admission of the Corporation's lack of foresight. RCA replied, however, by claiming that having also bought the Sun material at the time when they signed Presley, they were entirely within their rights to use such recordings in whatever manner they felt fit. Furthermore, one of the main reasons for the signing was the proven success of the distinctive Elvis Presley Sun sound, which RCA had done much to emulate in their own studio recordings, and it was logical for them to include examples of it on the first album. Whatever the pros and cons, the album became the classic, definitive, pioneering rock 'n' roll album, and was still selling, all over the world, forty years later.

Colonel Parker had quickly fixed up several important appearances at which Presley's magnetism as a live performer – revealed during his last year at Humes High School, and in his localised tours in 1955 – was demonstrated to a much wider audience. He appeared on television in California, but the constant travelling and live appearances took their toll. He collapsed in Jacksonville, Florida and was taken to hospital. He was warned to curtail his appearances, but he discharged himself within a day or so and continued the state-wide tour.

His live appearances made him a target for assault. Hundreds of screaming girls, raised to fever pitch by his stage movements and the exciting nature of the music itself, would frequently storm the stage, trying to grab him and tear his clothing. Presley said of such incidents '…if they want my shirt they can have it. After all, they put it on my back to start with!'

His hotel rooms were besieged, but not every appearance was received with such tumultuous enthusiasm. In many ways, his act was too unusual, and quite unlike anything most people older than teen-age had seen before. Colonel Parker made a rare error of judgement (or maybe it was just a plot to test the market) when he booked Elvis to appear at the Frontier Hotel, Las Vegas, in the early summer. The audience, mostly made up of middle-aged punters, received the sensation of rock 'n' roll in little more than stony, uncomprehending, silence. In the mid-1950s every aspect of his act was too different and disturbing for the usual customers of such venues. However, fifteen years later Elvis enjoyed some revenge, for by then he had become one of the biggest-drawing and most successful stars on the Las Vegas circuit.

But if Elvis had clearly not broken through to an older generation, no one could ignore the fanatical following he enjoyed within the new teenage market, which, the spearhead of what became known as the 'baby boom' generation, was a very large one in terms of numbers and therefore of record-buying potential. Hollywood – always on the look-out for new artists – became interested. Curiously enough, in the audience at those unsatisfactory performances at the Frontier Hotel was the famous producer Hal Wallis, who asked Colonel Parker to bring Elvis to the Paramount Pictures studios in Hollywood for a screen test.

Stories surrounding this test are legion, and for reasons that have never been satisfactorily explained, Presley was not asked to sing – perhaps Wallis was influenced by the reaction of the Las Vegas audiences. However, on the strength of this test, Wallis offered Presley a three-film contract, his screen début being scheduled for *The Rainmaker* which was to star Burt Lancaster and Katharine Hepburn. In this film, Presley was to play the part of a deranged youth, but in the event he was withdrawn. Perhaps those responsible felt the part might have been beyond his acting capability, or that it would have been wrong for his image as a new symbol for youth. The right part, in the event, was not long in coming.

Meanwhile in Hollywood, Elvis appeared on the Milton Berle television show on 6 June, which was seen by an estimated forty million viewers. This was just over one in five of the total population of the USA. The critics, however, not for the first time in popular music, and certainly not for the last, were in a minority in their condemnation of Presley's television performances. One said '…an unutterable bore… he can't sing a lick… like watching a male stripteaser and a malted milk machine at the same time...', but this pasting in the press meant nothing to the television moguls, who knew a hot property when they saw one. The new *Steve Allen Show* soon booked Elvis but insulted the fans in the process; for Allen got Presley to sing his new hit, 'Hound Dog', in evening dress to a real, if droopy looking, pooch. Although some may have felt (and probably, in retrospect, continue to feel) that Presley was ill-advised to do this, the fact was that the event generated an enormous amount of publicity.

The *Steve Allen Show* clashed with the more successful (in ratings terms) *Ed Sullivan Show* in being shown at the same time. It should be remembered that this was many years before the advent of home video recorders – a show missed was missed for ever. Sullivan had earlier publicly declared that under no circumstances would Elvis Presley ever appear on his show, but the ratings for Elvis's spot on the *Steve Allen Show* caused Sullivan to revise his opinion: Elvis was fast proving his audience-pulling prowess, and was becoming the most sought after musical act on television. The *Ed Sullivan Show*, having had second thoughts, booked Elvis to appear, but it was stipulated that the singer was only to be televised from the waist up, so that his body (and with it the gyratory hip movements that had caused so much concern to the guardians of the nation's morals) would not be seen. As a result (and because the Colonel knew how to make even the most censorial attitude towards his star into extra publicity, working on the principal that the more a thing is banned the more the public seems to want it), 54 million people watched this appearance – a thirty per cent increase on the staggering Milton Berle audience – a total viewing public not exceeded until the Beatles appeared on the same show eight years later.

Quite apart from his music, it was also becoming clear that Elvis's appearances were also beginning to affect young American fashion. His long slicked-back hair, and his casual out-door clothes worn on virtually every occasion, the collar of his shirt or jacket turned up at the back, together with his passion for fast cars, pool, pretty young girls and his generally aggressive stance all had the same kind of influence on young people which his contemporary young American film actors Marlon Brando and James Dean (the latter shortly to die in a horrendous car crash) had also exerted. But Colonel Parker was not slow to 'sell' Elvis Presley franchises to all kinds of manufacturing companies, and as a result bubble-gum cards, posters, pictures, books, magazines amid other paraphernalia – all devoted to Elvis – helped to promote his visual image in the way his records promoted his musical one, quite apart from the attractions of the added incremental income.

In another way, this extension of promotion and publicity was also used deliberately to make the public more aware of Elvis in visual terms in readiness for his imminent film début, so that by the time of his first film, he was almost as well known visually as his co-stars, whoever they might be. We have learned that Elvis had been released from *The Rainmaker*, and although he still had the Paramount Pictures contract, in the event his first film was for Twentieth-Century Fox. Originally entitled 'The Reno Brothers', under which it was shot, it was finally released as *Love Me Tender* – one suspects the hand of Colonel Parker in this change of title, for the song 'Love Me Tender' was to be Presley's next single, which he sang on a return appearance on the *Ed Sullivan Show* later in October of that year. Interestingly enough, the producer of the film was David Weisbart – a shrewed choice, for Weisbart had produced James Dean's most successful film, *Rebel Without A Cause*, a movie which reflected the youthful, inarticulate, rebelliousness of America's young generation, a year before.

Whatever success Dean had justifiably had in portraying the problems of inarticulate youth, Presley's success was anything but inarticulate. He broke off from filming to return to Tupelo, where the town had nominated an 'Elvis Presley Day'. The civic authorities gave him the freedom of the city and a gift of $5,000. With his growing fame and fortune, Elvis naturally wished to secure the future for himself and his parents. Later in 1956, he bought a green and white ranch on Audubon Drive, on the outskirts of the city of Memphis. He had a swimming-pool installed (mainly for decoration, as he was not a keen swimmer) and a garage had to be built to accommodate his three cars.

Three weeks before *Love Me Tender* opened at the Paramount Theater on Broadway – the day before it was simultaneously released at 550 cinemas throughout the United States – Elvis appeared on the *Ed Sullivan Show* to sing the title song of the film. Within days of his appearances, and the film's opening, the song was the biggest-selling record in the country and the film had recouped the Studios' investment. No one needed telling twice: less than three weeks later, Presley had begun work on his second film, *Loving You*. This was the first under his original three-film Paramount contract.

Elvis returned home to Memphis to celebrate Christmas with his family. While back in his adopted city, he dropped by the Sun Recording Studios to look up Sam Phillips and other friends. Whether appraised of his visit or not, also present on one occasion were Carl Perkins, Johnny Cash and Jerry Lee Lewis – artists whom Phillips had previously discovered and recorded – and Phillips actually taped five numbers performed by this star-studded quartet.

It would seem that this tape has been lost, for Johnny Cash recalls that some songs were recorded by all of them. There is photographic evidence that proves the four stars were all there at the same time, but Phillips did manage to record

43

many more numbers with Elvis, Carl Perkins and Jerry Lee Lewis – as it was near Christmas, there were a lot of religious songs recorded on that occasion. The labrynthine contractual problems associated with these artists prevented a major commercial issue of this material for many years. It was not until 1990, thirty-four years after the sessions took place, that the material was finally cleared for release.

By the beginning of the new year, 1957, virtually everything Elvis Presley did was news. The film studios had to cope with hundreds of letters every day and thousands of telephone calls, to say nothing of the incessant demands from the press for interviews and preview shots of the film. It is no doubt true to say that Elvis Presley received the most intensive publicity of any star at the time, and it says much for his inner strength of character that he was not only able to withstand this pressure so well, but also remain at heart the genuinely polite and – in company – shy, reserved person he had always been.

His acting, however, did not quite reveal him to be another James Dean. Although he was clearly much more than competent, his film appearances lacked the same creative dynamism as his singing. However, no one in show business could afford to ignore his enormous earning potential, which, thanks to RCA's world-wide connections, had been triumphantly demonstrated in many countries. In May 1957, Elvis began shooting his third film, the MGM production of *Jailhouse Rock*. This was a tougher proposition than either of his first two films: he had to be up each morning at 6.30 am, and the day's shooting did not finish before 6 pm. In the film, he was required to drive an excavator and dance, as well as play the most demanding role he had undertaken for the screen so far.

The result was an unqualified success. *Jailhouse Rock* remains the best of the first three films he made, for it has clearly stood the test of time. Part of its success has to be placed in the remarkable 'Jailhouse Rock' sequence, which has become one of the most potent visual images for 1950s rock music. Elvis received $250,000 for the film, plus half of the profits: over the years it made him millions. With the advance money, he bought a new residence to replace his home on Audubon Drive. This new – and bigger – property was located in a suburb of Memphis called Whitehaven, an exclusive residential district of the city, into which it became incorporated in 1969.

This new property, comprising thirteen-and-a-half acres, was named Graceland. It had been built some years before World War I – about the time of the birth of Elvis's grandfather Jessie, in fact – by a Dr Thomas Moore, who named it after his wife's aunt, Grace Toof, from whom the Moores' had inherited the land. The full address of Graceland was 3764 Highway 51 South at the time Elvis bought it – for $100,000, a sum which in those days was a high price for such a property.

At the end of September 1957, with the alterations to Graceland nearing completion, Elvis returned to Tupelo for a charity concert in aid of the city's Elvis Presley Recreational Center before flying to Hawaii for concerts at the Honolulu Stadium. This was his first journey outside mainland America, apart from an earlier tour of Canada, and he found himself very much taken by Hawaii. On his return to Graceland, indeed virtually before he had been able to live in his new home for any length of time, he received his Army call-up papers from the Memphis Draft Board, for induction into the United States Army. This was to serve his two years' compulsory national service, as part of the USA's contribution to the land forces of the fifteen-nation North Atlantic Treaty Organisation. He was scheduled to appear before the Draft Board on 20 January, 1958, which effectively would have been the day of his actually joining the Army, but he applied for a deferment on the grounds that he had begun work on what was his fourth film, *King Creole*, the second of the originally contracted Paramount Pictures movies. The deferment was granted, and a new date, 24 March, was set for his appearance before the Draft Board.

It should be remembered that there was nothing unusual in this deferment. Although every young man was legally liable for national service, there was no indication when the papers would be served; consequently, they could come at a time that was inconvenient to the recipient, and any number of reasons were acceptable to the Draft Board for deferment. Presley sought no special privilege, and none was given in this instance; very many young men of similar age were granted concessions.

King Creole was finished on time, and proved to be one of Presley's best films, for in it his natural acting ability is clearly revealed in a manner which is not true of his first two films. Indeed, if we consider *Jailhouse Rock* and *King Creole* side by side, it is surely obvious that he had more than found his acting feet, and was set fair to pursue a significant career in films. If we jump forward to the first two films he made following his Army discharge, *G.I. Blues* and *Flaming Star*, these consecutive films form a truly remarkable and impressive quartet of varied performances. We shall consider this aspect of his career in a later chapter, but we should mention now that had it not been for his forced military service, his film career might have taken a very different, and undoubtedly better, overall course.

However, the director of *King Creole*, Michael Curtiz, was much respected and highly experienced in Hollywood. He had made a considerable name for himself at Warner Brothers' studios; the addition of such stars as Walter Matthau, Dean Jagger and Carolyn Jones enhanced the appeal of this remarkable film. The story, loosely based on the best-selling novel *A Stone For Danny Fisher* by Harold

Robbins, was superior to those of Presley's first three films. When *King Creole* was released in June 1958, it was well reccived by the critics, even including those who had not previously given Elvis much credit for his acting. But by the date of the film's release Elvis had been in the American Army for over two months, and his careers – as a singer and film actor – were, temporarily at least, at an end.

Chapter Five

Soldier of fortune

When he woke up on the morning of 24 March, 1958 Elvis Presley was an American civilian, but when he eventually went to bed late that night he was an American soldier. He reported that day for his induction into the Army at Memphis Draft Board number 86. He was accompanied by his parents and by his friend Lamar Fike. Elvis stepped forward when his name was called, the step signifying his acceptance of Army induction, and he became Private Presley, E.A., no. 53310761. With that day's fellow draftees he boarded an Army bus, crossing the Mississippi River due west across the state line for Fort Chaffee, Arkansas, to commence his basic Army training.

The basic training was scheduled to last for six weeks, during which he – like all other draftees – was required to live on the camp. At the end of this time, his hair shorn to regulation length, his Army clothing tailored to fit, his skills added to by the ability to salute, march in order and fire both rifle and machine gun, he was transferred to Fort Hood, where his specialist Army training now commenced. During this longer period of training, and with the soldier now having passed out of the initial part of his service, Army personnel could be permitted to live out of camp, if members of their family lived within easy travelling distance. Elvis had rented a bungalow at Killean, a small town nearly, to which Vernon and Gladys moved so that he could join them early in May.

Despite the obvious upheaval that his Army service had caused to his career and his own life, Elvis was in good spirits. He had learned that his fourth film had achieved a great measure of success, and sales of his records (it should be remembered that by this time he had achieved something like ten consecutive number one records in the USA alone) had actually increased when he joined the

Army. During the previous few months, he had added another significant recording 'first' to his growing laurels – 'Jailhouse Rock', when released as a single in the UK, became the first ever such record to enter the charts at number one. At the very least, he knew that his loyal fans – now numbering millions world-wide – had not deserted him.

Once again, a change in Presley's life found him well able to cope. A year or two before, his phenomenal rise to stardom had left him, by all accounts, basically unchanged as a person. Now, thrown into a completely different environment, where his money meant nothing, yet constantly surrounded by publicity in almost everything he did, he again demonstrated his level-headedness. His response to Army life generally was a source of great relief to the Army authorities, who were concerned at the ballyhoo surrounding his enlistment. Some originally feared that he might throw the sort of tantrums associated with spoilt stars, or become emotionally disturbed by the authority to which he would be forced to submit. Other Army personnel thought he might have been better advised to have become part of the Army's Special Services Corps, reserved for those with outstanding skills as sportsmen, entertainers or artists, who were permitted to continue with their chosen professions, albeit within a military environment, in which their unique and creative activities would be placed at the service of the Army, and performed for the benefit of their fellow soldiers. As a world-famous entertainer, clearly Elvis would have been a prime contender for the Special Services Corps. But in a sense, such members were seen to receive special privileges, something which is invariably resented by other national servicemen. Elvis asked for no such special treatment, and became a much-liked trainee soldier, treated the same as all the others.

After he had completed the ten weeks of specialist training, he was granted his first full weekend pass. Colonel Parker, as well as RCA, had been waiting for this break from Army life for their artist. The opportunity was taken for Elvis to record some new songs at RCA's Nashville studios; this took place on 10 and 11 June. The result was very successful, for these sessions turned out to be two of his best up to that time, producing several major international hits.

However, in spite of these trouble-free months, family matters now began to concern Elvis. By the beginning of July, Gladys Presley was obviously unwell, and it was decided that she should return to Memphis by train, rather than by road or plane. There she was admitted to the Methodist Hospital where, four days later, hepatitis was diagnosed. By 11 August, her condition had deteriorated to the extent that Elvis could immediately apply for compassionate leave on the grounds of his mother's illness. He flew to Memphis – a brave step for him, as he had a deep fear of flying – and he began a round-the-clock vigil at his mother's bedside with Vernon. However, the course of the final stages of the disease was inexorable, and early in the morning of 14 August, 1958 Vernon broke the news to his son that Gladys had died of a heart attack, brought on by the hepatitis. By a particularly melancholy coincidence, the father of Elvis's High School friend, and now bodyguard, Red West, died eight hours later.

We have seen in some detail how close the bond had been between Elvis and his mother, and it is not difficult to imagine how profoundly the shock and deep distress her untimely death affected him. His reaction was traumatic, and years later those close to Elvis claimed that he never recovered from the shock of her death.

But the American Army, although sympathetic to the death of a close family member and giving all due compassionate leave to the soldier, waits for no man for ever. Elvis was now a fully trained soldier, who was required to serve his time as and where called upon to do so, and by the beginning of September, not quite three weeks after Gladys's death, he had been transferred to the 3rd Armored Division, prior to posting to West Germany as part of the US contribution to the NATO forces stationed there. Eventually, on 26 September, Elvis travelled by train with his fellow soldiers to the Brooklyn Naval Yard in New York City, to join the troopship USS *General Randall*. Even then, however, his embarkation brought about a cluster of radio and other interviews, duly taped by RCA and released on record, and the by-now customary photo calls on the dockside, prior to his embarkation for sailing to the West German port of Bremerhaven.

At the last moment, while on the quayside taking farewell of his family and friends, Elvis suddenly decided to get them to follow him to Germany within a few weeks, where they could all live together for the duration of his posting, invoking the same Army rule that had enabled him to live with his parents at Killean, near Fort Hood.

And so a month later Vernon, together with his mother Minnie Presley (then in her mid-sixties), Red West and Lamar Fike, joined Elvis in Germany. He had been stationed at Freiburg, in Baden-Württemberg (south-west Germany) situated near the River Rhine and the Black Forest. It is an old established city, a tourist attraction and cultural centre. His family and friends first stayed at the Grunewald Hotel in Bad Hauheim, and later they moved into a house on Goestrasse. Shortly afterwards, with Elvis made up to sergeant and enjoying the company of other senior NCOs, he invited Sergeant Bill Stanley and his wife Davada (Dee) home to meet his folks. Mr and Mrs Stanley had three sons, all under the age of six, and they all became great friends of the Presleys.

By all accounts, Elvis settled down well to his duties in Germany, and his fame did very little to disrupt his Army life. His fan mail, however, was prodigious, averaging over ten thousand letters a week. Colonel Parker (and RCA) had nothing to fear by his absence from admirers: they were clearly not deterred by his momentary official work elsewhere. Many of the letters were addressed simply to 'Elvis, Germany'. In some ways, his untroubled Army service was a bonus to the military authorities, for he demonstrated that there really was very little to it. He replied, in answer to a press question about the effect his Army service was having on his singing career, 'I'm in the Army, and that's my job at the moment.' For him, it was as simple as that; he did not ask for, and did not receive, any special treatment from the Army (if he had have done, it would have been world news, and bad news at that) and he also seemed to get on well with the local civilian population. He seemed genuinely to enjoy Army life, and one activity his military career introduced him to was karate – just how significant a part this was to play in his later private life no one could have foreseen at the time. However, Elvis soon developed a passion for karate, which he retained for the rest of his life, and on one occasion, when he was attacked on stage by a gang of thugs, it probably saved his life. Red West has reported that from time to time on Army manoeuvres Elvis and his fellow soldiers were issued with amphetamines to keep them awake for long periods. This was probably Elvis's first encounter with stimulants, to which some claimed he also developed an addiction, which lasted until his death.

While Sergeant Bill Stanley and his wife Dee were frequent and welcome visitors to the Presley household, their marriage had begun to deteriorate. After several months as friends of the Presleys, Bill and Dee separated, and were divorced not long afterwards. During this period, Dee and Vernon's friendship was blossoming into love. Elvis, meantime, had met the United States Army officer Captain Joseph P. Beaulieu, and through him his fourteen year old adopted daughter Priscilla, who was apparently already very mature for her age, both physically and mentally. It was not long before Elvis began calling at the Beaulieu home with some frequency.

During the eighteen months of Elvis's Army service in Germany, his duties were very similar to those of most other non-commissioned officers. He was a skilled shot, becoming a marksman and winning two medals for his ability. His main work at Freiburg centred around his role as an assistant squad leader, which entailed a great deal of jeep driving, on and off camp; in all, his Army career was reasonably uneventful, but he clearly enjoyed this enforced separation from his performing career, although he certainly sang frequently during this period, mainly for friends and associates.

His film career had been so successful that plans were being laid for the first film on his return to civilian life, the story being based on aspects of his – and therefore most of his contemporaries' – Army service. Paramount Pictures began filming location shots for the film in Germany. Those shots, which required Presley to seem to appear, were filmed using a stand-in; as his Army contract forbade any outside work, under no circumstances could he begin filming while still a soldier. However, the location shots meant that, on his discharge, the film could be quickly completed, which would also capitalise on the publicity generated by his return to civilian life.

At the beginning of 1960, with his discharge now merely weeks rather than months away, the commanding officer of the unit to which he was assigned decided to host a farewell party for their famous soldier. By an extraordinary coincidence, it was arranged and organised by Captain Marion Keisker – the very same Marion Keisker who had worked for Sam Phillips at Sun Records in the early

1950s, and who had been instrumental in pushing Elvis's name and getting Phillips to record him. Some years later, she left Memphis and joined the US Army; on being promoted to the rank of captain, she was posted to Germany where she met up again with 'her' singer. The party took place on 1 March; two days later Elvis returned to Fort Dix, New Jersey by plane. The aircraft landed at Prestwick in Scotland for refuelling, which entailed a stop of a little over an hour, and which enabled the military personnel on board to leave the plane for a while. In this way, Elvis managed to set foot, for the only time in his life, in the British Isles.

Elvis was formally discharged from the Army on 4 March, and the following day he returned to Graceland with his family and friends. He was now free to resume his career, and, having rested for a few weeks to consider his future – or, rather, the future Colonel Parker had outlined for him, a continuation of the record and film career, which had proved so successful before his military service.

In April, just over a month after his discharge, he made his first professional appearance in over two years by being a guest on Frank Sinatra's television show, the *Timex Special*. In addition to singing solo, he also sang duets with Sinatra. This was something new, for such an appearance could hardly have been considered by either singer prior to Elvis's Army career. In a sense, this was the first time that Elvis was calculated to aim at an older, and larger, audience through the most important medium of television. In spite of his recuperation, Elvis had already appeared in the recording studios, and on the film set, and he travelled to Hollywood, where the first priority was to finish *G.I. Blues*, the final title of the feature film based on his Army life.

It is clear that whoever was responsible for handling Elvis's public image while he was in the Army had done an outstanding job. Colonel Parker, of course, has to take much of the credit, for his publicity skills ensured that Elvis's discharge received enormous media coverage. The discharge itself was not particularly noteworthy; after all, Elvis could not remain in the Army for ever, and had to leave sometime. But the decision not to allow too much material to be released during his two years away meant that Presley was not over-exposed, at the same time as keeping his name in the public eye. In addition, it should be remembered that Elvis Presley was the first major popular singer in the western world to have served his national service in the Army, submitting to the two-year interruption in his performing career.

Furthermore, the public saw that Elvis had been prepared to do his service along with everyone else, with, as we have noted earlier, no special favours asked and none granted. In a sense, this was even more difficult for him, as anyone who is famous in the services almost has to be better than everyone else, merely in order to show that they are the same as everyone else. Presley had been a good soldier, and this led to a change of heart on the part of those members of the older generations to whom, before his Army career, he represented a somewhat dangerous public figure. For middle-class Americans, Elvis Presley had now matured into a good, all-round American boy.

51

In this way, therefore, his experience was also similar to those of millions of his contemporaries, who could readily relate to him, as now he could to them; his Army service proved to have been something of a blessing in disguise, a fact not lost on Colonel Parker, who was able to extract a significant amount of highly favourable publicity for his artist.

Another aspect of the infrequency of Presley recordings issued during his Army service was that during those two years Elvis was unable to develop his musicianship; if RCA had released any less than first-class recordings during this period (some comparatively poor material still being kept 'in the can') in order to keep the public reasonably happy, the result would almost certainly have done irreparable damage to the singer's long-term career. It may be claiming too much to suggest that all of these events were carefully planned, either by the Colonel or by RCA, or by both, but the fact remains that as things transpired, his national service – at that time – was probably the best thing that could have happened to him as far as his career was concerned.

Elvis Presley's homecoming therefore was in marked contrast to the reception he had been accorded by middle-class America four years before. In 1956, Billy Graham had said of Elvis: 'From what I've heard, I'm not sure I'd want my children to see him,' but in 1960 the State of Mississippi passed a resolution welcoming Presley back, citing him 'a legend and inspiration to tens of millions of Americans and hence he reaffirms a historic American ideal that success in our nation can be attained through individual initiative, hard work, and abiding faith in one's self and in the Creator.'

The train which carried the newly demobilised civilian from New Jersey in Hampshire to Memphis in Tennessee was delayed at every stop, being mobbed by thousands of fans en route, with the singer being called upon to appear on the platform of the last carriage, at whistle-stops, almost as if he were the latter-day equivalent of some earlier presidential candidate. When Elvis and his party finally arrived at Memphis Central Railroad Station, to something approaching a hero's welcome, the police escort of the entourage from the centre of the city to Elvis's Graceland home was immense, and for most of the rest of the day parts of Memphis were reduced to a traffic jam. Elvis had returned.

Chapter Six

Easy come, easy go

A few weeks after his return to Memphis, Elvis travelled to Nashville for is first post-army recording sessions. The sessions, as might perhaps have been expected, proved to be a very extensive series of recordings. What might not have been so immediately expected was the somewhat softer approach and overall tenor of the songs conveyed in them – by no means as raunchy or as revolutionary as his recordings had generally been in the two years prior to his Army call-up, those during 1956–58. It should be emphasised, however, that the dynamic of his recorded performances at these early April sessions remained utterly undiminished; although he had acquired an additional but thin veneer of softness in his ballad singing, the famous Presley power remained.

His television appearance with Frank Sinatra in April (for which Sinatra had paid the then astronomical sum of $125,000 in order for Elvis to sing just two songs) tended to emphasise this comparative lack of aggression. This point was reflected and commented upon in the review published in the show business weekly *Billboard*:

'...the expected dynamic was, to put it mildly, a bit over-rated.'

Elvis resumed his film career with the long-planned Paramount Pictures film, *G.I. Blues*, directed by Norman Taurog, and co-starring Juliet Prowse. One of his first post-Army single record releases, 'It's Now Or Never', an English language version of the famous old Neapolitan song, 'O Sole Mio', with some distinguished pianism from Floyd Cramer, proved to be a gigantic transcontinental hit, stemming as it did from the star's exposure to European influence during his

Army service. This was also reflected in the song 'Wooden Heart', recorded later in the summer of 1960 and used in the film, which was based on an old German folk-song: Elvis sings about a third of it in German. But his first new single for two years, 'Stuck On You', had been very much in his earlier vein, a hit to be sure, but perhaps almost predictably so in the circumstances.

However, this sustained record success (Elvis in the event had three consecutive number 1 records in Britain – the first artist ever to achieve this feat) meant that he now appealed to a new generation, reaching middle-of-the-road stations and radio shows. He was beginning to find a new audience among listeners who previously would not have heard a Presley single on their favourite radio show. His film acting, also, in *G.I. Blues* showed a different Presley from that portrayed in *Jailhouse Rock* or *King Creole*, as he now appeared with small children and even puppets, showing him to be more of an all-round entertainer. This aspect of his developing career might have proved beneficial to him, but it did not work out that way. Elvis's television appearance with Sinatra proved to be his last for over eight years.

On 3 July, 1960 Vernon Presley and Dee Stanley were finally married. Elvis, however, chose not to attend their wedding ceremony, which took place in Huntsville, Alabama. The event did not come as a surprise to Elvis, for Vernon and Dee had told him of their intention almost a year earlier, when they were all in Germany. Indeed, according to some reports, they actually asked Elvis for permission to marry – which he is reputed to have readily given, not wishing to stand in the way of his father's future happiness, but equally being somewhat nonplussed as Dee and Vernon were openly living together.

However, his decision not to attend the ceremony caused no little comment. On the one hand, there were those who felt privately that in some way Elvis resented Dee Stanley's entry into Vernon's life, and the circumstances that led to his remarriage. Equally, it was also clear that Elvis's attachment to his late mother's memory was so strong that he could not – so comparatively soon after her death – bring himself to attend the wedding of the woman who would, in certain circumstances, have to take Gladys's place in his life, and in all respects take her place in Vernon's. But on the other hand, as the 'official' explanation claimed, it ought to have been equally clear that having only just been discharged from the Army, Elvis's live appearances were still few and far between: the occasion of a wedding is essentially one dominated by the happy couple, and if Elvis Presley were to have attended the ceremony there is little doubt that his appearance would have caused something approaching a riot, detracting from the couple and possibly leading to an unfortunate incident – events that no one would wish to happen to mar a couple's wedding day.

In addition, at this time Elvis was completing the filming of *G.I. Blues*, and had had, even during the making of the picture, more than his share of attention. Visitors to the set included the King and Queen of Thailand and Scandinavian princesses from Sweden, Norway and Denmark, among other dignitaries. It would seem, therefore, that although feelings for his mother played some part in his decision not to attend Vernon and Dee's marriage, respect for his father's present and future happiness made up his mind for him. Elvis's innate sensitivity was here, we can be sure, demonstrated in its best light.

In any event, as soon as the film was finished, Elvis was required to return to the Twentieth-Century Fox studios to make what was in many ways the most remarkable film of his career. This was the western drama *Flaming Star*, directed by Don Siegel. In this film, Elvis plays a half-breed – with an Indian mother (Dolores Del Rio) and a white father (John McInture). The tension begins early on when a marauding band of Kiowa Indians massacres a white family, neighbours of Presley's own, an event that causes the townspeople to demand a choice of all members of Elvis's home as to where their allegiances lie. Elvis turned in what is clearly the finest acting performance of his career, but the film was comparatively unsuccessful. It should be remembered that the public expectation for Elvis's first post-Army film was immense, no matter what it was: *G.I. Blues* is a good film, cleverly punctuated with above average songs, and one that appealed to a wide audience. It fitted the demands of the time admirably, and proved to be enormously successful. With such self–evident popularity, Twentieth-Century Fox naturally wished to capitalise on the success of their competitors. *Flaming Star* was completed quickly, although the resultant film betrays no signs of haste, and was rushed out by Christmas of 1960, 20 December, two months to the day after the première of *G.I. Blues*, which was still doing phenomenal business.

The public, which had flocked to *G.I. Blues,* had not had their expectations dashed, and naturally went to see *Flaming Star*; but many were puzzled by the newer film. Whereas in *G.I. Blues* there were no less than ten songs, several of which became notable hits, in *Flaming Star* there were only two, the first of which is heard over the opening credits and the second within minutes of the start – and that, musically, was all. While the audience got from Elvis an acting role of astonishing promise, the lack of music (the story is serious drama; no other music could logically have been added without ruining the film) is said to have upset many fans who expected another musical – a not unnatural expectation in the circumstances.

But there is another reason, a social one, which is hardly ever remarked upon in discussions of this film. By 1960, the burgeoning civil rights movement in the United States had reached national proportions. The decade 1958–68, which culminated in the assassination of Martin Luther King in Memphis, was the most significant in the struggle for the rights of black people in America since the abolition of slavery. The racial undertones of *Flaming Star* with the bigotry and tension surrounding the mixed marriage of his screen parents, were so clearly delineated as to have struck a responsive chord in the audience – even though, it is safe to assume, not many would have been consciously aware of it. But it is significant that for thirty years, this film was banned in South Africa – the only Elvis film so to be. In addition, Presley himself was a Southerner, the region where the black struggle was to make itself more clearly felt.

One does not wish to make too much of the film's racial conflict, for it is very sensitively handled by the director and not made a dominant force in the story – although Elvis's brother (played by Steve Forrest) is shown to be fully white like their father, which causes some tension as a local girl prefers Forrest to Elvis for that very reason. Nevertheless, in the concluding third of the film, Elvis reverts almost completely to his Indian roots. The race element in the film was unacceptable to the lighter demands of public taste at the time.

Today, we are able to watch the film with our perceptions unaffected by those contemporary factors that led to its failure at the box-office. There is no doubt that Fox made a serious miscalculation in their handling of *Flaming Star*; they were contracted to do one more Presley film, but they never exercised this option, making no further movies with him. The comparative – but only comparative, for it did fair business, and made an adequate profit for Fox – lack of success of *Flaming Star* also led to back-pedalling from film-makers in casting Elvis in roles which demanded more acting than singing ability. This was a tragedy – akin to his lack of blues recordings, a genre in which he was an undoubted master – since both *King Creole* and *Flaming Star* showed that he possessed genuine acting talent.

As a result, the years 1960–65 saw Elvis Presley consolidate his wealth, but neither his musical nor his acting character. Those years at Graceland, in the company of a group of like-minded friends who came to be dubbed the 'Memphis Mafia' led – almost inevitably – to a certain indolence in his lifestyle, which at times certainly went too far. Yet at other times Elvis's natural warmth and generosity also went – by most standards – too far: the cars and lavish gifts, which he showered on the most casual of acquaintances, were many but his contributions to charities and deserving causes were almost always made anonymously, these donations having come to light only since his death.

The retrenchment in Elvis's career extended to his public appearances: his immediate post-Army success was not confined to the United States. In England, in particular, he had become without question the most important popular singer of his day, and as such was invited in 1961 to appear at the London Palladium before Her Majesty Queen Elizabeth II. But the conditions imposed by Colonel Parker – among which were that Presley would only accept if he could be presented to Her Majesty – meant that the invitation had to be withdrawn. Colonel Parker handled this badly: such a condition was completely out of the question, and in addition it demonstrated not only his ignorance of protocol but also his insensitivity in dealing with these matters. What was surely not pointed out to Colonel Parker was that the stars appearing in the show are almost invariably presented to the Royal party at the theatre. If Presley had accepted the invitation, there was every reason to believe that he would have met the Queen – indeed, there would have been a public outcry had he not been presented – but unfortunately the invitation could not be proceeded with, and he was consequently never asked to appear again in a show which is possibly the most prestigious variety event in the world.

In September 1961, Dee Presley became pregnant; she and Vernon told Elvis that he would shortly have a half-brother or sister. By some accounts he was outwardly pleased at the news, although to be twenty-seven years older than the infant was doubtless a sobering thought. However, shortly afterwards Dee suffered a miscarriage and never conceived again.

A few weeks later Elvis welcomed Priscilla Beaulieu to Graceland to stay with Vernon and Dee for Christmas. This was an unusual circumstance, for Priscilla was still only fifteen, and the idea of her staying at the Presley household would have raised several eyebrows. It was clearly explained that she would be chaperoned by Elvis's family, and she would be able to finish her schooling at a Catholic High School – the School of the Immaculate Conception – in Memphis. Her father had by then been promoted to the rank of major and had been posted to Travis Air Force Base, near San Francisco, but one other reason for his agreeing to let his daughter stay at Graceland was the clear undertaking given by Elvis that he intended to marry Priscilla. On that basis, Priscilla's stay with Vernon and Dee became permanent in January 1962.

From 1961 to 1968, Elvis Presley made twenty-one more feature films, none of which compares with the best of his previous screen work. This succession of films and their accompanying sound-track albums, led to less and less work in the recording studio. For over two years, in fact, from January 1964 to May 1966, Presley recorded nothing but sound-tracks for a collection of indifferent movies.

This was a flagrant waste of his talent: the question might be asked why he put up with it. He must have had, if only at an instinctive level, an estimation of his own worth as an artist. He wanted. He wanted to perform and to sing: after all, that was what he was born to do. But his upbringing, and the protection from the outside world which his lifestyle afforded him, to say nothing of the great wealth that he enjoyed, doubtless made him feel that any change in the creative routine might possibly be for the worse. Quite apart from anything else, he could not have remained immune from the massive transcontinental impact the Beatles and other major English rock bands were having in the five years from 1963–68. This was a new development, if in essence being nothing more than the musical break-out of the 'baby boom' generation – a greater reflection, ten years after the event, of Elvis's spearheading of the first rock and roll revolution – and was something that Elvis could do little to combat, even assuming he wished to do so. He was so firmly established as a certain type of singer – albeit of a very wide range of material – that the prevalent fashion for groups, almost all of whom were English, and who wrote and performed their own material to the virtual exclusion of any other songs, meant his style was eclipsed. Rather than change to meet the altered circumstances (which he could quite easily have done) he found himself being locked into a format that may have been financially secure but which creatively was extremely confining to him.

Presley's creative life, therefore, during this period fell into the routine of an average of three films a year, some made in as little as sixteen days, for which he received $1,000,000 a picture plus a share of the profits, accompanied by sound-track albums as his only record releases. With few exceptions, the films were as formula-filled as the familiar 'made-for-television' movies of the 1970s and 80s: they remained, however, the only means by which the public could hear and see Elvis Presley.

But such a formula inevitably led to a continuing fall-off in his record sales. RCA became concerned at the decline in revenue, and eventually persuaded Elvis to record a new religious album in Nashville in May 1966. This was his first major studio visit for over three years, and there is also no doubt that the success of the resultant album was both welcome and long overdue. But it was still some time before he returned to the recording studio again, although the subsequent changes in his film-making (a slowing-up in the number of films made, and a greater musical quality in the choice of material used) proved to be a wholly beneficial move.

Even Elvis Presley could not remain entirely immune to the changes then sending shock waves through the world of popular music. A visit to Hollywood by the Beatles in August 1965 led to Elvis hosting a party for the four Liverpudlians at his Hollywood home on the 27th of that month. Photographers were forbidden, but it is known that the five played and sang together, once they had all overcome their initial reserve. It is not entirely beyond the bounds of possibility that Elvis's home tape machine could have been switched on; but we must discount such speculation, for had it been the resultant tape would undoubtedly have surfaced by now. Equally, Presley's life was a private one, and he controlled his staff strictly. Who knows? A tape of just one song by Elvis Presley and the Beatles would represent all kinds of riches, but would even Elvis have had the temerity to have ensured such an impromptu session was recorded? At heart, he remained the shy country boy and would surely have hesitated to make such an arrangement.

Another aspect of his Southern upbringing, which also remained with him, was his strong affection for animals. In February 1967, he bought a ranch near Walls in DeSoto Country, Mississippi, just across the state line, ten miles south of Graceland. He named it Circle G and stocked it with thoroughbred horses. At Graceland in the early 1960s, he had a smaller collection of fine horses stabled behind the mansion, as well as a collection of peacocks strutting on the lawns. In addition, his pet dog Muffin endeared himself to his master although many friends and visitors reported that the animal was bad-tempered. Perhaps the most remarkable of Elvis's pets was Scatter, a chimpanzee with curious habits: he drank neat bourbon, was trained to use the bathroom, and had his own tailor-made clothes. Scatter was a great favourite with the 'Memphis Mafia', but some rumoured antics by the animal had better remain unreported. For all Elvis's enthusiasm for the Circle G ranch, demonstrated by his expenditure of over $500,000 within a few months, a more important event was beginning to occupy his mind, an event which in many ways was to dominate the rest of his life.

Chapter Seven

The last decade

At 9.41 am on 1 May, 1976 Elvis Presley and Priscilla Beaulieu were married in a private suite at the Aladdin Hotel in Las Vegas, Nevada. Judge David Zenoff, a Justice of the state's Supreme Court, performed the private ceremony, with only a few witnesses. The newlyweds then flew to Hollywood so that Elvis could complete his current film, *Clambake*. Two days later, Elvis and Priscilla returned to Memphis, where they hosted a lavish party for those friends and members of their staff who had not attended the wedding. Shortly after his marriage, Elvis bought a large house in Los Angeles, reputedly at a cost of $400,000, to be his permanent home when filming in Hollywood.

Nine months to the day after the wedding, on 1 February 1968, Priscilla gave birth to a daughter, who was christened Lisa Marie. In the event, she was to be Elvis and Priscilla's only child. This proved to be a particularly happy time for Elvis.

Recording sessions at the RCA studios in Nashville in September produced several important tracks, particularly 'Guitar Man' and 'Big Boss Man'; at the same time negotiations had been in train to bring to fruition another very important event, nothing less than his first television spectacular, to be screened by NBC and recorded in colour. This was not only the first such Presley special, but also the first time he had appeared before an audience – albeit via a telerecording – since his performances in Hawaii in 1961.

The director chosen to make the television show, Steve Binder, was keen to make not only a photographic record of Presley singing a selection of his hit records – something that had not really existed before – but also he wanted to recapture something of the electricity and excitement of the early rock 'n' roll era alongside big production numbers (at one stage Elvis appeared within his own name spelled out in lights twenty feet high).

The television special was to be a moment of truth for Elvis: and he knew it. He admitted to several friends before the filming that he was very nervous about appearing before an audience again – even though, in the studio, the number of people making up the audience would be small in comparison with his earlier pre-Army crowds, and would be drawn from a greater social cross-section than he had been used to appearing before (one couple in the second or third row were certainly well past retirement age, and occasionally can be seen discussing the performance taking place a few feet from them!). Presley was also anxious as to whether he would be able to engender the old excitement. But from his first dramatic entry, in a black all-leather outfit, the chemistry worked – even though one can see his hands visibly shaking at first. He proved himself once again to be a magisterial performer, an incomparable rock artist – and this, it should be remembered, at a time (1968) when the later rock explosion of the 1960s had made the dramatic presentation of music on stage a far more important aspect of performance than it had been ten years or so earlier. As the performance continues, one can sense a noticeable relaxation in Elvis's manner; he becomes more at ease, even humorous and faintly self-deprecatory; endearingly, it can be discerned that at heart he was the shy boy from Tupelo.

The success of this television programme did much to reaffirm Elvis's name in the forefront of popular music in the USA. His future, clearly signposted in this special, manifestly did not lie in the making of more of the pappy films of previous years. Although Elvis could command $1,000,000 per film, the Colonel could demand – and get – $100,000 for each performance, so ten performances would make the same money in less time and with less work. In addition, with RCA recording the live shows, the 'live' album could also replace the sound-track album, adding a lucrative sideline to the venture. Whether or not it was considered wise to speculate on the future of a succession of 'live' recordings – in the nature of which there would be a fair amount of duplicated material, with a consequential long-term fall in sales and revenue – this was the way in which Elvis's professional career was going to be directed in the immediate future.

By the beginning of 1969, therefore, Elvis's professional and private lives had changed markedly for the better. Married, and a father, he was much in demand to appear in live shows at the most exclusive and expensive venues. This was something short of the gigs of popular rock bands of the late-1960s, but it was nonetheless a step in the right direction – that of performing before an audience. Most important, Elvis was now again able to sing, and not merely to cavort in front of a camera. This increased freedom led also to Elvis expanding his repertoire significantly, for he now included in his act many songs by younger musicians and singer–songwriters.

Also, in March 1969, his best movie for several years, *Charro*, was released. The film – a National General production written, produced and directed by Charles Warren – was akin to the largely forgotten *Flaming Star*, in that it was a western with hardly any music – there was just the one title song – and in it Elvis appeared for the first and only time in his film career wearing a beard throughout. However, it failed to draw any significant praise form the critics, who had by that time become used merely to noting another new Presley movie rather than attempting to take it seriously. In truth, his acting in *Charro* appears somewhat stiff and wooden.

In spite of all this, it was nonetheless clear that an attempt was being made to undertake more significant work. By this time, Elvis had changed recording venues as well: he held an extended recording session in January and February of 1969 at the American Studios in Memphis. The significance of this move was that it was the first time he had made recordings – except those for film sound-tracks – since 1956 other than in an RCA studio. The opportunity of recording in his adopted home city was clearly beneficial, for the songs are by and large a fine collection which is, in total, brilliantly performed. It includes one of the very best performances from him for many years, the classic 'In The Ghetto', which again demonstrated to a welcoming world that Elvis's response to contemporary rock music was still as finely tuned as it had been fifteen years previously, given the chance.

However, in spite of this evident change of direction, Elvis was still contracted to make the last (as it turned out) of his formula films, a somewhat innocuous piece whose title *Change Of Habit* was perhaps more significant than anyone could have realised at the time. In July, the film completed, Elvis began exhausting rehearsals for another demanding event, a month-long engagement at the International Hotel, Las Vegas. This time, unlike the NBC special of the previous year, there was no chance to correct mistakes, to re-do anything that may need changing: every show was live, in front of a packed audience (the tickets were sold out within hours of the box-office opening) at the hotel's Showroom Internationale. The result, however, was a resounding success, professionally, personally and financially. Elvis gave two shows a night, seven days a week, for a month, during which time more than 100,000 people saw him perform. If Elvis could command – through Colonel Parker – $100,000 per show, then the gross payment for the month would be $6,000,000, a very large sum even today, but when amortised through each member of the audience, it would amount to less than $60 per person. They spent, on average, considerably more than that.

A return engagement was soon booked for January 1970, during the hotel's traditionally slack post-Christmas and New Year season, going against most of the established yardsticks for live appearances. It had been only five months after his previous sold-out appearances, and the shows were to take place during a month that was traditionally poor for business. But a week before he opened, fifty-eight performances – all but seven of the twenty-nine days – had been sold out; shortly afterwards, the remaining tickets had been sold. A mere three days after the end of this season Elvis and his entourage travelled to Houston for a series of twelve performances at the city's giant Astrodome. Around 44,500 people attended each of the shows – well over half-a-million in all – for which Elvis received a total, according to his fee of $100,000 per show, of $1,200,000 for a little over a week's work.

The tremendous interest generated by these appearances led naturally to their extension. It was crystal clear that the public wanted no more of the Presley films, but could not get enough of seeing him live. As the cinema could do more than television in creating an atmosphere, what better way could there be of reaching millions of people than by a full-length, spectacularly recorded documentary in colour of Presley, but issued and shown as a feature film? To direct such a film, the Oscar-winning Denis Sanders, whose *Czechoslovakia 1968* had catapulted him to the forefront of his profession, was chosen. The result, made for MGM, was a fine piece of work, which did its subject proud.

Early in 1971, rumours began to circulate concerning Presley's marriage and his alleged drug-taking. While the peripatetic nature of his profession placed strains on those at the centre, the problems between Elvis and Priscilla were probably exaggerated, although it is only since his death that their likely cause has come to light. It is also no secret that Priscilla did not take kindly to some members of the 'Memphis Mafia', nor they to her, and in a book published shortly before Elvis's death, three bodyguards claimed that he was by this time little short of a 'walking drug store'. However, against these claims should be set those by others who were equally close to him, and who strenuously denied such large-scale abuse, pointing also to Elvis's frequent and outspoken criticism of drug-takers and traffickers. Nor should it be forgotten that at the White House in 1971, President Nixon created Presley a member of the Federal Drug Enforcement Bureau, although the event has to be seen against the light of the protagonists' subsequent careers. Whatever the truth of Elvis's drug-taking, and it is difficult to believe that the truth will ever be entirely known, there can be little doubt that, from time to time during his demanding concert tours and appearances, Elvis resorted to stimulants.

In May of 1971, Elvis had undertaken another extensive recording session, this time in Nashville, which produced his classic blues recording, 'Merry Christmas,

Baby', as well as material of significantly less interest. There were, however, also three songs in which he accompanied himself on the piano, a rare glimpse indeed of his keyboard talents. His professional life, meantime, had more or less settled down to a succession of concert engagements along the lines of super cabaret. While this was fine up to a point, it also meant that he tended to neglect pure recording work. Every so often his concerts would be recorded, and bootleg versions of a fair number of them have tended to flood the record market in the USA.

In January 1972, a ten-mile portion of United States Highway 51, which runs past Graceland, was officially named 'Elvis Presley Boulevard'. This honour, however, can have provided little compensation for the events that followed soon after, which led to Elvis's entering the most unsettled and tragic period of his life.

It was during an engagement at the Las Vegas Hilton that Elvis was introduced to a karate expert, a professional bodyguard, named Mike Stone. Elvis had long been interested in karate, and was keen that Priscilla should learn the rudiments of the subject. At Elvis's insistence, Priscilla began to take karate lessons from Stone, but within a few weeks of her starting them, it became clear to friends of the couple that Priscilla's and Mike's relationship had become very close indeed. On 31 March, Stone's wife entered a divorce petition against her husband, and on 5 June it was granted. Later, Elvis and Priscilla announced officially that they had separated; about the same time, Elvis had met Linda Thompson, who was the reigning Miss Tennessee, and they became very close friends.

Elvis's most important engagement of the early 1970s was the *Elvis: Aloha from Hawaii* live television special, telecast on 14 January, 1973 and beamed direct to millions of viewers in many countries. It was also taped for future record release. The material, sufficient for a double album, was quickly released in the new JVC quadraphonic (four-channel) CD-4 system (the 'CD' having nothing to do with the later 'compact disc' format) and became the first million selling quadraphonic recording. A slightly earlier documentary, also for MGM but produced and directed by Pierre Adidge and Robert Abel, called *Elvis on Tour*, was also made in April 1972.

In October of 1973, Elvis and Priscilla's six-year marriage was dissolved in Santa Monica, California. Although by all accounts Elvis was deeply upset at the breakdown and collapse of his marriage, both parties always maintained that they held the greatest affection for each other. But early the following year, the Presley family's marital problems continued when Vernon and Dee separated.

As if to escape from any possible brooding over such matters, Elvis had meanwhile embarked on an extensive series of concert tours, which in turn presented something of a substantial problem for RCA. As their major artist was constantly on tour, it was becoming increasingly difficult to get him to learn new material. Furthermore, this had become imperative as sales of the resultant *Elvis Live* albums had fallen markedly: the fans just did not wish for ever to continue purchasing yet more performances of the same old material. In addition, the technical quality of many of these live recordings would often leave something to be desired, compared with the very high quality then demanded by other recording stars all over the world. By the end of 1975, it seemed likely that Presley was prevailed upon sufficiently to get him to take up proper studio recording work again, although it was becoming difficult to pin him down to dates. A single session in 1975, and two in 1976 – the last taking place at Graceland itself – required much overdubbing and post-recording cosmetic studio engineering to make them suitable for release – and even then they were not particularly outstanding. Such problems were doubtless a reflection of the crisis that the breakdown of his marriage and the subsequent lack of direction in his lifestyle had brought about.

In January 1975, Elvis celebrated his fortieth birthday, but by this time he had already undergone several stays in hospital for the treatment of various conditions, which became disturbingly more frequent. Whether these were connected psychosomatically with his emotional post-divorce problems or with whatever drug-taking he may or may not have been experimenting with, the physical manifestation that became most apparent was his weight problem. He had always been big-boned and was never really slim, but now he was getting fat, and getting fat quickly, to the extent that he had to crash-diet too frequently for his own good. There is no doubt that drugs were enlisted in these alarming crash diets, undertaken to make his bulging figure more presentable for his live concerts. In August 1975, he was back in the Baptist hospital, after breaking off a two-week engagement at the Las Vegas Hilton. As if this were not enough, at the same time Vernon suffered a serious heart attack.

But on New Year's Day 1976, Elvis Presley played to the biggest crowd of his career – over 60,000 – at a concert in Pontiac, Michigan. Shortly afterwards came an unusual development in his career – a business investment. A new company had been set up, Presley Center Sports Inc., to cater for the growing demand for racquet-ball, a sport in which he had become interested. This was the first (and only) time Elvis had allowed his name to be used for a business venture, but later the same year he left the company, which was renamed, although in 1977 Elvis was sued for $150,000 by his ex-business associates.

Another troublesome development was the firing of Elvis's bodyguards Red West, Sonny West and Dave Hebler by Vernon; according to Becky Yancey, Elvis's personal secretary and a staunch defender of his reputation against those who claimed he was a drug addict, Vernon had been forced to dismiss the men over their alleged rough handling of Presley fans at Graceland, which had led to a number of embarrassing and costly law suits. As if to compensate for these unhappy times, towards the end of 1976, Elvis met the attractive twenty year old Ginger Alden, who became his constant companion, and to whom he became engaged in January 1977.

But Elvis's troubles continued when on 21 March 1977 he cancelled an appearance at Baton Rouge, Louisiana, and flew back to Memphis, suffering from what his personal physician, Dr George Nichopoulos, diagnosed as fatigue and intestinal influenza with gastro-enteritis. Ex- President Nixon personally telephoned the hospital to enquire after the singer's condition and to wish him well. Elvis's illnesses were not all he had to contend with during these troubled months. In May of 1977, Vernon and Dee were divorced, and several weeks later a book ghosted for the three fired bodyguards caused something of a sensation with its author's disclosures of their allegations of Elvis's drug-taking.

In spite of these adverse pressures, a major television show was taped by CBS in June, and Elvis continued touring, his illnesses apparently behind him. It had been decided by RCA to issue a new album to coincide with the show's screening, after the tour had ended on 26 June in Indianapolis.

A further series of concerts had been planned to begin in late August, and on the 16th of that month Elvis and his entourage were preparing the final arrangements. At 2.30 pm, his friend Joe Esposito, having been summoned by Ginger Alden, who could not wake the singer, found Elvis lying on the floor of his bathroom-dressing room. Dr Nichopoulos was called immediately, as well as an ambulance and nearby medical staff, all of whom tried to revive Presley, both at Graceland and in the ambulance on the way to the Baptist Hospital at Memphis. Their efforts were in vain, and Elvis Presley was pronounced dead on arrival at 3.30 p m.

By 5 pm, a thousand fans had gathered outside the Graceland gates. An hour later there were three thousand, and by 6.30 pm almost twenty thousand. The following day, a Wednesday, thousands filed past his body. Over two hundred policemen and a medical team of 120 were on hand to control the crowd and to treat the many fans overcome by heat and emotional stress. On Thursday, with over 2,000 mourners standing vigil outside Graceland, a car smashed into the crowd at four in the morning killing Juanita Joan Johnson and Marie Alice Hovarter, and critically injuring Tammy Baiter. The driver, Treatise Wheeler, aged eighteen, was charged with multiple offences connected with the accident.

The pathologists' report was that Presley died of cardiac arrythmia – an irregular heartbeat. His body was laid to rest in a mausoleum at Forest Hills Cemetery, Memphis, close to his mother's grave.

In the days following Elvis's death, the population of Memphis had swollen by an estimated 200,000 visitors, a truly astonishing demonstration of the extent of his following. President Carter, in an unprecedented eulogy for a rock singer, said of him:

> *'Elvis Presley's death deprives our country of a part of itself. He was a symbol to the people of the world of the vitality, rebelliousness and good humour of this country.'*

Part II

The Music

Chapter Eight

The Sun recordings, 1954–55

The music of Elvis Presley is to be found entirely in his singing, and in nothing else. While he was a passable guitarist and pianist, no one would claim that his ability on these instruments was world-shattering. Nor – more exceptionally – was he a writer of songs, nor a composer, a singer-songwriter of later generations. The few songs to which his name is appended as co-writer hardly add a great deal to our understanding of him, and it may be that his contribution to the actual composition of such material was very small. There is nothing in the material of these songs that makes us say, 'That song was written by Elvis Presley, and by no one else.' But there is everything about any performance by him that causes us to say, after hearing only a few notes, 'That is Elvis Presley singing. It could be no one else.'

It is the nature of music – *any* music – that it exists through one thing only: performance. It is only by the performance of music that it reaches an audience, and it is the nature of performing genius to take music which, in the hands of less gifted interpreters, might not seem of much value, and to turn it, through the power of such genius, into a musical experience of great significance. Exactly what this significance is can be clearly stated: it is a musical experience to which we are compelled to return again and again.

The purpose of this study of Elvis Presley is to demonstrate, purely in musical terms, not only that he was a very great musical force, a very great artist, but also precisely what it was about his singing that made him such a performing genius. As a consequence, we have to sift through his recorded legacy, and the best way of doing this, as with any other musician – a classical composer, or opera singer, or concert pianist or violinist – is in chronological order, in sequence, from his earliest work to his last. In this way, we can better trace his artistic development.

We have seen in Part I that Elvis was not an artist who undertook world tours (when he was at the height of his career as a performing musician, 'world tours' did not exist in the way to which we have since become used). Therefore, the heart of his life's work is to be found solely in his recordings. We have also noted in Part I that Elvis, being such a naturally gifted singer, would often record a selection of songs in a period of time that today would be regarded as very quick. Not for him the poring over individual notes or balances, the adding of this or that to a basic beat or the thousand and one things that musicians today feel are the only ways in which music should be created in the studio. Forty years ago, musicians were invited to make records because the record company thought they could perform music: too often today, it seems, musicians use studio recording time not to put down takes of complete performances, but to practise music about which they were undecided before they got there. Consequently, the tapes of Elvis's sessions are almost always made up of complete takes and, by modern standards, not too many of them. By all accounts, Elvis would put down several takes of a song, usually the last one being the best, and when he felt he had done the best job he could, he and the musicians would move on to the next number.

There would, certainly in the early years of his recording career, be very little – if any – returning to the song later, and retaking this part or that, or overdubbing layers of new sound. Towards the end of his life, Elvis would make use of later techniques and recording practices, but at heart he remained a complete performer.

As a result, his recorded legacy is virtually that of whole performances – of which he was eventually the sole arbiter as to what was the best take to be released. In this regard, we have to respect Presley's final judgement, and that is why this book is primarily concerned with the commercially issued recordings of his career – the finished product by which he himself wished to be judged.

There remain, however, two other aspects of his recording career that have to be addressed. The first is that he was exclusively signed to one company, RCA. He was, therefore, largely in their hands with regard to the way in which his product was released. Not for him the total control over sequencing, release dates, cover design, merchandising spin-offs and all other aspects of modern-day marketing, which are essential for the record company to recoup their often hefty financial investment and for artists to ensure their work reaches the widest audience in the way they wish it to.

Elvis had no reason to be other than grateful for the work RCA did on his behalf, but it cannot be denied that occasionally the company let slip some golden opportunities (as we shall see), that RCA did not always realise the full musical potential of the Presley material they had, and the company also left in the vaults some fine performances, which certainly ought to have seen the light of day earlier. These 'unknown' recordings, most of them being 'out-takes', will, of their nature, often shed light on the way in which Presley approached the business of making records, as well as showing how his final performance was arrived at. We should remember that his releases were almost always geared to the single, and not to the album, with the result that his music-making was often confined on such occasions to segments of three minutes. Once he had decided on the best take, he would sometimes relax and enter into a jam session with the musicians, making music purely for the hell of it rather than for commercial, public consumption.

On rare occasions, RCA's engineers would keep the tape running, and these extended, 'unofficial' recordings will often shed extraordinary, fresh light upon his artistry. The other aspect is the existence of unofficial recordings of his live performances; in essence, these are little different from those just mentioned – with one exception. This is that the unofficial live tapes are of poor technical quality, and while the atmosphere is undeniable with regard to capturing the excitement of the occasion, they have to be heard in combination with the studio quality recordings of the same material. Only occasionally do these unreleased and unofficial recordings add much to our perception of Presley's performing greatness. For the sake of convenience, they will be referred to here, and in chapter sixteen, as bootlegs – although the subsequent release on RCA of hitherto unissued recordings will make them 'official'! At the time of writing, their release is 'unofficial'.

There have been several attempts to catalogue, so far as is practicable, Presley's complete recordings chronologically. An early publication in this field was *Elvis Recording Sessions* by Ernst Jorgensen, Erik Rasmussen and Johnny Mikkelsen (published in Denmark in 1977). But the book *Elvis Sessions: The Recorded Music Of Elvis Aron Presley (1953–1977)* by Joseph A. Tunzi, with an introduction by Scotty Moore (published in Chicago in 1993) is by far the most fully detailed of such publications. The enthusiast who wishes to have a complete list of every known Presley recording is strongly urged to acquire this very important book.

And so it is that we begin our study of Presley's legacy with the one recording that he paid for himself – all of $4 – which so fired Marion Keisker's imagination. We are in Memphis, Tennessee, one Saturday afternoon in 1953, and Elvis Presley has plucked up courage to make a record all by himself, in secret, to give to his mother as a birthday present...

71

1953 – exact date unknown
Venue: Memphis Recording Service, Sun Studios
Titles recorded: 'My Happiness', 'That's When Your Heartaches Begin'

This half-hour session (it could have taken no longer, and may have taken a lot less) is without question the single most important recording event in the history of rock 'n' roll. Marion Keisker must have heard dozens, if not hundreds, of potential hopefuls come and go in this 'make -a-record-yourself' manner, yet once Presley had started singing, she could hardly get to the tape machine quickly enough to capture his first-ever recorded performance for her boss to hear. The actual acetate has survived, despite being 'plumb near worn out' by Gladys Presley, and the performance of 'My Happiness' was first released officially almost forty years later before being reissued, along with its stable mate, 'That's When Your Heartaches Begin'. If anyone harboured doubts with regard to Elvis's natural vocal power and, it must be said, sensitivity, they are blown away by this 'home movies'-type disc: the nineteen year old's voice is fully formed, entirely unique and leaps from the old, worn grooves with a force that is literally astonishing. It is not only an important document in itself, but remains the only recording of Elvis performing alone, as he accompanies himself on the guitar, with no other musicians participating in the session. It has lately been rumoured that Elvis recorded three further titles – for another $4 – early in 1954 for the Memphis Recording Service at Sun, namely, 'I'll Never Stand In Your Way', 'Casual Love Affair', and 'Without You', but their whereabouts is unknown and, so far as can be ascertained, the likelihood of their existence, if they were ever recorded in the first place, is remote.

December, 1954
Venue: Sun Studios, Memphis
Titles recorded: 'Harbour Lights', 'You're Right, I'm Left, She's Gone',
'Milkcow Blues Boogie', 'You're A Heartbreaker'

There is considerable doubt that 'Harbour Lights' was recorded at these sessions: its use of all-acoustic guitar lends weight to July 1954 being its probable date. The recording was also rejected by Phillips, and first appeared only in 1976. Its main interest is that it is early Presley, although the song later became a hit for the Platters. Presley's voice sounds raw, and comes and goes in disconcerting fashion, as if he was moving around the microphone. It exposes his inexperience, which also points to the earlier dating.

The title of 'I'm Left, You're Right, She's Gone', has always been something of a mystery. This is how it is always referred to, but in the song Presley mainly sings 'you're right, I'm left, she's gone', which makes more sense as the title. Whatever the title, the addition of D.J. Fontana on drums gives a more solid backing, and the result is one of the beefiest Presley performances so far. This record was a moderate hit in Britain three years later, which says something for its undated sound; but it stands to one side of the rock mainstream, since it has a greater country feel than rock enthusiasts like.

'Milkcow Blues Boogie' is one of Presley's most important Sun recordings. It begins slowly, and very well, before Presley stops and says: 'Hold it fellas. That don't move me. Let's get real, real gone for a change!'. He then launches into a faster version, with a fine lengthy guitar solo, before the song fades out. This was the first Presley recording to adopt this trick. In 'You're A Heartbreaker', Presley's voice takes on a different quality: it is lower in pitch, and seems flawed by phasing and echo, which produce a washy and sibilant result.

January/February, 1955
Venue: Sun Studios, Memphis
Titles recorded: 'Baby, Let's Play House', 'I'll Never Let You Go',
'Mystery Train'

'Baby, Let's Play House' is a medium/fast rock number enlivened by raw and gutsy guitar work. Presley's repetition of 'Baby, baby, baby' is very exciting, and probably influenced Gene Vincent. With 'I'll Never Let You Go', we encounter one of the Sun recordings that resists pigeon-holing. It is very slow, wafted by acoustic guitar shakes and a soft bass line. Presley's voice is haunting: high, and veering on falsetto, until the end, which is faster. 'Mystery Train' is rock music, a fine fast number.

July, 1955
Venue: Sun Studios, Memphis
Titles recorded: 'I Forgot To Remember To Forget Her', 'Tomorrow Night',
'Trying To Get To You'

This last Sun session is not particularly memorable. 'I Forgot To Remember To Forget Her' is good early Presley; but his country roots are to the fore. The essence of his earlier rock records is absent. 'Tomorrow Night' was withheld by Phillips and RCA for ten years, until March 1965 when Chet Atkins supervised a new backing track for Presley's original vocal line. As the early Sun takes were not multitracked, the original backing had to be obliterated. Despite all this cosmetic surgery, the result is quite good, but it cannot be judged as an example of early Presley. Atkins was doubtless responsible for embellishing the voice with echo.

73

However, something of the excitement and passion of the early Presley shines through, qualities which were generally lacking at the time when Atkins resurrected the track. 'Trying To Get To You' also remained unreleased by Phillips, but was put out by RCA in April 1956, on Presley's first album.

Chapter Nine

The early RCA recordings, 1956–58

10/11 January, 1956
Venue: RCA Studio, Nashville
Titles recorded: 'Heartbreak Hotel', 'I Got A Woman', 'I'm Counting On You', 'I Was The One', 'Money Honey'

By the time Elvis Presley had signed with RCA, his musical style had been forged into a distinctive form, which was soon to take the world by storm. He was ready to go – and now he had the resources of one of the most important recording organisations in the world behind him. It is significant that Elvis Presley remained loyal to RCA for the rest of his life.

In the studio with him for this session were colleagues from the Sun days, as well as musicians with whom Elvis Presley had not previously worked. He knew Scotty Moore, Bill Black and D.J. Fontana, but Chet Atkins (a distinguished guitarist and manager of the RCA Nashville office) and pianist Floyd Cramer were newcomers. Also, three singers – Gordon Stoker and the Speer brothers, Ben and Brock – were booked to add backing vocals. This was a new departure for Presley. The result must have exceeded the dreams of everybody taking part, for 'Heartbreak Hotel' became one of the legendary rock performances. For many people, this *is* Elvis Presley, and it continues to excite and fascinate listeners.

'Heartbreak Hotel' is a classic performance, yet when it is analysed it appears so simple that one cannot recall a time when one did not know it. It is all the more effective for being so restrained. This may seem surprising in view of Presley's early image, but the beat is held back; the smouldering intensity and wounded defiance is conveyed entirely by the voice. 'Heartbreak Hotel' is a basic blues, with a syncopated throb. The key, E minor, fits Presley's voice like a glove, and when the bass guitar enters before 'Heartbreak' in the line '…down at the corner of Lonely Street at Heartbreak Hotel…', the interest quickens, leading to the second time, with quiet, insistent drums and guitar. Floyd Cramer's piano is ideal: it is impossible to imagine this song without his phrases high on the piano pattering like sad rain. The whole performance is outstanding.

'I Got A Woman', a fast, bouncy number, also begins with Presley alone, with a slurred 'weell'; but soon the rhythm has him moving around the microphone: his voice comes and goes as he moves this way and that, turning his head to encourage the other musicians. This was the first song Presley recorded for RCA. It has simple but effective guitar breaks, and an infectious feeling of musicianship. The sudden slow ending is brilliantly judged.

'I'm Counting On You' is a ballad, but Presley is still moving around, and the occasional syllable is lost. Like most ballads of the period, this chugs along over a triple beat; but Cramer's piano variations make the rhythms unpredictable. At no point can these musicians be taken for granted: there is always something interesting going on. 'I Was The One' is another ballad and the biggest sound on any song from these sessions. Presley's voice comes over more clearly here: it is full of inflections, from a plummy staccato to a sneering falsetto. At the time these recordings were made, there was no singer to compare with Presley for range and instrumental use of the voice. 'Money Honey' was recorded immediately after 'Heartbreak Hotel', and the sense of achievement in the earlier number had tumbled over into this performance. This is *real* rock 'n' roll. Later in 1956, Gene Vincent and the Blue Caps had a world-wide hit with 'Be-Bop-A-Lula', but Vincent's number was clearly influenced by Presley's 'Money Honey'. Cramer shows his prowess again: delicate glissandos, fast and insistent, flick from the top of the piano, punctuating Presley's deeply rhythmic performance, which is further enhanced by easy-paced guitar work.

30/31 January; February, 1956
Venue: RCA Studios, New York City
Titles recorded: 'Blue Suede Shoes', 'I'm Gonna Sit Right Down And Cry',
'Lawdy, Miss Clawdy', 'My Baby Left Me', 'One-Sided Love Affair', 'Shake,
Rattle And Roll', 'So Glad You're Mine', 'Tutti Frutti'

Twenty days after completing his first RCA session, Elvis Presley was in RCA's New York studios to record eight more songs. Chet Atkins, Floyd Cramer and the singers were absent, and Cramer was replaced by Shorty Long. Some cuts form this collection are in the same class as the first lessons.

'Blue Suede Shoes', with its driving rhythm, is a classic rock 'n' roll record. The barely controlled power of Presley's performance is made all the more enthralling by deliberate mispronunciation of some consonants. This gives the song a quality of bravado – a couldn't-care-less attitude – but it is clear that every quaver is sincerely meant by Presley. Scotty Moore's guitar is remarkable: he 'bends' chords flat to tilt the song in the rhythm and blues direction, and his guitar licks in verse two build the energy, until by the third verse it really burns.

'I'm Gonna Sit Right Down And Cry', another fast number, is punched along by a walking bass and insistent chord clusters from the piano. Presley is very close to the microphone, but the guitar solo is poor, and the song fails to ignite. 'Lawdy, Miss Clawdy' begins with fast piano chords – unusual, in view of the slow pulse. This is a genuine performance – a change from the spliced perfection of some artists – but there is hesitation in Presley's voice. I suspect he had not thoroughly absorbed the song. In 'My Baby Left Me', however, the message is faithfully reflected in the pitch of Presley's vocal line, which produces a whining effect, underpinned by an insidious beat. A very good rock number can be found in 'One Sided Love Affair'. Presley is in bouncy voice, with a 'hup' quality of humour and toe-tapping zest.

'Shake, Rattle And Roll' is a classic performance, which shows Presley's voice barely controlling its explosiveness. Other members of the band join Presley for the title each time it occurs, and the piano provides a major part of the texture. The chunky guitar solo is chordal, betraying the blue roots. Another fabulous take is 'So Glad You're Mine', especially in the original mono version. Later electronic interfering makes Presley's voice harsh and strident, but the original tapes show him in clean voice. The 'ooh-ee's simply tingle with life, echoed by good guitar work. Finally, 'Tutti Frutti' is another incomparable performance. Presley's vocal work is sensational; anybody who wants to be a rock singer should study each inflection of this recording. The fierce beat is sustained with solid power; above it the guitar flickers intermittently until it breaks out in the fiery solo. The ending – a genuine early touch of echo – is quite astonishing.

11 April, 1956
Venue: RCA Studio, Nashville
Titles recorded: 'I Want You, I Need You, I Love You'

Some problems must have surrounded this session, for this was the only song recorded. The result almost tells us as much, for in some transfers the first published take (itself spliced) subjects Presley's voice to severe mutilation. Although good recordings were by no means rare, this was still 1956, and some techniques were in their infancy. Presley is stuck back on a hefty wall of rhythm and echo. There is no light and shade in this ballad, but the alternative take, issued twenty years later, lets us hear Presley more as he was. As he made a mistake in the title in this alternative take, it was not issued at the time.

2 July, 1956
Venue: RCA Studios, New York City
Titles recorded: 'Any Way You Want Me', 'Don't Be Cruel', 'Hound Dog'

Presley sings 'Any Way You Want Me' with ringing power in the original recordings, although later 'stereo transcriptions' lacerate the ears. It is difficult to describe this song; perhaps 'smoochy rock' gets nearest. But Presley's performance is outstanding. At the end, the way in which he sings the word 'heart' is totally sincere; the sort of moment to make one want to play the song over and over again. 'Don't Be Cruel' is a classic cut, but it is more dated than other performances. Maybe the 'happy' inflection of Presley's voice has less appeal than his characteristic menacing form; and the song itself lacks grit. It remains, however, one of Presley's best recordings. 'Hound Dog' is truly sensational, with a pull that packs as big a punch decades after it was recorded. This is the young rebel revealed, rooted deep in the blues soil. Presley's 'Hound Dog', like 'Heartbreak Hotel' and a few others, is the essence of rock 'n' roll. It is the pull of conflicting harmonies that gives this song its aggressive quality; the song is in C major, the major chord of which (and on which Bill Black's bass line is based) is C, E and G. Presley erupts into the song with his never-to-be-forgotten opening in E *flat*. This sets up tremendous tension against the E natural in the bass, Presley spitting the words with contempt. Gordon Stoker, the singer from earlier sessions, is joined by Neal Matthews, Hoyt Hawkins and Hugh Jarrett, to form the Jordanaires; their singing adds great impact. Later in the song they clap, against solid drumming and inspired guitar licks.

August/September, 1956
Venue: Twentieth-Century Fox Studios, Hollywood
Titles recorded: 'Let Me Be', 'Poor Boy', 'We're Gonna Move'

This came before the 'sound-track album' concept, and the songs for Presley's first film were very different from those by which he achieved notoriety. This is just easy-paced country music, which fits the film's locale very well.

'Let Me Be' is pure country music. The song is hardly outstanding, but Presley's performance is so good that people could well be converted after hearing it. The title track, 'Love Me Tender', is a gentle, slow moving ballad, beautifully sung. The delayed entry of the word 'tender', when it first appears, is a magical touch, as is the close harmony of the backing vocals (the Ken Darby Trio) and their wistful final solo notes from the guitar .

78

'Poor Boy' is another good number, but contains too much of a 'squeeze box' effect. 'We're Gonna Move' is not, as might be expected, a rock number. The move in the title is a move of house.

1–3 September, 1956
Venue: Radio Recorders Studios, Hollywood
Titles recorded: 'Any Place Is Paradise', 'First In Line', 'How Do You Think I Feel?', 'How's The World Treating You?' 'Long Tall Sally', 'Love Me', 'Old Shep', 'Paralysed', 'Playing For Keeps', 'Ready, Teddy', 'Rip It Up', 'Too Much', 'When My Blue Moon Turns To Gold Again'

After recording the songs for his first film Elvis remained in Hollywood to make these recordings. Although his standard band was not used for the film, they played for this three-day session. The recording quality of 'Any Place Is Paradise' is not good, for an exaggerated echo has ruined the song. 'First In Line' is a long ballad but again the words are inaudible, owing to excessive echo. 'How Do You Think I Feel?' is not so swampily recorded. This fast number is one of the poorer tracks of Presley's early career. 'How's The World Treating You?' is much better; a sentimental ballad, with the Jordanaires much in evidence. Presley appears to sing this well, so far as one can judge through the wall of electronic hash.

The technical 'enhancement' does not matter in 'Long Tall Sally', a number which was soon to be a smash hit for Little Richard. Presley's performance has a raw, earthy, high-energy output. It is a classic, driving rock song, staggeringly performed. It plays for only one minute forty-nine seconds, but what dynamite is packed in! By contrast 'Love Me' is a slow, sentimental number. Presley makes the most of its pathos, by a natural break and fractional hesitancy. Only after it is over does one realise the song itself is mediocre, but Presley turns it into true art. The same can be said of 'Old Shep', the song that meant so much to him as a boy. The material is finer than 'Love Me', although it is possible to take exception to the sentiment. In its way, this is a classic performance, though it has little to do with rock 'n' roll. With 'Paralysed', we are back with the fast rockers, but the voice is almost lost. The energy of the song is the thing, and that is fully realised. 'Playing For Keeps' is a gently moving number, the lyrics of which are above average; and Presley makes the most of them.

'Ready, Teddy' – another Little Richard number – also gets a high-energy performance. This is a classic recording: Presley's voice tingles with vibrant life, and the beat drives along as fast as possible. The original mono tape is far preferable to 'stereo enhancement', which reduces the tight impact to infernal noise. 'Rip It Up' became an international smash for Bill Haley and the Comets. The hard rhythm of this performance is muted by echo on Presley's voice and the surrounding acoustic, but nothing can mask the 'throwaway' style essential to this classic rock number. The Jordanaires feature prominently in 'Too Much', a medium tempo shuffle, which is blues-based but thankfully has not been subjected to later studio hashings to the same degree as others from this session. Every word is crystal clear. The togetherness of Dudley Brooks's piano and Scotty Moore's guitar is beautifully judged. The engineers appear to have been up to their tricks on 'When My Blue Moon Turns To Gold Again', which is similar to 'Too Much', but Presley's voice is spoiled by echo, and poor balancing with the Jordanaires, who smother him. A pity.

December, 1956
Venue: Sun Studios, Memphis
Elvis Presley, Carl Perkins, Jerry Lee Lewis, Johnny Cash
Titles recorded: 'You Belong To My Heart', 'When God Dips His Love In My Heart', 'Just A Little Talk With Jesus', 'Jesus Walked That Lonesome Valley', 'I Shall Not Be Moved', 'Peace In The Valley', 'Down By The Riverside', 'I'm With A Crowd But So Alone', 'Farther Along', 'Blessed Jesus (Hold My Hand)', 'As We Travel Along On The Jericho Road', 'I Just Can't Make It By Myself', 'A Little Cabin Home On The Hill', 'Summertime Is Past And Gone', 'I Hear A Sweet Voice Calling', 'Sweetheart You Done Me Wrong', 'Keeper Of The Key', 'Crazy Arms', 'Don't Forbid Me', 'Too Much Monkey Business', 'Brown Eyed Handsome Man', 'Out Of Sight, Out Of Mind', 'Don't Be Cruel', 'Paralyzed', 'There's No Place Like Home', 'When The Saints Go Marching In', 'Softly And Tenderly', 'Is It So Strange', 'That's When Your Heartaches Begin', 'Rip It Up', 'I Gonna Bid My Blues Goodbye', 'That's My Desire', 'End Of The Road', 'Black Bottom Stomp', 'You're The Only Star In My Blue Heaven', 'Reconsider Baby'

The story of how these recordings came to be made is outlined in chapter four. By this time Elvis was under exclusive contract to RCA and strictly speaking he was in breach of his contract by making these recordings. However, it should be obvious to all that when four young men of great talent meet up together in a recording studio they are going to take advantage of the situation spontaneously to put down some tracks, which is what happened on this occasion.

The existence of these recordings has been known for very many years, but the contractual problems prove insurmountable. An album was released on the Sun label that sounds remarkably like the line-up shown above, although Presley's name was nowhere to be found on the album, but eventually – as had to happen – the recordings were released in 1990 by RCA. There is some disagreement as to whether Johnny Cash actually takes part on these particular songs; he clearly remembers making records with the other three, but this tape may have become lost.

What cannot be denied is that a great deal of musical electricity was generated on this occasion – as may well be expected – but technically the results are little more than passable. The main drawback, now that we have had the chance of hearing this legendary materials, is that the artists involved had not appeared together before, they had clearly not rehearsed, and none was entirely sure what any of the others was going to do at any one time. Even at this early stage in their careers, their individuality was such that they could not really blend as what must be thought of as the world's first 'supergroup'. Although these recordings are shown slightly out of chronological sequence in this book, it is more sensible that they be noted here, at the end of the Sun sessions. Whatever drawbacks there might be, the excitement and genuine musicianship of these four individual young masters on this December day in 1956 is brilliantly captured.

12/13 January, 1957
Venue: Radio Recorders Studios, Hollywood
Titles recorded: 'All Shook Up', 'Got A Lot O' Livin' To Do', 'I Beg Of You', 'I Believe', 'Mean Woman Blues', 'Peace In The Valley', 'Take My Hand, Precious Lord', 'Tell Me Why', 'That's When Your Heartaches Begin'
N B 'I Beg Of You' was not passed for release and was re-recorded 23 February

Presley's three appearances on the *Ed Sullivan Show* for CBS TV culminated on 6 January, 1957 with a performance of the religious song 'Peace In The Valley'. The public response was so strong that little time was lost in getting Presley into the studio to make a commercial recording of it. As Presley's previous chart success had been with rock numbers, 'All Shook Up' was chosen as his next single. Further songs were recorded to fill out the *Loving You* album, although the performances used in the film were not those recorded here. 'Tell Me Why' was not released for eight years, so this important session appeared piecemeal.

'All Shook Up' shows the early Presley at the height of his powers. This is a classic cut, brilliantly sung, a lesson to all aspiring rock 'n' roll singers, who should study every beat of Presley's performance. Note, too, Presley's use of the *back* of the guitar, almost as an additional drum. The medium-fast tempo of this rocker – Presley's first undisputed number one hit in Britain – is not punched out regardless. The sustained chords of the Jordanaires, the delicate touches from Moore, Black, Fontana and Brooks prove that basic rock 'n' roll is not all sound and fury. 'Got A Lot O' Livin' To Do' featured in *Loving You*, and influenced another white rock star, Jerry Lee Lewis. But Presley's suggestive 'c'mon baby' is even more smouldering than Jerry Lee's. Presley's voice is amazingly wide-ranging, as the final bars degenerate into scat singing of careless abandon. 'I Believe', the early 1950s Frankie Laine monster seller, was included for the *Peace In The Valley* collection, issued as an EP. Presley's performance, though sincere, is stiff and, as the first song recorded at the session, should have been re-made at the end, after everybody had played themselves in.

'Mean Woman Blues', also included in *Loving You*, is a rock classic by Claude Demetrius. Jerry Lee Lewis cut a timeless version of this, backing his world-wide hit 'Great Balls Of Fire', and by comparison Presley falls between two stools. On the one hand, the use of the Jordanaires detracts from the man-to-woman nature of the number, but their later clapping is just right. Presley's guitar licks are tremendous – something absent from Jerry Lee – but Dudley Brooks's piano, good as it is, has not the clattering boxiness of Lewis's. A fine Presley performance, although the revival atmosphere ultimately spoils it.

'Peace In The Valley', the main reason for the sessions, is a religious blues number. This is a remarkable recording: with no extraneous background effects, one can judge the quality of Presley's voice. He sings with great sincerity. His voice has great reserves of strength, yet is supple, and used with intelligence. The same is partly true of 'Take My Hand, Precious Lord', but the use of electric organ adds a distinctive new tone colour to the sound. Dudley Brooks plays this instrument with delicacy, and Presley, returning to his musical roots in a gentle revivalist number, is completely convincing. 'Tell Me Why', which was not released until 1965, is largely a country ballad. It stood outside the mainstream of Presley's success at that time, and was probably felt to lack commercial appeal. The performance, though, could hardly be improved upon. Neither could 'That's When Your Heartaches Begin', a slow song, with a wide-ranging melody. Presley sings with magisterial power phrasing and breath control and the difficult business of talking a middle section in a slow song is carried off perfectly.

19 January, 1957
Venue: Radio Recorders Studios, Hollywood
Titles recorded: 'Blueberry Hill', 'Have I Told You Lately That I Love You?', 'Is It So Strange', 'It Is No Secret'

A feature of the previous session was Presley's recording of material from other singers; in 'Blueberry Hill', he continued this. As Presley recorded his version, Fats Domino's inimitable recording was becoming a world-wide smash hit. Presley's performance is lower powered than Domino's, although Presley is in magnificent voice. Dudley Brooks's piano is distinctive and stylish; but as Domino was his own pianist, his version has the edge over Presley. 'Have I Told You Lately That I Love You?' is another familiar number, but Presley's performance is not outstanding. 'Is It So Strange' is not in the same class: the words are trite. 'It Is No

Secret' became the fourth song for the *Peace In The Valley* EP. Presley's restrained emotion, against a throbbing background, is most effective.

23/24 February, 1957
Venue: Radio Recorders Studios, Hollywood
Titles recorded: 'Don't Leave Me Now', 'I Beg Of You', 'I Need You So',
'Loving You', 'One Night', 'True Love', 'When It Rains, It Really Pours'

This is a mixed bag, and the release was as haphazard as the collection. 'Don't Leave Me Now' helped fill out the *Loving You* album: a slow predictable ballad, with a faintly 'bluesy' feel, it is well performed. 'I Beg Of You' is something else: a medium tempo 'soft' rocker, with the Jordanaires adding a distinctive background. Presley's voice is in good shape; he trumps a previous ace by his treatment of the word 'hold' in 'hold my hand' – he erupts suddenly on a long pitched growl, in true blues-shouter style.

'I Need You So' is a sentimental ballad, sung with great emotion, but lacking commercial appeal. A different proposition is 'Loving You', the title song of Presley's second film. This is another ballad, but not so sentimental. Apart form Presley's purely delivered melody, Brooks's contribution is the most important: his piano is stylish, apart from some out-of-character chords. The song ends magically. 'One Night' is another classic: a slow rocker, Presley's voice takes on a 'constricted' quality, which forces its way through the music. Presley's timing is held back until the break '...been too lonely too long', which is climactic in the best sense. Cole Porter's score for *High Society* was one of the most distinguished composed for the screen. The song 'True Love' was a major hit for Bing Crosby and Grace Kelly, and is a simple waltz. Presley gives a marvellous performance, outstandingly well sung, perfectly in tune, superbly phrased, with some telling Porter harmonies. A surprising success. 'When It Rains, It Really Pours', a blues power song, is very different musically, yet it remained unreleased for eight years.

February/March, 1957
Venue: Radio Recorders Studios, Hollywood
Titles recorded: 'Hot Dog', 'Lonesome Cowboy', 'Party', 'Teddy Bear'
N B In addition three previously recorded titles ('Loving You', 'Got A Lot O'
Livin' To Do' and 'Mean Woman Blues') were re-done for the film
sound-track of *Loving You*

This session was to lay down tracks for Presley's second film, *Loving You*. The three additional titles were not issued on disc, as they had already been recorded by RCA. Of the others, 'Hot Dog' is a fast 'train' number, with a locomotive whistle effect. The song is feeble, but Presley does something remarkable with it. Scotty Moore's guitar manages to quarry gold from the dross, and the fade-out is well managed. 'Lonesome Cowboy' is another inferior song, but 'Party' is better: a good up-tempo number with distinguished guitar breaks, but (at one minute twenty-seven seconds) it is too short. The gem of the set is 'Teddy Bear'. Its cheeky style extends to exaggerated slurring of words, and extending certain phrases beyond their usual length, catching up by shortening others. The voice has echo around it, but it works well. A classic of its kind.

May, 1957
Venue: MGM Studios, Hollywood (Culver City)
Titles recorded: 'Baby I Don't Care', 'Don't Leave Me Now', 'I Want To Be Free', 'Jailhouse Rock', 'Treat Me Nice', 'Young And Beautiful'
N B Two versions of 'Jailhouse Rock' were recorded, but only the first was issued commercially; 'Treat Me Nice' wasn't issued and was re-recorded the following September

This batch of songs was for Presley's third film, *Jailhouse Rock*. 'Baby I Don't Care' and 'Don't Leave Me Now' are contrasted: the first is a great rocking number, one of Presley's most infectious performances, 'Don't Leave Me Now' is different from that recorded the previous February in a studio session. Here it is more violent, aided by a recording quality that puts an added strain on Presley's voice. In the film Presley sings yet another version of this number, with simple accompaniment but no backing vocals.

'I Want To Be Free', despite the distinguished lyricist and composer (Lieber and Stoller), comes across poorly. The title track is another matter. This is a classic Presley recording and the film sequence is startling. Another Jerry Lieber–Mike Stoller number; the chords that grab the attention at the start and punctuate the song are among the most famous sounds in rock 'n' roll. Dudley Brooks's piano, high on the keyboard, is another never-to-be-forgotten sound, and the natural rock beat, with real bounce between the beats, is the epitome of controlled fire. The fire comparison continues with the burning guitar licks; but against this exciting instrumental sound, Presley's voice personifies youthful rebellion through the power of music. This performance is a true rock classic, and it is sobering to realise that within a short time Presley had committed to disc half-a-dozen or so of the most innovative statements in popular music this century. Now we have become used to the styles that evolved from this music, it is difficult to imagine how original this music was, and how it differed from other popular music of the mid-1950s. 'Jailhouse Rock', both as a song and a film, was a milestone. 'Young And Beautiful' is, by contrast, slow and sentimental, with the piano used not as a percussion instrument, but as a gentle tone colour, supported by soft wire-brush strokes on the drums and stylish close harmony from the Jordanaires.

5–7 September, 1957
Venue: Radio Recorders Studios, Hollywood
Titles recorded: 'Blue Christmas', 'Don't', 'Here Comes Santa Claus', 'I'll Be Home For Christmas', 'My Wish Came True', 'O Little Town Of Bethlehem', 'Santa Bring My Baby Back To Me', 'Santa Claus Is Back In Town', 'Silent Night', 'Treat Me Nice', 'White Christmas'

The titles give the reason for these sessions: Elvis's first *Christmas* LP, and his first album of religious material. In the event, the religious content is minimal, but the celebration of Christmas is there. 'Blue Christmas' is a slow ballad, the Jordanaires chromatic chord slides giving the song a strange feel, but Presley is here at his best, although absent from the middle eight, when the song sags. 'Don't' is another slow ballad, but incomparably better. Presley's voice is in commanding shape, and his breath control effortless, as he rides high in full power. Contrast is provided by 'Here Comes Santa Claus', a children's Christmas song, with a humorous lyric. Presley tantalises; his timing varies, though the song does not warrant such artistry. 'I'll Be Home For Christmas' is a slow ballad, with quiet drumming by D.J. Fontana. Presley sings the first line of verse two very well but his last phrase is hardly recognisable. Another slow ballad, 'My Wish Came True', is similar to 'Don't', but not so successful. The Jordanaires gospel harmonies take the spotlight. The setting of 'O Little Town Of Bethlehem' is better known in the United States than in other English-speaking countries, and is a genuine performance in which only the electric organ tends to obtrude. 'Santa Bring My Baby Back To Me' is worlds away: here we are in the mainstream of rock, and the result is a classic. A fast ostinato kicks the song into life, and the bravado of Presley's singing extends to verse two, which he begins flat, and verse three which, on repeat, is given a totally different vocal treatment. In short, this performance is a lesson in how to sing rock 'n' roll: Presley inflects the most straightforward lyrics with subtle undertones. 'Santa Clause Is Back In Town' is a classic blues-based number, proving again that Presley had an instinctive feel for the blues, but could also suggest double meanings without incurring the wrath of moral-protecting public figures.

'Silent Night' reveals another facet of Presley: it is a version of undoubted sincerity, and it would probably be more highly regarded if released by any other singer. One of the problems that beset Presley was that those who identified him with the blazing earthiness of rock could not accept that he could also sing a hymn with reverential calm. Every word in his performance is crystal clear and the only criticism is his splitting of the world 'Saviour' into two syllables.

'Treat Me Nice' is a complete contrast. It was not used on the *Christmas* album, but appeared in *Jailhouse Rock*. It is a bouncy number, with magical piano from Dudley Brooks. Worth a mention is the solid bass line, and the way in which Presley's voice dovetails perfectly with the Jordanaires in the baritone register. The final number, 'White Christmas', is the famous Irving Berlin song unforgettably recorded by Bing Crosby. As in 'True Love' Presley is genuine enough, but one senses the song is not really in his blood. The Crosby version remains the all-time classic performance.

January, 1958
Venue: Radio Recorders Studios, Hollywood
Titles recorded: 'As Long As I Have You', 'Crawfish', 'Danny', 'Dixieland Rock', 'Don't Ask Me Why', 'Hard Headed Woman', 'King Creole', 'Lover Doll', 'New Orleans', 'Steadfast, Loyal and True', 'Trouble', 'Young Dreams'

This session put down the songs for Elvis Presley's next film, Paramount Pictures' *King Creole*. The songs are a fine mixture, with some classic material. 'As Long As I Have You' is a slow ballad, which Presley sings well within his power, but with full voice. The pianist adds too much colour with his wide-spread phrases. The calypso style of Harry Belafonte had become a world-wide phenomenon the previous year with his string of smash hits, 'The Banana Boat Song', 'Island In The Sun', 'Coconut Woman', and 'Mary's Boy Child'. In *King Creole* (the film) 'Crawfish' clearly shows his influence. It is a street-call song, similar to the 'Strawberry Woman's Song' in Gershwin's *Porgy and Bess*. But Presley embraces this different material successfully. 'Danny' was recorded for inclusion in *King Creole*, but dropped from the film, and remained unreleased for over twenty years. It was finally issued on *A Legendary Performer* (vol 3). It is easy to see why it was dropped, for it would not have added to the film. It is slow with full backing vocals – Presley gets rather lost in the texture. In 'Dixieland Rock' however, one's worst fears are realised: it falls between two stools, the only point of interest being the insistent opening rhythm. 'Don't Ask Me Why' is more sure of itself; a slow throbbing ballad, well sung.

'Hard Headed Woman' is breathtaking in its surges of power. The use of brass, in true New Orleans style, makes sense, and the underlying rhythm is more interesting. The song is enlivened by shouts of 'Oh Yeah' from the Jordanaires, and there is an orchestral break that galvanises Presley into using his voice wordlessly, for all the world like a lead baritone sax. The final 'ah-ah-oo' leaves one gasping, but all the way through Presley has driven the song forward in unstoppable fashion.

If 'Hard Headed Woman' is a classic of its kind, then so is 'King Creole'. The menacing bass guitar builds an atmosphere of high tension, which is taken up by Presley. Only when his voice rises on the fourth line of each verse does it appear

86

that the caged tiger is about to escape. The guitar work by Scotty Moore is outstanding. Moore's acoustic guitar adds much to 'Lover Doll', a gentle, medium bounce number; but the song is not memorable. Nor is another jazz–rock infusion, 'New Orleans', which highlights the problem. Fast rock and New Orleans jazz do not mix. There is good trumpet work but the result remains a mere curiosity. 'Steadfast, Loyal And True' stands apart, but not for its musical qualities; for it is in essence a school song put in for the story line. 'Trouble' is more interesting. This is a slow medium tempo blues-based number, full of threatening gestures and a brooding, menacing quality, a testament to rebellious youth. Presley breaks his voice, like a yodel, as though to escape from the surroundings, and the doubling of the tempo by the drums is imaginative. The Creole jazz ending is startling, but works, and Presley's final whispered 'Yeah!' still shows defiance. Compared with this classic recording, 'Young Dreams' is best forgotten: a formula song, feeding on commonplace material.

1 February, 1958
Venue: Radio Recorders Studios, Hollywood
Titles recorded: 'Doncha' Think It's Time', 'My Wish Came True', 'Wear My Ring Around Your Neck', 'Your Cheatin' Heart'
N B 'My Wish Came True' was not issued

This was the last session Presley recorded before he joined the US Army, and it may have been difficult, for one of the songs remained unissued, and the others were all taken many times. 'Doncha' Think It's Time' and 'My Wish Came True' were both attempted on 23 January, 1958 but nothing came of them (although it is possible something from takes of 'Doncha' Think It's Time' was used on the issued version, which basically comes from the 1 February session).

The result is almost a parody of Presley. After forty takes, someone should have decided it was time for something else. 'Wear My Ring Around Your Neck' also disappoints, but for different reasons: here the recording is at fault, with Presley in the background, submerged beneath the powerhouse noise and hard-driving rhythm of this fast rocker. It is almost impossible to believe that this song was recorded in the same studios, by the same musicians, a matter of days after similar material ('Hard Headed Woman' and 'King Creole') had been successfully captured on tape. The same is true of Hank Williams's great number, 'Your Cheatin' Heart': the performance is disappointing and should have been re-made.

10/11 June, 1958
Venue: RCA Studios, Nashville
Titles recorded: 'A Big Hunk O' Love', 'A Fool Such As I', 'Ain't That Lovin' You Baby', 'I Got Stung', 'I Need Your Love Tonight'

Compared with the unsatisfactory recordings made earlier in 1958, the dynamism returned here with redoubled force. 'A Big Hunk O' Love' is a classic rocker. Presley is at the top of his form. Although the recording is smothered with echo, it is in keeping with the song. 'A Fool Such As I', a medium 'walk' number, is very different, with the Jordanaires better integrated. Ray Walker took over from Hugh Jarret as bass singer in the Jordanaires for these sessions, and the low Cs are astounding. The recording is better, too: its fatter sound tends to bury Presley on occasion, but his classic qualities shine through. 'Ain't That Lovin' You Baby' is a marching tempo song, constructed along the lines of 'Heartbreak Hotel', but with a happier message, with Presley letting his hair down.

Another classic cut is 'I Got Stung': the vitality is remarkable, with the song driving along in top gear. Even Presley gets a little lost in the general *melee*, but when he surfaces his magic blazes through as he kicks the rhythm along. Finally (although it was the first to be recorded) 'I Need Your Love Tonight' is another classic rocker. It is fast, but not frenetic, with Presley's voice little short of amazing: all the earlier qualities are there, and most importantly his control of vocal technique. Hank Garland's surging guitar work is especially fine.

Chapter Ten

From Nashville to Hollywood, 1960–66

20/21 March, 1960
Venue: RCA Studios, Nashville
Titles recorded: 'A Mess Of Blues', 'Fame And Fortune', 'It Feels So Right',
'Make Me Know It', 'Soldier Boy', 'Stuck On You'

The first sessions after Presley's Army discharge continue where he left off twenty-one months before. The band was virtually the same, the venue was the same, but the recording techniques had improved enormously. Stereo, previously seldom used in popular music recordings, was now a matter of course, and its greater fidelity brought a more natural sound and a more creative approach to recording pop and rock.

'A Mess Of Blues' is a classic Presley recording: curiously, his voice sounds different from other numbers at the same session. He sings with his tongue further back in his mouth. But Presley is fully in front, giving each word its due; he drives the song forwards, matching the lyrics and giving urgent shape to the number. The final falsetto is a master touch. With 'Fame And Fortune', the tempo seems too slow, so that the overall effect is droopy. 'It Feels So Right' is unusual. It has a slow powerful pulse, which Presley throws out at the top of his register. 'Make Me Know It' is in medium-fast rock tempo; Presley's performance makes something interesting out of less than top-drawer material – and the fine recording helps.

'Soldier Boy', a natural choice for Presley's first session after his Army service, is moderately slow: this came before the 'protest songs' of the early 1960s, but is sung with real intensity. Another fine performance is 'Stuck On You'. This has a rock tempo, more gentle than the rockers of the 1950s. It is attractive, and beautifully recorded with everything balanced and clear. Presley sings in a relaxed manner, totally in command, and this recording has achieved classic status.

3/4 April, 1960
Venue: RCA Studios, Nashville
Titles recorded: 'Are You Lonesome Tonight?', 'Dirty, Dirty Feeling', 'Fever', 'Girl Next Door Went A'Walking', 'I Gotta Know', 'I Will Be Home Again', 'It's Now Or Never', 'Like A Baby', 'Reconsider Baby', 'Such A Night', 'The Girl Of My Best Friend', 'The Thrill Of Your Love'

The first sessions after Presley's Army discharge had gone well, possibly better than many would have thought, and it was clear he was as dynamic as ever. This session reinforced that view, for Presley now recorded some of his greatest performances and his biggest-selling individual record, 'Are You Lonesome Tonight?', marks a startling change of direction: it is a slow-moving ballad, gentle, caring, beautifully sung, with the kind of voice Presley had already shown on 'Silent Night' – natural, unforced, dead in tune, and totally distinctive. This classic song is enhanced by the extended 'talking' section in the middle – a difficult procedure to bring off, but here, surrounded by echo, it succeeds. This single sold over five million copies. In 'Dirty, Dirty Feeling' a fast, bouncy, musically dated number, Presley sounds like one of his favourite singers, Bobby Darin. 'Fever' is incomparably better. Presley's performance is totally restrained and full of subdued but insistent strength, outstandingly recorded. 'The Girl Next Door Went A'Walking' is also unusual: to judge by Presley's perfectly proportioned performance, he liked it. Another good popular number, but one which now sounds faded, is 'I Gotta Know', a medium tempo bounce. Again, the beat is infectious, and Presley is having a high old time against the vocal counterpoint of Ray Walker. 'I Will Be Home Again' is a sop to the venue: a classic recording of its type, this slow ballad, sung in duet with Charlie Hodge, has limited appeal other than to Nashville enthusiasts.

With 'It's Now Or Never' we come to one of Presley's greatest performances. This song sold around ten million copies as a single, and is an English version of the Neapolitan song, 'O Sole Mio'. After a gentle introduction Presley's first, stirring top E, strong and manly, sets the scene, and the ensuing singing, abetted by Floyd Cramer's graceful piano, adds to the atmosphere. The steady beat is just right and the climax, with Presley soaring up to an incredible top G sharp, is pure magic. Another very fine performance is 'Like A Baby', which is helped by the controlled backing. Boots Randolph's saxophone solo is memorable; dirty and bluesy, oozing with sexual undertones.

In spite of the major successes of 'Are You Lonesome Tonight?' and 'It's Now Or Never', a possibly more lasting example of Presley's genius is to be found in 'Reconsider Baby'. This is a basic blues, not contaminated by other types of music or commercial pressures. It is clear that he was a blues singer of importance. It is tragic that he never cut a blues album, but performances such as this give a tantalising glimpse of what might have been. This is a classic blues performance; timeless and awe-inspiring in its power and emotion. Boots Randolph's contribution is staggering and everyone on this take struck musical sparks from the others. This track is a refutation of those who do not recognise what a phenomenal artist Presley was.

Vastly different material is found on 'Such A Night' – a curious choice, for it had been a world-wide hit for Johnnie Ray half-a-dozen or more years earlier. Presley's performance is disappointing: had he recorded this number before he went into the Army, then he would have made a better job of it. Presley had trouble recording this, which accounts for the nature of the standard release. On *A Legendary Performer* (vol 2), two false starts, where he has difficulty getting the beat right are included. 'The Girl Of My Best Friend' is a very good song of its day, which has also stood the test of time. A medium-bounce tempo, the lyrics are far from mundane, and the Jordanaires backing contributes to Presley's tale of woe. The song is distinguished, and superbly recorded.

27/28 April; 6 May, 1960
Venue: RCA Studios, Hollywood (April) and Radio Recorders Studios, Hollywood (May)
Titles recorded: 'Big Boots', 'Blue Suede Shoes', 'Didja Ever', 'Doin' The Best I Can', 'Frankfurt Special', 'G.I. Blues', 'Pocketful Of Rainbows', 'Shoppin' Around', 'Tonight Is So Right For Love', 'Tonight's All Right For Love', 'What's She Really Like?', 'Wooden Heart'
N B The session on 6 May was to re-record the songs that were unsuccessful in April

These sessions were to lay down the tracks for Elvis Presley's first film after his Army discharge, *G.I. Blues*. Two songs with almost identical titles, 'Tonight Is So Right For Love', and 'Tonight's All Right For Love' were necessary, as the first was unable for copyright reasons to be released at that time in Europe. The film deals with US Army life in Germany as part of NATO, which Presley had experienced during his service. 'Big Boots', however, is a lullaby to a dozing child, and is well sung in Presley's quiet manner. The use of celeste in the backing is just right, but the song is over before it has got going. 'Blue Suede Shoes' is good, but it lacks the rawness of the performance of January 1956. 'Didja Ever' is an 'Army'-type song. It has add-on lyrics to a tune that is basically on 'open' notes, which are those of a bugle call. The use of a baritone tuba is another big plus, but it is Presley's performance which grows in strength with each line.

'Doin' The Best I Can' is a slow ballad, written by Doc Pomus and Mort Shuman. Presley sings this well and with sensitivity. But it is last on the *G.I. Blues* album, which thereby comes to an end on a sorrowful note. 'Frankfurt Special' (always spelled Frankfort) is a tremendously successful song, a fast 'train' number, kicked into life by Presley's tight entry, 'Is this train the Frankfurt Special?'. From that opening it drives forward, each verse rising by a semitone from the previous one. 'G.I. Blues' itself moves to a march rhythm – the Jordanaires' 'Hup, two, three, four' – and is a successful mixing of a blues beat with the march, but with little independent life. The same cannot be said for 'Pocketful Of Rainbows', which is very attractive: soft, with gentle percussion, and quiet accordion and guitar work. Presley sings this to perfection, as he also does 'Shoppin' Around', a medium-fast rocker with strong country bias. 'Tonight Is So Right For Love' uses the 'Barcarolle' from Offenbach's opera *The Tales of Hoffmann*, whereas 'Tonight's All Right For Love' takes a tune form Johann Strauss's *Tales From the Vienna Woods* as its basis.

The Offenbach tune stands up better to this treatment than the Strauss. 'What's She Really Like?' is a catchy number, of medium-bounce tempo, sung in appropriately easy-going style. Finally, 'Wooden Heart', which is a beautifully touching medium-slow ballad, very attractive in itself, and fascinatingly scored with an almost Bavarian gentility in the backing instrumentation, is a song that brought out some of the best of Elvis Presley's singing – delicate, restrained, finely controlled with its breathing and *mezzo-voce* ('half voice'), and relaxed: a very fine example of an aspect of this singer's art. In *A Legendary Performer* (vol 3) a faster take of 'Frankfurt Special' is issued: it is preferable to that used in the film, but the speed was probably too fast for the set. This collection of songs for *G.I. Blues* constitutes one of the best for a film made by Presley. His next film – and his next recordings – were vastly different.

12 August, 1960
Venue: Twentieth-Century Fox Studios, (?) Hollywood
Titles recorded: 'Britches', 'A Cane And A High-Starched Collar', 'Flaming Star', 'Summer Kisses, Winter Tears'

These four titles were recorded for Presley's next film, the dramatic western, *Flaming Star*, in which he gives the finest acting performance of his career. In the event, owing to the dramatic nature of the film only two songs were used, the title song (played over the opening credits) and 'A Cane And A High-Starched Collar'. Curiously enough, only the title song and 'Summer Kisses, Winter Tears' were issued before 1976, when 'A Cane And A High-Starched Collar' was released on volume 2 of the *Legendary Performer* series. 'Britches' did not appear until 1978, on volume 3 of the same series.

It is not surprising that the songs have a country, almost hill-billy flavour to them. 'Britches' is a medium up-tempo number, with a pretty tune, enhanced by Presley's 'Yo-de-o-de-o' refrain. It is short – only one minute thirty-nine seconds – but attractive. 'A Cane And A High-Starched Collar' is sung almost at the start of the film, at a family dance gathering, before a horrifying murder plunges the story into a black atmosphere, from which it never escapes. The issue on volume 2 of the *Legendary Performer* series is fascinating, because it starts with take two – announced – and lets us hear the breakdown, Presley's comments, and the announcement of and complete take three. Presley may have had some trouble with the words in take one – which we do not hear – and in take two he breaks down in laughter at the line 'I'll be your darling Jenny'. On the complete take, the accordionist messes up his chords, so these faults (which could have been easily edited out) possibly prevented the earlier release of the song.

'Flaming Star' itself is striking – it has a Red Indian feel (as befits the story – Presley plays a half breed). It uses low unpitched drums as an ostinato. This song recalls the musical atmosphere of Johnny Preston's big hit of early 1960, 'Running Bear', also with a Red Indian background, and was possibly influenced by it. The stereophonic recording enables us to hear the wide and deep backing. 'Summer Kisses, Winter Tears', which *was* issued at the time, although not used in the film, has an air of nostalgia about it, but is too based on formulas to have independent life.

October, 1960
Venue: Twentieth-Century Fox Studios (?), Hollywood
Titles recorded: 'Forget Me Never', 'In My Way', 'I Slipped, I Stumbled, I Fell', 'Lonely Man', 'Wild In The Country'

These recordings were to tape the songs for Elvis Presley's next film, *Wild In The Country*. This film, too, shows more of Presley's acting than his singing, but the music does feature more prominently than in *Flaming Star*.

'Husky Dusky Day', used in the film, was never issued commercially: it was recorded on the sound set, not in a studio, and of those listed above, 'Forget Me Never' was not used in the film. It is a gentle, softly swaying song with a quiet acoustic guitar accompaniment. It is a haunting number. 'In My Way' is similar: slow, accompanied by acoustic guitar. The recording is strange: there is a distracting buzz. 'I Slipped, I Stumbled, I Fell' is a hard rocker, spoiled by echo: there is no 'air' around Presley or the instruments. 'Lonely Man' is very fine indeed. It has great emotional appeal, and Presley's performance is one of the best of his career. A neglected song, it deserves to be better known. 'Wild In The Country', another gentle number, is heard over the credits in the film, where its hypnotic movement creates the film's atmosphere.

93

30/31 October, 1960

Venue: RCA Studios, Nashville

Titles recorded: 'Crying In The Chapel', 'His Hand In Mine', 'I Believe In The Man In The Sky', 'If We Never Meet Again', 'I'm Gonna Walk Dem Golden Stairs', 'In My Father's House', 'Jesus Knows Just What I Need', 'Joshua Fit The Battle', 'Known Only To Him', 'Mansion Over The Hilltop', 'Milky White Way', 'Surrender', 'Swing Down, Sweet Chariot', 'Working On The Building'

As can be seen, this session was set up to make a new religious album. The result is remarkable: one can understand that his church upbringing had given Presley a deep love and reverence for these songs. The charge of sentimentality can be levelled against a few of these items, but Presley's sincerity is never in doubt. 'Crying In The Chapel' – the most successful of these recordings, but not released for five years – veers near these waters, but the pulse is slow, with harmonies (superbly realised by the Jordanaires) that carry the beat. It is sung by Presley with tenderness and a fine feeling for the words. In 'His Hand In Mine', Presley sings beautifully against the vocal backing. Although the instrumentalists are unknown, it is possible the distinctive piano stylist is Floyd Cramer. The tasteful arrangements on most of the songs recorded are best shown in 'I Believe In The Man In The Sky', a medium-fast religious song, and 'If We Never Meet Again, in 3/4 time – a slow song with fetching melody, although it cannot escape the charge of stiffness. The accusation cannot be levelled against 'I'm Gonna Walk Dem Golden Stairs', a fast revival number. Presley sings below full power, but enough to keep the song moving. The waltz tempo is apparent in 'In My Father's House'. Presley, the Jordanaires and Millie Kirkham blend, with a lovely quality to Presley's voice. Ray Walker takes a verse to contrast, and the diction and phrasing of all singers are exemplary. The harmonies, a feature of these sessions, are heard to excellent effect in 'Jesus Knows Just What I Need', a slowish medium tempo song. Unusually, the piano has a gently insistent 'oom-pah' part. In complete contrast, the spiritual 'Joshua Fit The Battle' is fast and bouncy, with soft, swing piano and drums. The Jordanaires shine here. 'Known Only To Him' returns to slow 3/4 time, an expressive song, performed with great tenderness. 'Mansion Over The Hilltop' lacks distinction, although it is effective enough. It is the Jordanaires who shine in 'Milk White Way' (the first song recorded at the sessions) against Presley's relaxed, balanced solos.

The enormous success of 'It's Now Or Never' demanded a follow-up, and 'Surrender' attempts to repeat the formula. The Neapolitan song, 'Come Back To Sorrento' is transferred to bossa nova rhythm, with fast guitar chords. It does not quite come off – although Presley sings the arrangement to perfection, with a dazzling top B flat full of powerful head-tone. The arrangement of 'Swing Down, Sweet Chariot' is in fast, close harmony style. Presley threads through the intricate vocal tapestry effectively here and in 'Working On The Building', a bouncy revival number. Presley leads without shouting and the second verse begins with Presley in duet with a descant. The Jordanaires' clapping adds to the growing religious fervour.

12/13 March, 1961
Venue: RCA Studios, Nashville
Titles recorded: 'Gently', 'Give Me The Right', 'I Feel So Bad', 'I Want You With Me', 'I'm Comin' Home', 'In Your Arms', 'It's A Sin', 'Judy', 'Put The Blame On Me', 'Sentimental Me', 'Starting Today', 'There's Always Me'

A new album was the reason for these sessions, and 'Gently' sets the overall tone. It is remarkable for Presley's soft vocal line as well as guitar work, which threads its way against his voice. There are some nice harmonies and a quiet, superbly balanced, bass line. 'Give Me The Right' is not top-drawer material: a slow, heavy ballad with a surprisingly free saxophone solo from Boots Randolph. 'I Feel So Bad' is quite different, with phrases from guitar and piano propelling it. 'I Want You With Me' is a standard rock number of its time, and Bobby Darin also made a fine recording of hit on his otherwise best-forgotten album *For Teenagers Only*. What makes the Presley track less appealing is the recording. Presley gets lost in the general uproar. With 'I'm Comin' Home', a Charlie Rich number, driven with fast drumming, Cramer's piano is still not well balanced. 'In Your Arms' has Presley's voice better balanced, but the Jordanaires and Millie Kirkham have too much echo. This time, Boots Randolph is too distant! But as the song is not up to much, this is no great disaster. The slow, delicate number 'It's A Sin' begins with a soft falsetto from Presley – a good example of his ability to handle this tricky part of the voice. Poor balancing spoils 'Judy', where the guitar never stops and is so far forward that it overshadows the song. It is difficult to hear Presley while this clatter is going on just behind him. 'Put The Blame On Me' is a good arrangement, a good performance – though it is a mediocre number.

'Sentimental Me' is a better song – slow, with a gently throbbing beat. Presley gets round this one, but it lacks conviction. 'Starting Today' is much better: Floyd Cramer's gentle, haunting piano is ideally balanced. This is a really beautiful song, delicately performed by Presley and the Jordanaires. Finally, 'There's Always Me' is a superb performance: the opening is magical, with much achieved with little effort. A fine track, of which any singer would feel proud.

21–23 March, 1961
Venue: Radio Recorders Studios, Hollywood
Titles recorded: 'Almost Always True', 'Aloha-oe', 'Beach Boy Blues', 'Blue Hawaii', 'Can't Help Falling In Love', 'Hawaiian Sunset', 'Hawaiian Wedding Song', 'Island Of Love', 'Ito Eats', 'Ku-u-i-po', 'Moonlight Swim', 'No More', 'Rock-A-Hula-Baby', 'Slicin' Sand', 'Steppin' Out Of Line'

These tracks make up the songs for Elvis Presley's next film, Paramount Pictures' *Blue Hawaii*. A succession of Hawaiian songs provided a challenge: the distinctive sound of Hawaiian music places constrictions on songwriters, and a variety is not always achieved. 'Almost Always True' is a situation song, of a *frère-Jacques* construction. It has a long saxophone introduction from Boots Randolph, but is not memorable for anything else. Presley arranged the traditional Hawaiian song 'Aloha-oe', which is well sung by him in Hawaiian. The strange thing is that all the backing vocals are on the left-hand channel; an unimaginative use of stereo. Little need be said about 'Beach Boy Blues', which appeared before Californian surfers became famous. It is a feeble song, indifferently performed. Much the same is true of 'Blue Hawaii', but this undistinguished song is enhanced by unusual instrumentation, and Presley's soft high note at the end. 'Can't Help Falling In Love' can only be better; the melody is another classical theme, the 'Plaisir d'Amour' by Martini (*Il Tedesco*). This is sung with very good breath control by Presley: the breaks in the vocal line are natural and effective. 'Hawaiian Sunset' is the best of the Hawaiian-type numbers: it is well sung, with nice harmonies in the arrangement. Most striking is the unusual melody line. The famous tune 'Hawaiian Wedding Song' is tastefully done, but less so is 'Island Of Love' written by the composers of 'Hawaiian Sunset' (Tepper and Bennett), who offer a watered-down version of that song.

In such surroundings, it was natural that a Belafonte-style number should surface and his influence is obvious in 'Ito Eats'. It even includes 'day-day' repeats, and the final line shows its indebtedness. There is, however, a relaxed feel, and the use of unpitched drums is effective. The slow, gently bouncing number, 'Ku-u-i-po', is also well sung, with fine use by Presley of his *mezzo-voce*. The song itself hardly merits attention, and neither does 'Moonlight Swim', a gentle but innocuous number. 'No More' is a good song, which Presley seems to believe in and enjoys singing. He doubtless got a lot of fun from 'Rock-A-Hula-Baby', an impossible fusion of Hawaiian and rock; a slick, fun piece. The nearest to a genuine rocker in the collection is 'Slicin' Sand', which is of the 'Blue Suede Shoes' variety, but it does not stand up on its own. The final song 'Steppin' Out of Line' was originally written to be a part of the film sound-track, but was dropped. It was eventually released on the album *Pot Luck* the following year.

25/26 June, 1961
Venue: RCA Studios, Nashville
Titles recorded: 'His Latest Flame', 'I'm Yours', 'Kiss Me Quick', 'Little Sister', 'That's Someone You Never Forget'

These sessions – spread over two days – produced only five songs, but included some outstanding hit material. 'His Latest Flame', a classic recording of a fine song by Doc Pomus and Mort Shuman, tells a story – like 'The Girl Of My

Best Friend'. It is propelled by an original rocking beat, and the words are more important than in most rockers. Presley sings with power and ease. The piano part (presumably Floyd Cramer) adds the finishing touch. 'I'm Yours' is outstanding: a slow arrangement of this fine song. Floyd Cramer, this time on organ, adds a superb part. Cramer also appears on 'Kiss Me Quick', a medium bounce to a soft rock beat – but hardly hit material.

'Little Sister' is another classic Presley performance. There is a 'dirty' feel, a smouldering innuendo in Presley's voice, which is cut through by electric guitar phrases. This has a mesmerising effect, helped by the song being contained within a few notes. The final number, 'That's Someone You Never Forget' is excellent. It is slow and moves with block harmonies: a haunting song, beautifully sung.

5 July, 1961
Venue: RCA Studios, Nashville
Titles recorded: 'Angel', 'A Whistling Tune', 'Follow That Dream', 'I'm Not The Marrying Kind', 'Sound Advice', 'What A Wonderful Life'
N B 'A Whistling Tune' was not issued

These five songs, recorded under studio conditions by RCA, made up the sound-track for Presley's film *Follow That Dream*, an innocuous vehicle enlivened by Presley (as Toby Kwimper) displaying judo skills. In the event, 'A Whistling Tune' was not used and turned up (in a different recording) in Presley's next film.

'Angel' has a slow, exotic atmosphere, with an attractive echo answer from Millie Kirkham. The song, however, is barely passable. The title song, 'Follow That Dream', is happy, with an infectious bounce. 'I'm Not The Marrying Kind' is a quiet, bouncy number, with a slow introduction. It is effective in its restrained piano. Much the same is true of 'Sound Advice' but it is well undistinguished. The final song, 'What A Wonderful Life' is better, and Presley appears more moved by it, missing no trick to give point to the words.

15/16 October, 1961
Venue: RCA Studios, Nashville
Titles recorded: 'Anything That's Part Of You', 'For The Millionth And Last Time', 'Good Luck Charm', 'I Met Her Today'
N B 'Night Rider' was recorded at these sessions, but was unsatisfactory and re-recorded the following March

RCA was looking for a new single and found one with 'Good Luck Charm'. 'Anything That's Part Of You', a ballad, is one of the most underestimated Presley recordings. Floyd Cramer's piano is to the fore and through it an acoustic guitar weaves delicate embroidery. Presley's performance builds to hypnotic effect. 'For The Millionth And Last Time' is undistinguished, and although set to a cha-cha-cha rhythm, is enervating. 'Good Luck Charm' was a big hit throughout the world, (number one in Britain) but, heard from a distance of almost thirty years, does not stand up. It is a medium tempo bounce, elevated to hit status by the musicianship lavished upon it. Presley's genius as a singer stems partly form his ability to give a totally committed performance, bringing out the song's best qualities, so that one feels the song is better than it really is.

The same comments apply to 'I Met Her Today'. This ordinary ballad is so well sung that one listens to Presley's voice rather than to what he is singing about.

October/November, 1961
Venue: Radio Recorders Studios, Hollywood
Titles recorded: 'A Whistling Tune', 'Home Is Where The Heart Is', 'I Got Lucky', 'King Of The Whole Wide World', 'Riding The Rainbow', 'This Is Living'

These sessions provided the songs for Presley's next film *Kid Galahad*, about a boxer. 'A Whistling Tune' is precisely what it says: a catchy number, but little more. 'Home Is Where The Heart Is', is a good song, and Presley sings with great feeling for the vocal line. 'I Got Lucky' is unusual in that the drum follows Presley's vocal line. It is a happy song, but not particularly memorable. 'King Of The Whole Wide World' is outstanding: a good rock number, with chunky piano and burning saxophone. Presley's vocal range is quite fantastic – from a *mezzo-voce* in one octave to a powerful *fortissimo* in another, with only a fractional gap between. Tremendously successful, the song tingles with well-being. 'Riding The Rainbow' is another rocker, but not so good. It is lightly arranged, and the piano is featured, but it does not add up to much. Neither does the final song, 'This Is Living'; another fast rocking tempo, with a strong boogie bass, Presley's duetting against the Jordanaires is well done, but it cannot rescue the song.

18/19 March, 1962
Venue: RCA Studios, Nashville
Titles recorded: 'Easy Question', 'Fountain Of Love', 'Gonna Get Back Home Somehow', 'I Feel That I've Known You Forever', 'Just For Old Times' Sake', 'Just Tell Her Jim Said Hello', 'Night Rider', 'She's Not You', 'Something Blue', 'Suspicion', 'You'll Be Gone'

These sessions produced a new album and a single, but the songs are variable in quality, and none shows Presley at his greatest. The first song, 'Easy Question', is too innocuous, and the second, 'Fountain Of Love', too uncertain in style, to be successful. This is not a criticism of Presley, who sings both numbers superbly, but of the material. 'Fountain Of Love' is an unsuccessful mixture. 'Gonna Get Back Home Somehow' is better: a fast, infectious number, whose variety of vocal colouring produces inimitable results. 'I Fell That I've Known You Forever', a slow waltz, builds to a finely controlled climax, but lacks power. The sentimental slow ballad, 'Just For Old Times' Sake' has the merits of a restrained arrangement and distinctive harmonies. Presley sings this with great feeling, but 'Just Tell Her Jim Said Hello' is disappointing. The arrangement is fussy: the triangle sounds like a nagging door-bell, and the recording is poorly balanced. The bass is too far forward, and the final chord cuts off as the song fades.

'Night Rider', a fast number, has dirty, raucous saxophone commentary, but is poor material. Presley sounds uncommitted in 'She's Not You'. 'Something Blue' is better, for this features imaginative piano from Floyd Cramer. 'Suspicion', a fine number, which was a big hit for Terry Stafford in 1964, is not the outstanding performance Presley could have given. The final song, 'You'll Be Gone', is another unusual number; it has the flavour of a Mexican beguine, and is notable for stylish guitar work. There is too much echo around Presley's voice, but one can appreciate his breath control. An underrated recording.

March, 1962
Venue: Radio Recorders Studios, Hollywood
Titles recorded: 'A Boy Like Me, A Girl Like You', 'Because Of Love', 'Earth Boy', 'Girls! Girls! Girls!', 'I Don't Wanna Be Tied', 'I Don't Want To', 'Return To Sender', 'Song Of The Shrimp', 'Thanks To The Rolling Sea', 'The Walls Have Ears', 'We'll Be Together', 'We're Coming In Loaded', 'Where Do You Come From?'

These songs constitute the numbers for Presley's film for Paramount Pictures, *Girls! Girls! Girls!*, and are the usual mixture of situation numbers, formula offerings and outstanding songs. The songs featured in the majority of Presley's films for the next seven years or so are rarely noteworthy. The surprising thing is that, with so many second- and third-rate songs, Presley was able to do anything. 'A Boy Like Me, A Girl Like You' is light years away from the classic Presley recordings of the 1950s and the early 1960s. It is without any distinguishing characteristics. 'Because Of Love' is even worse: an instrumental backing so feeble and lacking in fibre that it sounds childish compared with Presley's sterling work on the vocal line. 'Earth Boy' is another formula song, but has a pinch of oriental flavouring. The title track 'Girls! Girls! Girls!' is a fast and bouncy number, and it has the virtues of fun and an extended Boots Randolph saxophone riff. 'I Don't Wanna Be Tied' recalls one of Presley's favourite singers – Bobby Darin. It would be good juke-box material, and has an unusual slow ending, but does not bear repetition. 'I Don't Want To' is good of its type, and will be familiar to those who know 'The Party's Over'. Well sung, this ought to have achieved success, and could still prove to be a posthumous hit for Presley.

But 'Return To Sender' is a classic cut, an outstanding example of Presley's art at its best. The song is difficult to bring off, but Presley treads its vocal tightrope superbly. Not for a second do the repetitions of the title seem too many, and the unusual words are commandingly put across. The beat is exactly right and, although nothing to do with rock, this is Presley at his best. 'Song Of The Shrimp' is very strange. This unusual song is beautifully written, clearly recorded, tastefully arranged and endearingly performed, giving an outstanding result. But it is still a song about a shrimp! 'Thanks To The Rolling Sea', another Darin-type performance, is a superior plot-song. Its use of drums gives it a 'chain-gang' feel. 'The Walls Have Ears' might have been effective on the screen, but heard by itself it is best forgotten. 'We'll Be Together' is also poor material, as is 'We're Coming In Loaded'. The unusual arrangement has a flickering bass line, but the song is feeble. The final song, 'Where Do You Come From?' is not much better, but has its moments, although it adds little to our perception of the singer.

Autumn, 1962
Venue: Hollywood
Titles recorded: 'A World Of Our Own', 'Beyond The Bend', 'Cotton Candy Land', 'Happy Ending', 'How Would You Like To Be', 'I'm Falling In Love Tonight', 'One Broken Heart For Sale', 'Relax', 'Take Me To The Fair', 'They Remind Me Too Much Of You'

These were recorded for the MGM film *It Happened At The World's Fair*. This continues the formula of *Girls! Girls! Girls!* and the songs are of variable quality. 'A World Of Our Own' is pleasant enough, but mediocre, hampered by a wooden backing. 'Beyond The Bend' is another undistinguished song, and not even inventive guitar playing can rescue it. Although some admire the performance, it is sad that Presley performed this material. 'Cotton Candy Land' is a kind of oriental lullaby, beautifully done but with no life outside of the film. With 'Happy Ending' we are back to a fast rocker with an infectious beat, but the song has no guts. 'How Would You Like To Be' is a children's song enlivened by a military drum. The middle eight is in polka dots manner, but the song is too long. 'I Am Falling In Love Tonight' is better material, a slow ballad with imaginative work from organ and piano. Elvis begins the song unaccompanied, dictated by the demands of the film; but it makes a very effective, compelling beginning. 'One Broken Heart For Sale' is a better number than most of the other songs. It is a fast bouncer in 'Return To Sender' style but it has a second-hand air. The song is marred by poor recording; the sound is tight and the acoustic has a squashed image. Perhaps the best number is 'Relax', which is dramatic yet quiet and dreamy, written in a style not unlike 'Fever'. There is a gently picking guitar thread against Presley's Darin-ish style. But the song tends to lose its way in the middle section. 'Take Me To The Fair' is hardly worth mentioning. Presley's singing is good in the final song, 'They Remind Me Too Much Of You'. Again, the song does not quite make it; but with a fine piano contribution and Presley's superb phrasing the result is an object lesson to ballad singers.

22/23 January, 1963
Venue: Radio Recorders Studios, Hollywood
Titles recorded: 'Bossa Nova Baby', 'The Bullfighter Was A Lady', 'El Toro',
'Fun In Acapulco', 'Guadalajara', 'I Think I'm Gonna Like It Here',
'Marguerita', 'Mexico', 'There's No Room To Rhumba In A Sports Car', 'Vino,
Dinero Y Amor', 'You Can't Say No In Acapulco'

Eleven days after MGM handed over the song tapes for *It Happened At The World's Fair* to RCA, Presley was back in Hollywood to put down these titles for his next film. This was for Paramount Pictures, and was his second location film, *Fun In Acapulco*.

The Acapulco setting naturally demanded a collection of songs with local atmosphere. With one or two exceptions, the composers did not find inspiration in the Mexican location. It seems as though Presley was unhappy. He re-recorded a number of these songs, and an alternative take of 'Guadalajara', taped on 27 February, 1963, is included on *A Legendary Performer* (vol 3). The first song, 'Bossa Nova Baby', is something like the old Presley, and contrasts with the inferior material he had previously used in his films. This is a fast, modern record, notably because of its use of organ. There is a touch of rock about the song, together with a bossa nova feel which is magical. In spite of the fast pace, every word is crystal clear and in its way this is a classic recording. The remaining songs are little more than aural wallpaper. 'The Bullfighter Was A Lady' is best merely imagined; 'El Toro' is feeble, and 'Fun In Acapulco' is distorted by the recording engineers. Elvis begins the song very loudly, which surprised the engineers. They turn down the volume, and do not adjust it, ruining the sound of Presley's voice.

There are no problems with 'Guadalajara', which is a curiosity. Presley sings it in Mexican Spanish, and very well, for his diction enables every word to be heard. The same cannot be said of 'I Think I'm Gonna Like It Here', another feeble number without the benefit of good orchestral backing. 'Marguerita' is a better song, and begins arrestingly with two trumpets. Unfortunately the engineers have compressed the sound, making it sound bland. The orchestration in 'Mexico' is its best feature; this is another forgettable number. A blind should also be drawn over 'There's No Room To Rhumba In A Sports Car', in spite of Presley's vain attempts to infuse life into it. The Mexican number 'Vino, Dinero Y Amor' brings this poor collection to a close. It is a wild number, very fast, but as the backing consists of what appears to be the entire population of Mexico, it is difficult to appreciate. 'You Can't Say No In Acapulco' is what used to be termed a 'novelty' number, and of its type it had some attractive qualities. The general fantasy feeling of an endlessly enjoyable holiday mood is well caught and projected here.

26/27 May, 1963
Venue: RCA Studios, Nashville
Titles recorded: 'Blue River', 'Devil In Disguise', 'Echoes Of Love', 'Finders Keepers, Losers Weepers', 'Long Lonely Highway', 'Love Me Tonight', 'Never Ending', 'Please Don't Drag That String Around', 'Slowly But Surely', 'Western Union', 'What Now, What Next, Where To?', 'Witchcraft'

These were required for a new album, but were issued in haphazard fashion. It may be that Presley's films, with their sound-track albums, made RCA feel they were pushing out too much Presley material. 'Devil In Disguise' is a very unusual song: the guitar and piano introduction is contradicted by the subsequent cha-cha rhythm, and when the chorus arrives the beat has changed to a fast pulse. A solid bass from Bob Moore joins in and the song takes off when clapping suddenly appears. 'Echoes Of Love' is a medium tempo song with repeated phrases on piano and unusual use of vibes. Presley is relaxed and easy-going like the song itself, which is good pop but little more. 'Finders Keepers, Losers Weepers' is humorous, but too flippant to bear repetition. The distinctive characteristic, apart from the medium bounce in Presley's voice, is Boots Randolph's saxophone. In 'Long Lonely Highway', a 'travel' song of blues extraction, there is an unusual catchy rhythm, similar to 'Devil In Disguise'. 'Love Me Tonight' is a slow ballad with a gentle piano which features prominently. Elvis is in good voice, and sings in a simple manner. A similar song is 'Never Ending', but it is not distinctive material. 'Please Don't Drag That String Around' is a good up-tempo number pushed along by a fruity saxophone line. In spite of its qualities, this song lacks an immediate hook, as one might expect from a number used as a fill-up in a film sound-track. 'Slowly But Surely' is disappointing, apart from the guitar lick that opens it. 'Western Union' is a novelty number, designed to recapture the style of 'Return To Sender'. Like most such attempts it is a pale imitation of the original.

'What Now, What Next, Where To?' despite its clumsy title, is one of the best numbers from these sessions. Presley is abetted by Floyd Cramer on piano, but the engineers have surrounded his voice with echo. The final song, 'Witchcraft', is a fast blues number. The opening is a standard bass line, but when Boots Randolph joins Presley, a great jive record results.

July, 1963
Venue: Hollywood
Titles recorded: 'C'mon Everybody', 'Do The Vega', 'If You Think I Don't Need You', 'I Need Somebody To Lean On', 'Night Life', 'Santa Lucia', 'Today, Tomorrow And Forever', 'Viva Las Vegas', 'What'd I Say', 'Yellow Rose Of Texas'/'The Eyes Of Texas'
N B 'Do The Vega' and 'Night Life' were not used in the film

These songs were for Presley's next film *Viva Las Vegas*. In Britain, the title was changed to *Love In Las Vegas*. This is one of the best collection of songs in a Presley film since *G.I. Blues*, three years before. 'C'mon Everybody' is not the same as the great Eddie Cochran number. It is a medium-fast song with good breaks. 'Do The Vega' shows the influence of the samba-type song 'La Bamba'. 'If You Think I Don't Need You' has a big-band backing, tight and hard-driven, with another outstanding saxophone break. This fine song deserves to be better known, as does the Doc Pomus/Mort Shuman number 'I Need Somebody To Lean On'. In spite of filigree guitar work and gentle piano backing, there is too much echo on the voice, and the instruments are too far back. This song has a similar atmosphere to another underrated number a few years before, 'Was There A Call For Me?' by Woody Harris and Mary Holmes. 'Night Life' is not in this class: it begins with a sinuous 'night-club' atmosphere from baritone saxophone and a mean electric bass. The change of key (to the supertonic) is standard formula, but effective. The Neapolitan song 'Santa Lucia' is a surprise choice, but Presley rises to the challenge. His strong baritone voice copes well with this classic, but he is not Caruso. As the song only lasts one minute eleven seconds, it is over before it has begun. 'Today, Tomorrow and Forever' is another piece of classical music, this time Liszt's *Liebestraum*. In spite of the distinctive tune, this is ruined by out-of-tune singing from the Jordanaires at the end. Somebody in the studio agreed, for at the end of the take you can hear a lone 'Yuch'!

'What'd I Say' is the great rhythm and blues hit for Jerry Lee Lewis of two years before. Presley returns to his roots with exciting singing. Unfortunately his voice is harsh here, and buried in the general uproar. This cannot be because he was tired, as it was only the second song recorded at these sessions. The final number (or rather numbers) is the 'Yellow Rose Of Texas'/'The Eyes Of Texas'. This is an average arrangement sung without conviction.

October, 1963
Venue: RCA Studios, Nashville
Titles recorded: 'Anyone', 'Barefoot Ballad', 'Catchin' On Fast', 'Kissin' Cousins', 'Kissin' Cousins' (No. 2), 'Once Is Enough', 'One Boy, Two Little Girls', 'Smokey Mountain Boy', 'Tender Feeling', 'There's Gold In The Mountains'

These songs were possibly recorded in October, but exact details are not available. They were for Presley's next film *Kissin' Cousins*, in which he plays two parts. The first song 'Anyone' is poor, a ballad, well sung but undistinguished. The country style is more to the fore in 'Barefoot Ballad', with violin, banjo and possibly a nose flute in the background. Presley's voice sounds unlike anything heard before, but it fits the song and the film. 'Catchin' On Fast' is a very good song, with drums featured prominently, although it is possible to be put off by the sudden ending. It is difficult not to be confused by the two versions of 'Kissin' Cousins'. 'Kissin' Cousins' (No. 1) is an underrated song. It has a bluesy feel, with sensational drumming. 'Kissin' Cousins' (No. 2) is different: the playing is poor by comparison. Three mediocre songs included are 'Once Is Enough', in rockabilly style; 'One Boy, Two Little Girls', a gentle bouncy number, and 'Smokey Mountain Boy', which has a march rhythm and a whistling introduction. 'Tender Feeling', using the song 'Shenandoah', is a stylish arrangement with effective lyrics. It is well sung, and reminds us what a great natural singer Elvis Presley was. The final song, 'There's Gold In The Mountains' is enlivened by good piano and guitar work, but is undistinguished.

12 January, 1964
Venue: RCA Studios, Nashville
Titles recorded: 'Ask Me', 'It Hurts Me', 'Memphis Tennessee'
N B 'Ask Me' and 'Memphis Tennessee' were recorded at the big sessions on 26/27 May, 1963 but were unsuccessful; they were re-recorded at this session

'Ask Me' has Floyd Cramer on organ, which adds a distinctive tone colour, but detracts from Presley's voice. 'It Hurts Me' is a slow ballad, with Elvis more controlled than for some time. Parts of the song are almost whispered, and others are given at full power. The result is dramatic and compelling. There is another take issued early in 1979, without the Jordanaires, but the song is improved by the additional voices. 'Memphis Tennessee' was a hit in 1963 for both Chuck Berry and (in Britain) Dave Berry. It is a pity that Presley's previous recording in May was unsuccessful. This is a superb performance, with the right quality of restrained unhappiness.

24 and 28 February; 2 and 6 March, 1964
Venue: Radio Recorders, Hollywood
Titles recorded: 'Big Love, Big Heartache', 'Carny Town', 'Hard Knocks', 'It's A Wonderful World', 'It's Carnival Time', 'Little Egypt', 'One Track Heart', 'Poison Ivy League', 'Roustabout', 'There's A Brand New Day On The Horizon', 'Wheels On My Heels'

These songs made up the tracks for Presley's Paramount film *Roustabout*, and show a marked decline in quality. Whatever Presley thought of this material, he attempts to give the least worthy song the best chance. He cannot avoid sounding uninterested in 'Big Love, Big Heartache', 'Carny Town' (very poor), 'Hard Knock' (quite undistinguished) and 'It's A Wonderful World', which has a fast tempo but a slow-moving voice part. 'It's Carnival Time' is based on the harmonies from Fucick's 'Entry of the Gladiators' (the theme song for every circus). 'Little Egypt' is a song about a belly dancer. 'Poison Ivy League' is a cynical view of co-eds. 'Roustabout' matches the free-wheeling mood of the title and is another song in fast tempo with a slow melody. 'John Brown's Body' forms the harmony for 'There's A Brand New Day On The Horizon', and the final song, 'Wheels On My Heels', is nothing to write home about.

July, 1964
Venue: Hollywood
Titles recorded: 'Cross My Heart And Hope To Die', 'Do Not Disturb', 'Do The Clam', 'Fort Lauderdale Chamber Of Commerce', 'Girl Happy', 'I've Got To Find My Baby', 'The Meanest Girl In Town', 'Puppet On A String', 'Spring Fever', 'Startin' Tonight', 'Wolf Call'

These songs constitute the sound-track recordings for MGM's *Girl Happy*. They are better than those used for *Roustabout*. 'Cross My Heart And Hope To Die' has a jazz feel in its introduction, but fails to live up to this opening. 'Do Not Disturb' is a slow song, so well sung it almost makes one forget the poor material. 'Do The Clam' begins with soft drums and guitar, and is a speciality dance number, effective in the film, but not on disc, in spite of the use of stereo distance. The unusually titled 'Fort Lauderdale Chamber Of Commerce' is a good song, well put over. It is a 'plot' song with a cha-cha-cha beat, and the hook around the title is very effective.

In 'Girl Happy' there is a quality reminiscent of Jimmy Justice to Presley's voice, which may be due to the engineers. 'I've Got To Find My Baby' has a dramatic opening in fast shouting style. 'The Meanest Girl In Town' is a fast song characterised by unimaginative use of backing vocals. In 'Puppet On A String', the Floyd Cramer-like piano introduction is atmospheric, but the song is average. So is 'Spring Fever', a fast bouncy number, and 'Startin' Tonight' is cut off suddenly. The final song, 'Wolf Call' is a good novelty number with a more committed performance, but once again the mixing sounds false and unnatural.

February, 1965
Venue: RCA Studios, Nashville
Titles recorded: 'Animal Instinct', 'Go East, Young Man', 'Golden Coins', 'Harem Holiday', 'Hey Little Girl', 'Kismet', 'Mirage', 'My Desert Serenade', 'Shake That Tambourine', 'So Close, Yet So Far', 'Wisdom Of The Ages'
N B 'Animal Instinct' and 'Wisdom Of The Ages' were not included in the film

This collection was required for Elvis Presley's first film of 1965, the MGM studio production of *Harum Scarum* (titled *Harem Holiday* in Europe). Although no one would pretend Elvis Presley's films up to this time had made any significant contribution to the history of the cinema, with this one his credibility took a sharp downward turn. Almost all the songs in this film are mediocre, and scarcely bear serious attention.

By chance, the first song 'Animal Instinct' is quite good, enlivened by fascinating touches from flute and percussion with the accent falling on the second beat. Although this song has merit, it was removed from the film! 'Go East, Young Man' has an attractive cha-cha backing, but is otherwise unremarkable. With 'Golden Coins' we touch rock bottom. 'Harem Holiday' has no melodic appeal, and the accompaniment is divorced from the melody. By far the best is 'Hey Little Girl', a rocking number with intriguing use of piano. This also gets a committed performance from Presley.

The film's Middle East setting enables the arrangers to include appropriate orchestral backing in 'Kismet' (a slow cha-cha). The song is made more interesting by the use of an oboe (although it sounds sour), and two antique cymbals. 'Mirage' is another feeble song, and so is 'My Desert Serenade', which can be best described as oriental rock. When one considers what George Harrison was shortly to achieve by fusing Eastern influences with rock, this song pales into insignificance. 'Shake That Tambourine' is in fast-rocker tempo, but is mediocre, and the last two, 'So Close, Yet So Far' and 'Wisdom Of The Ages' do not deserve to be heard more than once. This collection can only be regarded as bitterly disappointing.

May, 1965
Venue: Hollywood
Titles recorded: 'Beginner's Luck', 'Chesay', 'Come Along', 'Down By The Riverside'/'When The Saints Go Marching In', 'Everybody Come Aboard', 'Frankie And Johnny', 'Hard Luck', 'Look Out Broadway', 'Petunia The Gardener's Daughter', 'Please Don't Stop Loving Me', 'Shout It Out', 'What Every Woman Lives For'

These sessions produced the songs for the second of Presley's three films of 1965, the United Artists' production of *Frankie and Johnny*. The first song, 'Beginner's Luck', is in medium-slow tempo, and is a quiet, restrained number of great gentleness. Presley sings it to perfection and the result is streets ahead of what he had done recently. 'Chesay' is best appreciated by reference to the film, which explains the European feel of the number. For those who do not know it the effect is of a Russo–Greek gypsy drinking-song. The song begins slow, and gets faster and faster; it is very effective. Unfortunately the same cannot be said of 'Come Along', another undistinguished piece.

'Down By The Riverside'/'When The Saints Go Marching In', traditional material, is well sung with a good bounce, but Presley's performance lacks the conviction. 'Everybody Come Aboard' is razzmatazz, but the writer's attempt to capture the right atmosphere has led him to rely on formulas. In 'Frankie And Johnny' Presley seems uninterested. Although well done, it is not a considered performance, and one can only assume it was an off-day. 'Hard Luck' has a mouth-organ introduction to set the scene and Presley gives the most committed singing of the set. But even he cannot redeem the words (Toodle-Oo)! 'Look Out Broadway' is another plot number with Presley in duet with Donna Douglas. It almost becomes a trio with persistent Mr Bass-Man. Although the Showboat atmosphere is well caught, the song does not stand up. 'Petunia, The Gardener's Daughter' begins with a honky-tonk opening from the band, and a relaxed, improvised introduction by Presley against the piano. He also duets with Donna Douglas on this song, which offers a faded charm. 'Please Don't Stop Loving Me' is a formula number of poor quality. 'Shout It Out' is fast but unmemorable. As an example of what Presley could do with less than first-class material 'What Every Woman Lives For' is one of the best; this slow ballad has a prominent blues piano backing. Presley sings it well, and tries to make it a better number than it is.

26/27 July; 2 and 4 August, 1965
Venue: Radio Recorders Studio, Hollywood
Titles recorded: 'Datin'', 'Dog's Life', 'Drum Of The Islands', 'A House Of Sand', 'Paradise, Hawaiian Style', 'Queenie Wahine's Papaya', 'Sand Castles', 'Scratch My Back', 'Stop Where You Are', 'This Is My Heaven'
N B 'Sand Castles' was not included in the film

These songs form the sound-track numbers for Presley's third film of 1965, *Paradise, Hawaiian Style*. This is clearly an attempt by Paramount Pictures to repeat the success of *Blue Hawaii* (1961), but in no way does this film approach the earlier one. The songs are well sung and played by the distinguished musicians assembled. The root cause of the problem is the undistinguished material that they had to work with. The first song, 'Datin'', is well projected by Presley and his backing musicians, but is poor material. The next 'Dog's Life', is far better and gets a much more committed performance. One can sense the interest in his voice from the arresting opening to the striking conclusion. 'Drums Of The Islands' is sung by the male voice chorus in unison with Presley, but is let down by the material, as is 'House Of Sand' and 'Paradise, Hawaiian Style' in which Presley shows signs of strain.

With 'Queenie Wahine's Papaya' we encounter a plot song, but for all the unusual lyrics and instrumentation, and the tongue-twisting the song accelerates, it remains indifferent. 'Sand Castles' (which was not included in the film) is probably the best of the lot; it has plenty of atmosphere, and this gentle song receives a fine performance from Presley. 'Scratch My Back' is better than most but is not worthy of Presley's talent – the same is true of 'Stop Where You Are'. This has an unusual, rhythmic opening, but the ending is trite. The final song, a slow ballad, 'This Is My Heaven', receives the best performance in the entire film. Presley lavishes all his artistry on it, but the song remains, sadly, rooted to the spot.

February, 1966
Venue: Unknown
Titles recorded: 'Adam And Evil', 'All That I Am', 'Am I Ready?', 'Beach Shack',
'I'll Be Back', 'Never Say Yes', 'Smorgasbord', 'Stop, Look And Listen',
'Spinout'

These sessions, which may have taken place in either Nashville or Hollywood, were to tape the songs for Presley's next film, *Spinout* (in Britain, *California Holiday*). There are some interesting touches in 'Adam And Evil': Mr Bass-Man is in evidence as the drums begin a fast and intricate beat. Presley sings in his 'teddy bear' voice, but divorced from the film the song hardly bears repetition. 'All That I Am' is a slow bossa nova, with a Spanish guitar opening, very well sung, as is 'Am I Ready?' a slow ballad, but manifestly not a good song. In 'Beach Shack' Presley returns to Belafonte-style material, in a light and airy song that recalls 'La Bamba'. 'I'll Be Back' is a feeble number, of interest only to Presley fans, but in 'Never Say Yes' the engineers appear to have interfered with the natural balance. For some reason this fast rocker has a messy sound, and the track a confused feel.

'Smorgasbord' has Presley picking women as though they were courses on a smorgasbord – a novel twist – and the song has merit. In 'Stop, Look And Listen' we have one of the better songs in the film, let down only by the electric organ. Once more, Presley has a touch of Darin in his performance, and the surprise ending is very attractive. The original title track, 'Spinout', is undistinguished with another too-prominent organ part in the middle section.

Chapter Eleven

Change of habit

25 and 28 May, 1966
Venue: RCA Studios, Nashville
Titles recorded: 'By And By', 'Come What May', 'Down In The Alley', 'Farther Along', 'Fools Fall In Love', 'How Great Thou Art', 'If The Lord Wasn't Walking By My Side', 'In The Garden', 'Love Letters', 'Run On', 'So High', 'Somebody Bigger Than You And I', 'Stand By Me', 'Tomorrow Is A Long Time', 'Where Could I Go But To The Lord?', 'Where No One Stands Alone', 'Without Him'

This major session proved to be a turning point in Presley's career. The material drew from him performances of incomparable stature. Presley's following during the previous ten years had been among the most loyal of any singer. But a singer can only retain the respect of his fans by recognising that they demand both a continuation of the songs that established his reputation and an acknowledgement that popular music is continuously evolving. So far, Presley had appeared unwilling or unable to sense the change in popular music that had occurred with the arrival of the Beatles. The necessary change for Presley began with these sessions; although he continued to make poor films, we can clearly see the improvement in the choice of material.

'By And By' has a bright 'Sunday morning' revival atmosphere. Presley does not shout, but sings, forcing the attention towards the attractiveness of the song, rather than its simple religious message. With 'Come What May' we encounter a song that was out of date even when it was recorded. It is a fast rocker, but the production, to a generation used to the sounds of Phil Spector, is raw and messy. In 'Down In The Alley' we have another revival shouter, a fierce rock–blues song which makes a powerful impact – but the words are far from religious! Nothing could be more different than 'Farther Along', a restrained song in waltz time. Presley sings this in a sincere manner. Another surprising number is 'Fools Fall In Love'. This is fast, with hefty brass and big vocal backing, which Presley sings *mezzo– voce*.

In 'How Great Thou Art' we have one of Presley's finest recorded performances. It is sung almost throughout in his low register, with deep rumblings from piano, timpani and male voice singers. The overall effect is overwhelming. Presley brings a magical top F at the end. 'If The Lord Wasn't Walking By My Side' is a bouncy number, sung in strict missionary manner, but it is unlikely any of the preachers in the First Assembly Of God Church could have matched Presley's fire and brimstone. This revivalist style continues with 'In The Garden', a slow song with real gospel feel. This is not raw and gutsy, but suitably reverent. In 'Love Letters', Presley revives the Ketty Lester hit of 1962. The result is a magnificent performance, featuring piano and organ, although it is difficult to accept this young man's song. 'Run On' has a blues introduction and although not particularly memorable, is a successful kind of 'gospel-rock'. Presley's performance is compelling, but in 'So High' the effect tends to rely more on the arrangement than on his singing. The arrangement is good; after a while, clapping adds the icing to the cake, but even this cannot rescue the number. A fine slow song, 'Somebody Bigger Than You And I' provides a welcome contrast, and for this Presley sings in his deep baritone register. His breath control and phrasing are outstanding, and the same is true of 'Stand By Me'. In this performance Elvis returns to the church of his youth, for he leads the choir in this magnificent version of a very moving song. In 'Tomorrow Is A Long Time' we enter a new, and completely different world. This was the first song by Bob Dylan that Presley recorded, and it gives a tantalising glimpse of what might have been, had he recorded an album of Dylan compositions instead of being side-tracked into a succession of formula films. It is a superb performance, maintained over nearly five-and-a-half minutes. It is softly insistent yet civilised, and the half lights of the backing contribute to Presley's restrained interpretation. This gradually exerts a hypnotic fascination. But this masterly performance was used as a fill-up to the album of Presley's recently completed film *Spinout*! It sticks out like a Mozart quartet discovered beneath a pile of Austrian drinking-songs. More superb singing, closer to the majority of songs recorded at this time, is to be found on the hymn-like 'Where Could I Go But To The Lord?'. Presley does not force his tone, and sings well within himself. He adds a faint blues inflection, which gives the right ethnic touch. Another tremendous performance is 'Where No One Stands Alone'. This is also a slow 3/4 song, which leads from an inexorable build-up to a thrilling climax. The way in which Presley sings this suggests that the words had personal significance. The final song, 'Without Him', is notable for the light backing, confined mainly to organ and piano, and is performed with burning sincerity, entirely without mawkishness.

10 June, 1966
Venue: RCA Studios, Nashville
Titles recorded: 'If Every Day Was Like Christmas', 'I'll Remember You',
'Indescribably Blue'

These three titles completed the lengthy sessions of the previous month, recorded for the Christmas market. 'If Every Day Was Like Christmas' is not the usual innocuous number, but a surprisingly serious song partly written by Red West. 'I'll Remember You' is not to be confused with the song 'I Remember You', revived by Frank Ifield in 1962. It begins with a too-fussy arrangement, although Presley sings with sincerity and conviction using superb breath control and inflection in the lyrics. By far the best of these three is 'Indescribably Blue', a slow ballad which begins in Mediterranean style with tremulous guitar. This powerful song is sung appropriately. The solo female singer (possibly Millie Kirkham) adds a poignant touch, and Henry Slaughter on organ gives further instrumental colour. This is one of the most 'manly' performances Presley recorded.

June, 1966
Venue: Hollywood
Titles recorded: 'Baby If You'll Give Me All Your Love', 'City By Night', 'Could I Fall In Love', 'Double Trouble', 'I Love Only One Girl', 'It Won't Be Long', 'Long-Legged Girl', 'Old MacDonald', 'There Is So Much World To See'
N B 'It Won't Be Long' was not included in the film

These songs constitute the sound-track recordings for Presley's next film, the MGM studio production of *Double Trouble*. Although by this time overdubbing was standard practice, of Presley's sound-track recordings this is one of the most 'produced'. The result lacks the feel of a standard studio recording, and the natural ambience of undoctored sound. The songs do not show much advance over Presley's previous film material.

The first song 'Baby If You'll Give Me All Your Love' is a fast rocker, well sung, but of poor quality. The next, 'City By Night', is better; a medium tempo 'walking' blues, with imaginative use of brass. It is dramatic in its effect, and Presley sustains the menacing atmosphere with dark vocal quality. 'Could I Fall In Love' is another good song. One of its surprising features is the use of a string quartet, and it is possible that we hear Charlie Hodge in duet with Presley. 'Double Trouble' lacks coherent style; the backing is confused and messy, possibly the result of too much technical alteration. In 'I Love Only One Girl', the old French marching song 'Auprès de Ma Blonde', is transposed with unusual and not inappropriate effect. 'It Won't Be Long' is a totally forgettable number. 'Long-Legged Girl' begins in fierce stomping manner; it is well done, but lacks originality. With the old song 'Old MacDonald', Elvis lets himself go and gives a fun-filled performance. The final song, 'There Is So Much World To See', falls between several styles – and fails. The arrangement is fussy and heavy, and although the lyrics are slick, the tune is poor.

28/29 September, 1966
Venue: Radio Recorders Studio, Hollywood
Titles recorded: 'Easy Come, Easy Go', 'I'll Take Love', 'The Love Machine', 'She's A Machine', 'Sing You Children', 'Yoga Is As Yoga Does', 'You Gonna Stop'

A further collection of mediocre songs, this set was recorded for Presley's next film, Paramount's *Easy Come, Easy Go*. There is an occasional flash of inspiration in the odd guitar lick during the song 'Easy Come, Easy Go', but the side drum is incessant and unbearably off-beat. 'I'll Take Love' wallows in banality, and although Presley does his considerable best with this and 'The Love Machine', he cannot disguise his uncommitted performance. 'She's A Machine' is mildly interesting: it has a fast backing, but the vocal line is slow. A brilliant arrangement (featuring trumpets) also attempts to rescue 'Sing You Children', a fast gospel-type number. 'Yoga Is As Yoga Does' is so badly recorded as to scarcely deserve a mention. 'You Gotta Stop' is more interesting; it has a slow introduction, and an unusual backing, once the frantic pace starts, with sudden breaks and fragmentary solos. Presley rises to this difficult challenge and rides the music, but it remains undistinguished.

21 February, 1967
Venue: RCA Studios, Nashville
Titles recorded: 'Clambake', 'Confidence', 'The Girl I Never Loved', 'Hey, Hey, Hey', 'A House That Has Everything', 'How Can You Lose What You Never Had?', 'Who Needs Money?' 'You Don't Know Me'
N B 'How Can You Lose What You Never Had?' was not included in the film; 'You Don't Know Me' was specially recorded for disc

Compared with *Easy Come, Easy Go* these songs for Presley's next film, United Artist's *Clambake*, are an improvement. But one must question the judgement of whoever was responsible for contracting Presley to record material of such low quality. The title song, 'Clambake', receives a fine performance and has an unusual bass line. It appears to be founded on 'Shortnin' Bread'. 'Confidence' is a children's song, but is unlikely to appeal to any child. 'The Girl I Never Loved' is another example of a third-rate song well done. 'Hey, Hey, Hey' is a typical pop song of the mid-1960s. This uses formulas of the time, but is so well done it has its own validity. Unfortunately the recording is bad: Presley appears overdubbed, and his first entry seems to come from another studio. 'A House That Has Everything' is a forgettable slow cha-cha, and 'How Can You Lose What You Never Had?' surely shows further interference by the technicians. It has an imaginative organ part, but Presley is ill at ease. 'Who Needs Money?' reflects the character of the song; everyone involved appears money-mad. Presley duets with Willie Hutchins on this fast number, but the song is dreary. Presley is heard to much better effect on the last song 'You Don't Know Me', a slow ballad, good and well sung. Once more the engineers must be faulted, as Floyd Cramer's fluent piano appears several miles away.

20 March, 1967
Venue: RCA Studios, Nashville
Titles recorded: 'Suppose'

On 20 March, 1967 Presley, with his usual coterie of musicians, arrived at the RCA Studios in Nashville. Something must have gone seriously wrong, for only one song, 'Suppose', was recorded, and this was never issued. Later, in June, it was re-recorded for Presley's next film *Speedway*.

June, 1967
Venue: Hollywood
Titles recorded: 'Five Sleepy Heads', 'He's Your Uncle Not Your Dad', 'Let Yourself Go', 'Speedway', 'Suppose', 'There Ain't Nothing Like A Song', 'Who Are You?', 'Your Time Hasn't Come Yet Baby'
N B 'Five Sleepy Heads' and 'Suppose' were not included in the film

These songs were for Presley's next film, MGM's *Speedway*. We have noted the change of direction in Presley's career emanating from the May 1966 sessions, but the songs for this film unfortunately it does not carry much conviction. 'Five Sleepy Heads' was cut from the film. It is a bedtime story, sung to Brahms's 'Lullaby'. Although the original tune is a distinct improvement over most of Presley's film songs, the arrangement does not work. 'He's Your Uncle Not Your Dad' is not worthy of Presley. 'Let Yourself Go', however, a mean blues-type song, is a characteristic of the title track 'Speedway', which results from outstanding drum work. The song drives, and there is a nice use of tambourine, but Presley's first entry is subdued and his voice rarely in focus. 'Suppose' (attempted the previous March in Nashville) is unusual: it is slow and darkly dramatic, well projected by Presley. An unusual feature of the backing track is the double bass played with the bow. 'There Ain't Nothing Like A Song' again has Presley too far back. For a fast-moving song put over with drive and gusto, this is a serious technical fault, and even the presence of Nancy Sinatra for a few lines does not redeem it. 'Who Are You?' is worse: a slow samba, it is very poor material. 'Your Time Hasn't Come Yet Baby' can only justify its soft, bouncy existence in the context of the film.

10 and 12 September, 1967
Venue: RCA Studios, Nashville
Titles recorded: 'Big Boss Man', 'Guitar Man', 'High Heel Sneakers', 'Just Call Me Lonesome', 'Mine', 'Singing Tree', 'We Call On Him', 'You Don't Know Me', 'You'll Never Walk Alone'

This unusually varied group of songs was not recorded with any definite project in mind, but includes some of the most important songs Presley recorded for years.

A good example is 'Big Boss Man'. This is given a superb performance by all concerned and the overwhelming impression is of a powerfully driven song. The guitar work, possibly by Jerry Reed, is outstanding, and there are imaginative touches from Charlie McCoy's harmonica. The same is true of 'Guitar Man', which is a finely driven country song, with Presley relishing the almost autobiographical lyrics. With 'High Heel Sneakers' (a hit in Britain for Tommy Tucker three years before), Presley's performance, to use the then-current jargon, is more 'rocker' than 'mod'. The song does not stand up to this treatment, and although the atmosphere is subtle and erotic, its cleverness means Presley has little chance to get going. Presley is also ill-at-ease in 'Just Call Me Lonesome' and 'Mine'. The first is poor, for it lies too high. 'Mine' is a slow ballad, distinguished by Floyd Cramer's piano, but Presley's uncertainty can be noticed in a tremulous quality in his voice. No complaints can be levelled against 'Singing Tree', which is beautifully sung. Especially effective are the duet harmonies, but the song has little strength. 'We Call On Him' is a gentle number, but lacks distinction. In 'You Don't Know Me', Presley re-recorded a song which he had already taped for the film *Clambake*. The fine song was a hit for Ray Charles in 1962, and the re-recording is outstanding, with superb breath control from Presley, and the Jordanaires on top form. Apart from these virtues, Floyd Cramer's fine pianism is audible. Finally, 'You'll Never Walk Alone', an astonishing hit for Gerry Marsden (of Gerry and the Pacemakers) in 1963. Although Presley's performance is sincere, and possibly influenced by the Liverpool singer, the sound is out of focus and the result not compelling.

2 October, 1967
Venue: RCA Studios, Nashville.
Titles recorded: 'All I Needed Was The Rain', 'Going Home', 'Stay Away', 'Stay Away, Joe'

The above four titles were recorded for Presley's next film for MGM, *Stay Away, Joe*. Presley also recorded the song 'Dominic', which was never released. It is not known whether the performance was unsatisfactory or if it was ever completed. The songs released show a vast improvement over Presley's previous film numbers. 'All I Needed Was The Rain' is a very good country blues, soft, with a faintly moaning harmonica threading its way through a complex acoustic guitar pattern. This receives an exceptionally fine performance from Presley. If fault can be found, the song fades out too soon, breaking the spell. In 'Going Home' there is more interesting use of guitars.

There was confusion in earlier pressings between 'Stay Away' and 'Stay Away, Joe'. This is understandable, but the songs are very different. The first, 'Stay Away', is an adaptation of the English folk-song 'Greensleeves', but the words and arrangement do not come up to the haunting quality of the original. This is a pity, for this could have become a big hit for Presley. He is more at ease in 'Stay Away, Joe'. All through this hill-billy stomp there is a genuine laugh in Presley's voice, which is quite infectious.

15 and 17 January, 1968
Venue: RCA Studios, Nashville
Titles recorded: 'Too Much Monkey Business', 'US Male'

Confusion surrounds this session. There were rumours that many more numbers were put down, but so far as can be ascertained these two were the only titles completed. 'Too Much Monkey Business' is a medium-fast rocker, which had already been a hit for Chuck Berry. It is a curiosity from Presley. Apparently he asked for new lyrics, but the flippant references to Vietnam in January 1968 are in bad taste. In 'US Male' Presley is again out of touch with contemporary thought. This is full of male chauvinism, and sung in a style that does not come off, although it became a hit.

March, 1968
Venue: Hollywood
Titles recorded: 'Almost In Love', 'Edge Of Reality', 'A Little Less
Conversation', 'Wonderful World'

These four songs are from Presley's next film, MGM's *Live A Little, Love A Little*. They are more successful than any of Presley's film recordings for a long time. 'Almost In Love', a medium tempo bossa nova, has a fine arrangement, including strings, trombones and vibraphone. It is a surprisingly successful mixture, as this was not Presley's *mètier*. This song, which is not so well known as it ought to be, shows a new facet of Presley's musical personality. 'Edge of Reality' is another interesting number. It begins with a chromatic choral introduction, and the use of brass is noteworthy. 'A Little Less Conversation' has a rocking feel, typical of the best of the late 1960s. It is fast, with florid drumming, powerful brass and a heavy, active bass. Presley's performance is one of his best: there is a throb and arrogance in his singing which is irresistible. Given the right song, Presley was still capable of putting a performance difficult to surpass. 'Wonderful World' suffers by comparison: it is a kind of fast waltz but not a great song, with a fussy backing.

Chapter Twelve

The return of the master, 1968–69

After the television spectacular for NBC recorded in June 1968, Elvis Presley's career seemed set fair to enter a new and vital phase. The success of the show, with its immensely wide-ranging material, demonstrated for the first time in many years Presley's command of the rock idiom. Here was no ageing star, brought out for teenagers of the 1950s who now found themselves the carpet-slippered, television-addicted parents of the late 1960s. Presley was a paradox on this show: he had not changed at all with regard to his earlier material, but he had changed with regard to his stage presence and choice of fresh material.

27–30 June, 1968
Venue: NBC Studios, Burbank, Los Angeles
Titles recorded: 'All Shook Up', 'Are You Lonesome Tonight?', 'Baby, What You Want Me To Do' (two versions), 'Big Boss Man', 'Blue Christmas', 'Blue Suede Shoes', 'Can't Help Falling In Love', 'Don't Be Cruel' (not released), 'Guitar Man' (two versions), 'Heartbreak Hotel', 'Hound Dog', 'If I Can Dream', 'It Hurts Me' (not released), 'Jailhouse Rock', 'Lawdy, Miss Clawdy', 'Let Yourself Go' (not released), 'Little Egypt', 'Love Me', 'Love Me Tender', 'Memories', 'Nothingville', 'One Night', 'Santa Claus Is Back In Town' (not released), 'Saved', 'That's All Right' (not released), 'Tiger Man', 'Trouble' (two versions), 'Trying To Get To You', 'Up Above My Head', 'When My Blue Moon Turns To Gold Again' (not released), 'Where Could I Go But To The Lord?'

This extended series of recordings was to tape Presley's NBC TV spectacular, an hour-long show which marked his comeback. The television film was well

117

done, and makes fascinating viewing, but divorced from the screen, the sound-track album is in many ways a very disappointing Presley issue. In spite of the large number of titles recorded, it is best to deal with them in order of appearance on the record as they are strung together with linking dialogue, which makes it difficult to pick out individual songs.

The main drawback is the atrocious quality of the recording. It is almost unbelievable that in 1968 these recordings were made only in mono. For those interested in Presley's speaking voice, the record contains many examples of his chatting to the audience, but the recording quality is very poor. Of course, a 'sound-track' from a videotaped show had to be mono as it was only possible to record sound in mono on videotape. But it must have been patently obvious that an album would be issued, and simultaneous stereo recording ought to have been employed. In addition, the mono microphones were almost continuously overloaded – although some backing tracks were pre-recorded so this should have been foreseen. Finally, Elvis and some accompanying musicians kept moving 'off mike' – but this also ought to have been dealt with at the planning stage by using more microphones.

Generally speaking, the songs make up a selection of Presley's hits of the previous dozen years, and the album begins with a fine version of 'Trouble', which originally appeared in *King Creole*. In this new version, the opening New Orleans riff is cut out, and Presley's singing is not as eruptive as earlier. This segues into 'Guitar Man', which appears as a recurring theme on the record and gets a tremendous performance full of dark surging qualities form Presley; and the orchestra, helped by squealing high trumpets, is fabulous. It is a different story with 'Lawdy, Miss Clawdy', full of extraneous noise and atmosphere where it is difficult to appreciate Presley through the screams, bumps, slurps and bad balancing. This segues into 'Baby, What You Want Me To Do?', which is an edited version of a lengthy take in the film (part of the long guitar solo is included on *A Legendary Performer* – vol 2), but the confused sound has all the attraction of a home movie.

The album moves into a medley of 'Heartbreak Hotel', 'Hound Dog' and 'All Shook Up', but the technical disaster goes from bad to worse. In 'Heartbreak Hotel' Presley's voice, full of power and conviction, is all but drowned in applause. 'Hound Dog' is also well performed, with powerful orchestral brass, but the recording is bass heavy, and the sound is made worse by an extraordinary recording fault. This is an apparent electrical feedback on B Flat, due to which this note gets louder and louder, and blares through 'All Shook Up'. The result is an unmitigated disaster; no self-respecting artist should have had to lend his name to this.

The next three songs are a little better. 'Can't Help Falling In Love' suffers from poor balance and overpowering overdubbed strings later. 'Jailhouse Rock', one of the rawest songs Presley ever recorded, fares better in these circumstances, but Don Randi's stodgy organ playing draws back the rhythm.

Presley can do nothing to lift this song, and the final section degenerates into a welter of noise. 'Love Me Tender' is not fit to be compared with his earlier version.

We now enter a different world. 'Where Could I Go To But To The Lord?' was the first song recorded on 28 June. It appears that the engineers had been listening to the previous day's disasters, for the sound is much better; it is clean and clear, and the backing musicians seem more committed. Presley's voice, now we can hear it, is in good shape, the only criticism being that acoustically he is set a little too far back. This segues into a fine, sincere performance of 'Up Above My Head', which in turn leads into 'Saved'. This is a brilliant performance of a staggering gospel-rock number by Lieber and Stoller, which gets better as it proceeds up the scale. In 'Blue Christmas' we are back to the confusion of 27 June, with both song and performance lost in acoustic gloom. 'One Night' starts in ludicrous fashion, but Presley turns this sonic dross into vocal gold. 'Memories' is a fine song, well performed, with a shimmering orchestral tapestry in the background. The crude recording techniques are not too obvious here. In 'Nothingville' a haunting atmosphere is created, full of dark and lonely foreboding. Presley gives a marvellous performance, but it is over too soon! It segues into 'Big Boss Man', where the drawbacks of the orchestra ought to have stopped the release of this take. Presley is very good, but the NBC orchestra is badly out of synchronisation. Curiously enough, Presley revives 'Little Egypt', from *Roustabout*, and the dozen or so bars of this funny little song contrast with the reprise of 'Trouble' and 'Guitar Man', which are little more than reminiscences. The album ends with 'If I Can Dream', which was Presley's current hit. This slow beefy ballad was clearly *not* recorded at the sessions that produced the earlier confusion, for it is well recorded, with Presley's voice full of power and gravel. It is extraordinary that he used this style of singing, for his voice is almost unlike anything in the earlier part of his career. The song moves to a powerful climax, with a slow brass build-up which makes a fine ending to an uneven and exasperating record.

Of the other songs recorded in these sessions, but issued later, it is better to deal with them in alphabetical order. 'Are You Lonesome Tonight?' comes from the poor sessions of 27 June, and is only interesting for the atmosphere and rapport between the singer and the audience. The extended instrumental version of 'Baby, What You Want Me To Do?' also appears on *A Legendary Performer* (vol 2) where it 'highlights Elvis on lead guitar'. This is the only merit on the take. In 'Blue Suede Shoes', the poor recording nonetheless has undeniable drive. The second verse is much better, for at least Presley can be heard, and the guitar is not so obtrusive. 'Love Me' is another messy piece of work, for all its atmosphere. 'Tiger Man' attempts to recapture the early days of rock 'n' roll, but the recording is so dismal that the performance has little significance. 'Trying To Get to You' is a great improvement, for Presley is much better balanced.

119

7 July, 1968
Venue: Possibly Hollywood
Titles recorded: 'Charro'

This is the only song in Presley's next film, the National General Pictures' *Charro*. The film, hardly one of his more compelling performances, shows a desire to tap Presley's under-used acting ability. The title song, heard over the credits, is unusual and dramatic, with a big orchestral backing used sparingly by the arranger, Hugo Montenegro whose use of strings, piano and horns in the early part is striking. Montenegro was then enjoying an international hit with his theme from the Clint Eastwood film, *The Good, The Bad And The Ugly*. But 'Charro', for all its qualities, feeds on the more commonplace characteristics of the earlier tune. It is an unusual song and gives a tantalising glimpse of Presley's feel for the big dramatic ballad, something largely denied him up to this time.

October, 1968
Venue: Hollywood
Titles recorded: 'Almost', 'Clean Up Your Own Backyard'
N B 'Aura Lee', 'Sign Of The Zodiac' and 'Swing Down, Sweet Chariot' were also recorded at these sessions, but were unsuccessful were not issued at the time.

These songs were for the film sound-track of Presley's next film *The Trouble With Girls*, for MGM. In the event only 'Almost' and 'Clean Up Your Own Backyard' were released on disc. 'Aura Lee' and 'Sign Of The Zodiac' were probably recorded on the film set. 'Almost' shows poor overdubbing, for Presley is not well balanced with the instruments. A very obtrusive piano begins the song, and tends to smother Presley later. 'Clean Up Your Own Backyard' is quite different. This is a good number, with a gentle but solid beat, and receives a superb performance from Presley. Every inflection can be heard and savoured, and the overdubbing of brass and female voices enhances the gospel feel of the song.

13–23 January, 1969
Venue: American Studios, Memphis
Titles recorded: 'A Little Bit Of Green', 'Come Out', 'Don't Cry Daddy', 'From A Jack To A King', 'Gentle On My Mind', 'Hey Jude', 'I'll Be There', 'I'll Hold You In My Heart', 'I'm Movin' On', 'Inherit The Wind', 'In The Ghetto', 'Long Black Limousine', 'Mama Liked The Roses', 'My Little Friend', 'Poor Man's Gold', 'Rubberneckin'', 'Suspicious Minds', 'This Is The Story', 'Wearin' That Loved On Look', 'Without Love', 'You'll Think Of Me'
N B 'Come Out' and 'Poor Man's Gold' were not released

These extended sessions, which took ten days, together with the following sessions in February (spread over six days), produced a new batch of material, which was intended to capitalise on the success of the album of the TV special. Although that album left much to be desired from the technical viewpoint, these recordings, the first Presley had made in Memphis since the Sun days fifteen years before, show a great advance. The material is generally speaking good, as are the natural, yet unimaginative, recordings. For once it is possible to listen with pleasure, without having to make allowances for inferior material or inadequate engineering.

'A Little Bit Of Green' displays a restrained yet insistent beat. Curiously, this is not one of the better songs from these sessions. 'Don't Cry Baby' is a difficult song to put across: it can seem mawkishly sentimental, but Presley's alterations make no sense in the song 'From A Jck To A King', which was a hit for Ned Miller in 1963. This old number is chewed over by him as if he were a dog gnawwing away at a meaty bone. Presley reveals unsuspected depths in the lyrics of the Dean Martin hit 'Gentle On My Mind': Presley is rugged as opposed to the blandsophistication of Martin. The brass work here is fascinating, as is the rest of the backing. But also remarkable are the restrained use of female voices and Presley's seriousness – the result is a very fine performance. In 'Hey Jude' Presley turns to the Beatles. Just as the 'Gentle On My Mind' performance is different from that generally known, so 'Hey Jude' is so unlike the original as to make it a different song. He performs it in a high voice, as tough half-whispering to a friend, but this strange atmosphere exerts a fascination.

'I'll Be There' is unusual, in that Presley vocalises for much of the time, almost in a bluegrass way. The song is hardly a world-shaker, but it is pleasant enough. A notable feature of the instrumental backing is the varied and colourful arrangement, which almost makes the song sound better than it is. 'I'll Hold You In My Heart' has dated. The recording is not well balanced, for the drumming is too far forward and obtrudes on Presley's plastic singing. But what breath control! 'I'm Movin' On' is superb. The performance is delicate, yet solid, and the strength and tenderness of 'travel' country-based music is fully revealed. The jangly piano and solid, driving brass are quite hypnotic in their build-up and growth. 'Inherit The Wind' is another fine performance, but the vocal quality seems strained. This was the first song recorded on 16 June, and a certain stiffness is noticeable.

When we come to 'In The Ghetto' we encounter a classic Presley recording. It is essentially a protest song and nobody listening to this performance can remain unmoved. Every word is crystal clear, and Presley's manly voice has both authority and tenderness. The subject of the song is the plight of those who live in ghettos, and the bare, insistent, unchanging harmonies mirror this, as the singer is trapped by their pull.

With 'Long Black Limousine' we enter an unusual atmosphere. Solemn bells intone this morbid funeral song. In spite of the dark tragedy behind the number, the drumming and bass line are both superb, and Presley feeds off them and to them. His voice is in great shape; he takes quite extended phrases in one breath, and the song shows a fine use of recording technique.

'Mama Liked The Roses' is a female equivalent of 'Don't Cry Daddy'. Presley is doubtless sincere, but this has to be listened to with indulgence. 'My Little Friend' is a weak song, and although the arrangement is good, Presley's voice sounds a little querulous. Unfortunately, the overdubbing of strings is not good, for the playing is poor and out of tune. 'Rubberneckin'' is a fun song, sung by Presley with an attractive 'tight' quality. The brass playing is good and the atmosphere, urgent and zappy, becomes very infectious. 'Suspicious Minds' became one of Presley's signature tunes, for he recorded four versions. This, the first, became a major hit for him towards the end of 1969. The song is outstanding, and the fast yet menacing atmosphere is ideally caught. The later versions are live, but there is no doubt that the clean nature of this first version enables more to be heard. 'This Is The Story' is a strange song. It has a 'still' introduction, modern, yet with hardly a change of tempo or harmony. The string overdubbing is poor, as on 'My Little Friend'.

'Wearin' That Loved On Look' is outstanding. It opens in rhythm-and-blues slow style, with Presley in staggering voice. He admired the Welsh singer Tom Jones, and there is more than a hint of Jones in Presley's performance. Apart from Presley's magnificent singing, the instrumentation deserves mention. The organ – way on the right-hand channel – is imaginatively used, and the drumming subtly attractive. Rich contributions from the backing vocals and a clangy piano, together with a thumping bass line, make the whole thing irresistible. Tom Jones recorded 'Without Love' sometime after Presley and went on to have a big hit with it, so in this instance he returned the compliment. It is a sentimental song, sung with great conviction by Presley. It is a pity this was not released as a single, for it could easily have been a hit for him. In the last song, 'You'll Think Of Me', there is a strangely disconnected opening which gradually builds to the basic tempo. The song, which lasts almost four minutes, is long for the material, but Presley manages to hold it together through the layers of sound.

17–22 February, 1969
Venue: American Studios, Memphis
Titles recorded: 'After Loving You', 'And The Grass Won't Pay No Mind', 'Any Day Now', 'Do You Know Who I Am?', 'If I'm A Fool', 'It Keeps Right On A-Hurtin'', 'Kentucky Rain', 'Memory Revival', 'Only The Strong Survive', 'Power Of My Love', 'Stranger In My Own Home Town', 'The Fair's Moving On', 'True Love Travels On A Gravel Road', 'Who Am I?'
NB 'Memory Revival' was not released

This is a mixed collection of much the same quality as the previous month's sessions. 'After Loving You' is an example of Presley at his best. The song holds no surprises for those who know 'Blueberry Hill', but Presley creates something passionate and dark from second-rate material. Amazingly, he makes it work – and does so alone, for the backing offers no help. Only a great performer could have achieved this, but the song is not allowed to fade out naturally; it is snipped off before the end by the engineers. 'And The Grass Won't Pay No Mind' is another excellent performance. This Neil Diamond song features some fine string writing. Presley sings with a delicacy, in a restrained and intimate manner. The song is difficult, ranging over two octaves. At first Presley appears to have trouble with the lowest notes, but overall this is a fine performance. 'Any Day Now' is another fine song, with music by Burt Bacharach. Typically, the melody has unusual contours, and the arrangement produces strange sonorities from the orchestra: now an oboe solo, now a few bars of solo violin, now the deep and solid brass sound. Presley gives a staggering performance: powerful, wide-ranging, full of expression. Another unusual song is 'Do You Know Who I Am?'. This is not a typical ballad, for it has unconnected changes of key (which makes the song difficult to sing), but Presley rises to the challenge. Another interesting feature is the occasional use of a string quartet.

'If I'm A Fool' is a straightforward country song, with a soft feel about it. This kind of material is easy to dismiss; but it should be remembered that songs of this type were close to Presley's heart. Familiarity is apparent in a Johnny Tillotson number 'It Keep Right On A-Hurtin'. Presley turns in a moderate performance, which is well recorded. 'Kentucky Rain' is sung with passion and conviction, but as it is a despairing number the effect is enervating. Presley enters into the spirit of the song, and it is doubtful if he ever sounded more miserable on record. 'Only The Strong Survive' is a dramatic song from the Gamble–Huff stable. This is one occasion where Presley appears unfamiliar with the material, for the performance is too slow. 'Power Of My Love' is worlds away. It is remarkable in that it is both old-school rock 'n' roll and in 3/4 time. Solid and raunchy, Presley's performance is irresistible: full of shy innuendoes and *double entendres*. There are a few singers who can manage this, yet it stems from the Presley of 1954/55. It is explosive, breathy and rich, with an extraordinary ending. 'Stranger In My Own Home Town', a Curtis Mayfield number, begins with a superb orchestral opening. The big orchestral backing is fused with basic rhythm and blues. Presley moves around the music, like a collector savouring his possessions, and this electrifying performance is an outstanding example of Presley's art. 'The Fair's Moving On' is akin to the Eartha Kitt song 'The Day That The Circus Left Town'. Both are in slow 3/4 time, and Presley puts it over clearly and simply; but he cannot disguise the song's lack of distinction. 'True Love Travels On A Gravel Road' is full of fire, with a wide-ranging vocal line, well arranged and recorded, but in the last analysis not out of the top drawer. 'Who Am I?' is a straightforward song, restrained and sincere. It is also well arranged and features more organ than other tracks: Presley sings it simply and appealingly.

5/6 March, 1969
Venue: Universal Studios, Hollywood
Titles recorded: 'Change Of Habit', 'Have A Happy', 'Let's Be Friends', 'Let's Forget About The Stars', 'Let Us Pray'

These songs were for Presley's last feature film, Universal Pictures' *Change Of Habit*. They contain an unusual song, 'Let's Forget About The Stars'. It could not have been recorded then, as it is in mono.

'Change Of Habit' is a beefy number with a funky bass line. It is possibly too long, lasting three-and-a-quarter minutes, but in its favour are Presley's committed performance, a light and airy piano part, and an infectious rhythm. 'Have A Happy' shows an unwelcome return to the standards of Presley's least attractive earlier films, and is undistinguished. In spite of its strange background 'Let's Forget About The Stars' is feeble, and Presley appears bored and ill-at-ease with this unworthy material. The final song 'Let Us Pray', a surprisingly fast rocking number, is helped by staccato drumming and Presley's light voice. Although some commentators dismiss this, possibly Presley was more involved in this number than the others.

Chapter Thirteen

On stage, 1969–74

Beginning with the live performances of August 1969 at the International Hotel, Las Vegas, Presley was able to rid himself of the succession of mediocre films. Although it was nine years since he had last performed in public, any doubts he may have had were swept away by the tremendous success of the engagements. Return bookings were obligatory and naturally RCA wished to record them on disc. What few people seemed to realise was that what makes a fine concert (variety of material, to show the performer's range of abilities) does not necessarily make a fine record, where the purchaser would expect to find songs of a similar nature. This is not to say that all the songs must be the same; but the album has to have its own identity. Listening at home is different to being at a concert.

Presley's success as a live performer was partly because his concerts were carefully chosen, and rehearsed to perfection. On the LP *Sergeant Pepper's Lonely Hearts Club Band* two years before, the Beatles had demonstrated the total concept album, whereby the forty minutes' or so playing time is used to make musical statements which themselves add up to a total greater than the individual songs. In time, the album as a mere collection of songs became a thing of the past. With Presley's ability and resources, it is a tragedy that the record-buying public was denied for years a Presley studio album as carefully put together and rehearsed as his live concerts.

To the record-buying public in foreign countries, the constant flow of similar Presley material was exasperating. The millions of followers outside the USA had no chance to attend his live performances; their needs were completely ignored on discs.

One technical disadvantage of a live recording is the lack of opportunity to correct mistakes. For safety's sake, RCA tended to record two performances on the same day. The better performance was released; but for every released track from these live performances there was at least one unreleased. Since Presley's death, the number of unauthorised albums has risen to around one hundred, and many of these used tapes which were rejected by RCA. However, in spite of the fact that RCA often possessed two or more performances of the same song, there might well be flaws in each of them which would prevent their release on a commercial album. Consequently, there would appear to be little point in listing all the titles which were recorded at these sessions, when a great many of them have not been released, and probably will not be released in the future. For the sake of clarity, only songs which have been released are listed and discussed.

22–26 August, 1969
Venue: International Hotel, Las Vegas
Titles released: 'All Shook Up', 'Are You Lonesome Tonight?', 'Blue Suede Shoes', 'Can't Help Falling In Love', 'Hound Dog', 'I Can't Stop Loving You', 'In The Ghetto', 'Johnnie B. Goode', 'My Baby', 'Mystery Train'/'Tiger Man', 'Runaway', 'Suspicious Minds', 'Words', 'Yesterday'

The majority of these recordings were issued on the first album of the two-record set 'From Memphis To Vegas, From Vegas To Memphis'. 'All Shook Up' was the first song released from these performances, being taped at the evening performance on 22 August. This is a fine performance, with Presley's 'plummy' voice suiting the song, although this could be due to his nervousness. This is clearly the case in 'Are You Lonesome Tonight?'; but once he begins singing (after a hesitant spoken introduction) the magic of the performance overrides any tension. This is a good version of this classic number, from which only the faintly hysterical and too closely balanced backing singers detract. 'Blue Suede Shoes' is disappointing. Presley seems uneasy, but James Burton's guitar work is outstanding. 'Can't Help Falling In Love' is better; a fine performance. 'Hound Dog' is a poor parody. It sounds as if the engineers have cut from an introduction (possibly 26 August) to a performance on another day (possibly 22 August). Presley's voice is too far back, and he is nervous. 'I Can't Stop Loving You' is good enough, but Presley sounds as if he's been caught on an off-night. The audience interruption at the end adds its own excitement. 'In The Ghetto' is reported to have been recorded immediately after 'I Can't Stop Loving You', but the result is superior. James Burton's guitar spins 'Johnnie B. Goode' into life, but this is from a batch of songs that places Presley's voice too distant in image. Presley's voice suited 'My Babe' very well. This dark song receives a formidable performance; and in the 'Mystery Train'/'Tiger Man' medley Presley is helped by the band, who are in good form.

'Runaway' was a major hit for Del Shannon in 1961, since when it has become a classic rock number. Presley had never performed it before. However much he

126

may have admired the song, his voice is not at its best and his 'hammy' use of the microphone causes his voice to fade out at odd moments. The strain continues in 'Suspicious Minds'; this is faster than the earlier studio performance and may have been pitched too high for Presley at this time. It is also too long. The Bee Gees' number 'Words', which followed 'Suspicious Minds' in the show, is far better. It is slightly faster than the Bee Gees' version, and shows Presley receptive to influences; he gives a superb performance, free from strain and tension. Mention must be made of James Burton's astonishing guitar work, and fine backing musicianship from pianist Larry Muhoberac in Lennon and McCartney's 'Yesterday'. In the show Presley followed this with 'Hey Jude', but this was cut out before release.

16–19 February, 1970
Venue: International Hotel, Las Vegas
Titles released: 'Let It Be Me', 'Polk Salad Annie', 'Proud Mary', 'Release Me', 'See See Rider', 'Sweet Caroline', 'The Wonder Of You', 'Walk A Mile In My Shoes'

Following the success of the August appearances, Presley returned in February for another series. The material released shows that RCA were anxious to find fresh numbers, although at the same time they recorded many songs Presley had done before. 'Let It Be Me' is a fine Gilbert Becaud song; it receives a hymn-like performance, with a massive sound backing. This is hardly hit material, but Presley clearly enjoyed it. 'Polk Salad Annie' is fabulous; Presley speaks over the 'till ready' introduction, during which James Burton's guitar flicks malevolently until it catches fire. This is a marvellous song and it receives a hypnotic performance; there is more than a hint of James Brown's influence here.

In 'Proud Mary', a hit in the previous year for Creedence Clearwater Revival, Presley turns in a solid version, with fine backing from the band. This song shortly became a rock classic, and Presley included it in a number of shows. Three years before, Engelbert Humperdinck's 'Release Me' first entered the British charts, to remain in the Top 50 for fifty-five consecutive weeks. This oozing melody is not well done by Presley. His voice sounds raw and his blues-tight shouting in the top register adds nothing to the cloying melody. 'See See Rider' became a favourite of Presley's and he frequently included it in his live shows. It is a marvellous performance, full of power and dark strength, and the hard-driving guitar work from James Burton is fine. A studio performance probably would have enhanced 'Sweet Caroline'. This fine Neil Diamond song is well sung by Presley, but is too fast for the song to 'breathe' as it should. It preceded 'Release Me' in performance on 18 February; Presley's voice had probably not yet settled for the performance. 'The Wonder Of You' is outstanding. This is the only song released from the performance of 19 February and became a number one hit for Presley in the summer of 1970. (In some charts it was Presley's first number one hit in Britain for five years.) The strain in this case is appropriate, and the conviction and power of the performance are overwhelming. 'Walk A Mile In My Shoes' is unusual, not least in regard to the lyrics; but Presley gives a subtle performance. It is impossible not to be delighted by this example of popular music at its best.

4–8 June, 1970
Venue: RCA Studios, Nashville
Titles recorded: 'Bridge Over Troubled Water', 'Cindy, Cindy', 'Faded Love', 'Funny How Time Slips Away', 'Got My Mojo Working'/'Keep Your Hands Off', 'Heart Of Rome', 'How The Web Was Woven', 'I'll Never Know', 'I Really Don't Want To Know', 'I Was Born About 10,000 Years Ago', 'I Washed My Hands In Muddy Water', 'If I Were You', 'It Ain't No Big Thing', 'It's Your Baby, You Rock It', 'I've Lost You', 'Just Pretend', 'Life', 'Little Cabin On The Hill', 'Love Letters', 'Make The World Go Away', 'Mary In The Morning', 'Only Believe', 'Patch It Up', 'Sound Of Your Cry', 'Stranger In The Crowd', 'Sylvia', 'The Fool', 'The Next Step Is Love', 'There Goes My Everything', 'This Is Our Dance', 'Tomorrow Never Comes', 'Twenty Days And Twenty Nights', 'When I'm Over You', 'You Don't Have To Say You Love Me'

This series of recordings is one of the most interesting of Presley's career because of the consistency of material and the quality of recording. For the first time in years people could hear Presley in a natural acoustic, singing material of remarkable range and sympathy.

'Bridge Over Troubled Water', the classic Simon and Garfunkel song, was released on the mainly live *That's The Way It Is* album, when the final bars of a live version were spliced onto the studio recording to give the illusion of a live show. This fails on two counts: first the audience, had it been a live show, would not have refrained from applause once they realised what the song was; and second the sound image changes suddenly on the last chord. It is impossible to believe that *two* pianos were used at the sessions – but there are two on the final tape, one on each channel. This would not matter much, were it not that they are neither in tune, nor in tempo. In spite of this meddling, Presley's outstanding singing is not disguised. This is a fabulous version, burning with sincerity and power, and finding depths in the song not revealed by the composers. It is a pity Presley's great version had been tampered with in this way.

'Cindy, Cindy' is worlds away: crude and lacking commitment. The heavy arrangement is notable in 'Faded Love', a standard country number. 'Funny How Time Slips Away' is different again. Singing without strain, Presley is the arch-stylist, at times stepping back to allow other musicians their day in the sun. 'Got My Mojo Working' is sensational; it was cut in after it had actually begun, but whoever had the presence of mind to switch on the tape machine deserves a medal. Presley is enjoying himself to the hilt and urging the other musicians to do likewise. One hopes there are more tapes of this kind. Different again is 'Heart Of

Elvis with father, Vernon and mother, Gladys. The bond between mother and son is clearly visible in this picture taken shortly before her death in 1958.

"The Million Dollar Quartet", Sun Studios in 1956. From left; Jerry Lee Lewis, Carl Perkins, Elvis Presley and Johnny Cash.

Elvis rehearsing at the keyboard in 1958.

Performing in 1956 with his backing group; the Jordannaires. From left; Hugh Jarrett, Hoyt Hawkins, Neal Matthews and Gordon Stocker.

"Elvis has left the building…". After a rousing performance Elvis would be whisked away to a waiting car by security, before his fans became aware that he had left the building.

Elvis in concert with four of his guitars: (above) Gibson J200 with tooled leather decorative and protective jacket; (below) playing a Gibson Super 400; (opposite top) Playing a modified or customised Gibson Dove; (opposite below) Elvis with a Martin D18 with a tooled leather and protective jacket.

Elvis's return to live entertainment was heralded with a sponsored television programme for NBC in 1968. (Affectionately known as the "'68 Special")

Elvis with Ed Parker, his Hawaiian karate instructor.
(On a point of interest, Ed was the little boy who reputedly sounded the alarm when the attack on Pearl Harbor began in 1941.)

Behind the scenes with Sammy
Davis Jnr and Red West at the
Hilton International Hotel on
opening night (above).

Backstage in July 1969. The
King's style had now changed
from sharp suits to a more
comfortable look, with high
collars and jumpsuits. Scarves
also featured highly and after
being worn for a short time
they would be tossed to his
adoring fans (right).

Scene from the film "On Tour" made in 1972.

Rome', almost Neapolitan, well done in every respect. However, the song itself does not merit attention. The same applied to 'How The Web Was Woven', a medium-slow ballad, with a softly insistent beat. Another change of material is found in 'I'll Never Know', a beautiful ballad which never manages to take flight, but which deserves to be better known.

'I Really Don't Want To Know' is another slow ballad, in waltz tempo. This is not as heavily arranged as some of the other songs. 'I Was Born About 10,000 Years Ago' was first cut into pieces and used as linking material for the *Elvis Country* album. It was later issued *in toto*, and the result is a fine track – fast, brilliantly imagined, and full of delightful touches. The only drawback is the lyric, which is too parochial.

'I Washed My Hands In Muddy Water' has a similar feel; a toe-tapping number which Presley sings in great style. 'If I were You' is good, commercial Nashville with acknowledged influences from the 1960s. Presley makes the most of less-than-compelling lyrics in 'It Ain't No Big Thing'. 'It's Your Baby, You Rock It' also falls into this category, with Presley adopting his 'Tom Jones' manner; and although 'I've Lost You' is a powerful ballad, its qualities are not best revealed here. This is strong stuff, but something of the tragedy is lost. The version recorded two months later in Las Vegas is better.

'Just Pretend' and 'Life' are similar: massive, slow and uninspired in both material and execution. These were recorded towards the end of the 6 June session; perhaps Presley was tired. 'Little Cabin On The Hill' is a happy country song, with brilliant harmonica work by Charlie McCoy. Presley gives an irresistible performance, which almost disguises the forgettable material. In 'Love Letters' Presley recorded a second version of the Ketty Lester hit, which he recorded brilliantly in 1966. The first version, so good in every way, is nevertheless eclipsed by the later take. Colonel Parker's earlier artist, Eddy Arnold, had a big hit in 1966 for RCA with 'Make The World Go Away', but Presley's version does not compare. Presley seems uninterested.

'Mary In The Morning' lacks subtlety. The song is over four minutes long and, although parts are outstanding, the backing is over-done, shattering the fragile song. 'Only Believe' is a religious song of insufferable boredom, and 'Patch It Up' was better recorded later in August. Here the recording is badly balanced, reducing to inaudibility the efforts of many musicians, to ensure that the 'beat' comes through. 'Sound Of Your Cry' is an unusual ballad, which Presley sings particularly well, but the song alone could never have made it. 'Stranger In The Crowd' has a fast rhythm, masterfully built into a catchy beat. 'Sylvia' is not in the same class, although it has imaginative touches, including a string quartet. Presley is too far back to 'tell', and gets lost in the sound.

'The Fool' is strangely compelling; fast, with a bluesy feel, half-sung by Presley in a threatening moody manner. Charlie McCoy's harmonica is again worthy of note. 'The Next Step Is Love' is another fascinating track, the essence of Presley at his most 'laid back'; everything is so casual it has almost a Perry Como influence.

'There Goes My Everything', a country waltz, had been a big hit for Engelbert Humperdinck in 1967, and this success was repeated by Elvis in March 1971, when his version entered the charts. So far as the United Kingdom, where it reached number six, was concerned, it was again a hit. Presley's breath control is amazing, and the recording quality too is fine. 'This Is Our Dance' is another fine song, and could prove a posthumous hit for Presley, should this masculine, gentle, romantic style become popular again. 'Tomorrow Never Comes' is another beautiful song, performed with sincerity and consistency of voice. The wide image of the recording is remarkable – the side drum comes so far from the left that the player could be in the next studio! 'Twenty Days And Twenty Nights' is a slow ballad with strings and brass overdubbed. Once more, the arrangement is impressive, as is Presley's performance; but the song lacks distinction.

'When I'm Over You' is weak; but 'You Don't Have To Say You Love Me', – the 1966 Dusty Springfield hit – is quite different. Although his treatment of this number is naturally beefier than Ms Springfield's, Presley appears to have been subjected to phasing by the engineers, for his voice is sibilant and unnatural. A pity, for this is a very good performance.

13–15 August, 1970
Venue: International Hotel, Las Vegas
Titles recorded: 'Bridge Over Troubled Water', 'I Just Can't Help Believing', 'I've Lost You', 'Patch It Up', 'You've Lost That Loving Feeling'
N B 'Bridge Over Troubled Water' was not released

These recordings were used in the documentary film *That's The Way It Is*, and show Presley's genius as a live performer. 'Bridge Over Troubled Water' has not been issued; if it is anything like the other recordings, it must be outstanding. In 'I Just Can't Help Believing' Presley is enthralling: he is in good voice, relaxed yet powerful, and the orchestration is all that could be desired. In particular, his singing of the word 'girl' at the end of the first verse is almost unbelievable. In its way, this performance is a classic. So is 'I've Lost You', in which another fine performance of a haunting song is enhanced by marvellous orchestral backing. In particular, Ronnie Tutt's drumming and the fine piano of Glen Harding deserve mention, as well as the anonymous oboe player. 'Patch It Up' is in fast rocker style, enlivened by middle-register keyboard work and rhythmic clapping. This is a good song with plenty of drive, but it is not so fine a performance. It goes on too long, and the ending is inconclusive. With 'You've Lost That Loving Feeling' we have both the virtues and disadvantages of live recordings. This class song, a double hit (in 1965 and 1969) for the Righteous Brothers, and for Cilla Black (in 1965), is staggeringly performed by Presley. Unfortunately the audience recognise the song (and then applaud the recognition) eight bars after it has begun. The atmosphere, carefully built up and magically created, is completely broken. This is a pity, for the orchestration is fabulous – especially low pedal Ds on trombones; but later Presley lowers the temperature by half-singing, 'I'd get down on my knees for you – if this suit was not too tight!'.

22 September, 1970
Venue: RCA Studios, Nashville
Titles recorded: 'Rags To Riches', 'Snowbird', 'Where Did They Go, Lord?', 'Whole Lotta Shakin' Goin' On'

For some reason 'Rags To Riches' was only issued in mono on LP at first. However, the single version in mono was a hit for Presley in 1971, but lacks a definite Presley image. It is a slow ballad, suitably beefy, but not one of his best. 'Snowbird' is well arranged and recorded, and sung in fine country style. 'Where Did They Go, Lord?' has a sombre opening to its dark, prayerful character, abetted by sudden flashes from the guitar.

The fine rocker, 'Whole Lotta Shakin' Goin' On', is updated by fluent drumming – not accenting the off-beat – and the constant pulse of the bass. Sam Phillips would have approved. This is enhanced by Charlie McCoy's organ playing, which dates it somewhat; but the result is so infectious, so exhilarating, that criticism is silenced.

15 March, 1971
Venue: RCA Studios, Nashville
Titles recorded: 'Amazing Grace', 'Early Morning Rain', 'For Loving Me', 'The First Time Ever I Saw Your Face'

These sessions should have been longer, but after one day Presley contracted an eye infection, and the remaining sessions were cancelled. This is a pity, for these four titles are excellent, and the following sessions could have developed into a first-class collection of material.

'Amazing Grace' was one of the remarkable successes of the early 1970s. Earlier in the year Judy Collins had had a major international hit with the traditional lament, and the following year the Band Of The Royal Scots Dragoon Guards repeated the success, eclipsing Miss Collins. At the same time, her version was re-issued and succeeded in becoming anther hit the second time around, only fifteen months after it had first entered the charts. It is one of the great melodies, and it was natural that Presley should have been attracted by it. It was probably the Judy Collins version that led Presley to include female voices, but the result is not an entire success, for they obtrude too much. It would have been better had he sung it in an uncluttered arrangement. 'Early Morning Rain' is by Gordon Lightfoot; this begins with fine acoustic guitar and receives a marvellous performance from Presley. It is warm and intimate capturing exactly the spirit of the song. It is enhanced by excellent harmonica work by Charlie McCoy, and is a classic performance. 'For Loving Me' is another delicious performance; it is beautifully recorded, with Presley in full command. This is Nashville at its best, a wholly musical realisation of the song. McCoy's harmonica and James Burton's admired guitar give additional lustre to Presley's performance.

'The First Time Ever I Saw Your Face' became a big hit for Roberta Flack the following year. This is a song that everyone admires and many singers performed, yet was not a hit when it first appeared. It is surprising that Presley's was not the hit single. But it was the first song recorded, and the result is stiff and inflexible. The song needs a fluent, plastic performance and its best qualities are not apparent here.

15–21 May, 1971
Venue: RCA Studios, Nashville
Titles recorded: 'An Evening Prayer', 'A Thing Called Love', 'Don't Think Twice, It's All Right', 'Fools Rush In', 'He Touched Me', 'Help Me Make It Through The Night', 'Holly Leaves And Christmas Trees', 'If I Get Home On Christmas Day', 'I'll Be Home On Christmas Day', 'I'll Take You Home Again, Kathleen', 'I'm Leavin'', 'It's Only Love', 'It's Still Here', 'It Won't Seem Like Christmas', 'I've Got Confidence', 'I Will Be True', 'Lead Me, Guide Me,' 'Love Me, Love The Life I Lead', 'Merry Christmas Baby', 'Miracle Of The Rosary', 'O Come, All Ye Faithful', 'On A Snowy Christmas Night', 'Padre', 'Seeing Is Believing', 'Silver Bells', 'The First Noel', 'The Wonderful World Of Christmas', 'Until It's Time For You To Go', 'We Can Make The Morning', 'Winter Wonderland'

This major recording session, during which no less than thirty titles were recorded, made a welcome return to the studio for Presley. A glance at the titles will show that one of the ideas behind the sessions was to put together a new Christmas album; but the first song 'An Evening Prayer' was released the following year as part of a sacred album *He Touched Me*. We have noted before that Presley's performances of religious songs are marked by a deep and genuine sincerity, and 'An Evening Prayer' is no exception. Every word is crystal clear, and the performance is very moving, especially the concluding 'Amen'.

'A Thing Called Love' is a curious mixture of country material, above a walking bass, married to a Christmas cake arrangement, the result is unsuccessful. Towards the end of the session on 16 May, Presley put down a version of Dylan's 'Don't Think Twice, It's All Right', which lasts over eight minutes. For release it was cut to less than three minutes. When one considers the quality of some of the other songs at these sessions (especially 'Merry Christmas Baby') it is to be hoped that the complete take of 'Don't Think Twice, It's All Right' will eventually be released. As it happens, the engineers have done their best. As the song suddenly fades in, the listener is catapulted into the fluid world of the session. As well as Presley's fabulous singing, James Burton's superb guitar work should be mentioned. One must hope the complete take will appear sometime. 'Fools Rush

In', the Johnny Mercer number, does not show Presley at his best, but it was possibly included with an eye to the Las Vegas market. It is slick, clean, but antiseptic. 'He Touched Me', the title track of the religious album, had doubtless been in Presley's mind for a long time. It is the kind of hymn he had known from his youth, and the performance is effective and moving. In 'Help Me Make It Through The Night', the classic song by Kris Kristofferson, Presley commits a rare error of judgement. The song, which is a cry for help, is sung by Presley in a beefy way which destroys the fragile melody line.

'Holly Leaves And Christmas Trees' is feeble, as is 'If I Get Home On Christmas Day'. Presley seems uninterested, his lack of power in his top register is as if he could not be bothered. The similarly titled 'I'll Be Home On Christmas Day' is different. It is 'bluesy', and Presley forces his voice, to produce a sense of strain. The song is interesting and receives a more committed performance. 'I'll Take You Home Again, Kathleen' is fascinating, for this traditional song was originally recorded with Presley accompanying himself on the piano, the other instruments being overdubbed. As Presley's piano playing here is uninteresting, the procedure is justified.

'I'm Leavin'' is a remarkable performance of an unusual song. The title was in tune with the times and his performance is startling. Presley changes the quality of his voice to emphasise the despairing nature of the lyrics. This performance deserves to be better known. 'It's Only Love' is an attempt to produce a commercial number in the current style, but it fails. The material is not good enough, and Presley is unwilling to drive the song along. It is, however, a fascinating performance. 'It's Still Here' is another song accompanied by Presley on the piano. Here, Presley reveals himself to be a stylish and talented pianist, far from the chord strumming that passes as piano playing by some performers. It is a simple song, sensitively performed, and the odd fluff in ensemble enhances its appeal. In 'It Won't Seem Like Christmas' we return to Yuletide material. Presley performs this 3/4 country song in a simple manner, making extensive use of his natural vibrato. 'I've Got Confidence' is in revival/gospel style. It ends as it begins to get going, and is not the success is could have been. 'I Will Be True' is the third number with Presley on piano, but the song lacks distinction. 'Lead Me, Guide Me' is more convincing, though the arrangement is so basic it can only be regarded as an album track. 'Love Me, Love The Life I Lead' is a number Presley might have heard Tom Jones sing, and its slow medium tempo gives full opportunity for Presley's powerfully straining emotion.

In 'Merry Christmas Baby' we encounter not only the finest recorded performance of these seven days, but one of the greatest Presley performances committed to disc. It is a blues, and once again his natural feel for this difficult medium is apparent. The blues is a simple harmonic structure. This simplicity means almost any singer can *sing*, but only a handful can *perform*, the blues. It is clear that Presley is one of this handful. It is a tragedy that he never recorded a blues album.

133

'Miracle Of The Rosary' is doubtless sincere, but it is the sort of religious song that would turn many people into atheists. It is in poor taste, and Presley sounds ill-at-ease. 'O Come, All Ye Faithful' is a beautiful performance, carefully arranged by Presley himself. The first verse is almost Lutheran in its four-part harmony, almost entirely unaccompanied; and in the second verse (with female descant) the cumulative effect is remarkable. The same cannot be said of 'On A Snowy Christmas Night', a slowish, mediocre ballad, and 'Padre' also lacks distinction. 'Seeing Is Believing' is unusual: it is a driving rocker, but has a fervent religious message and the rhythm is so irresistible it could have become a major hit. 'Silver Bells', in contrast, did not even deserve to be recorded. 'The First Noel' is too high for Presley's voice. This forces him to strain, a fact he attempts to disguise by exaggerating words, with the result that a simple carol is made unusually heavy (in the worse sense). 'The Wonderful World Of Christmas' is another uninteresting song but it is well performed. 'Until It's Time For You To Go' became a classic hit for Presley, and this performance is one of his best. He infuses each word with an added meaning.

'We Can Make The Morning', a straightforward ballad, is badly recorded, with Presley out of focus and uncertain. The final song, 'Winter Wonderland', has a baritone quality, but Presley is too heavy for this simple material.

8/9 June, 1971
Venue: RCA Studios, Nashville
Titles recorded: 'Bosom Of Abraham', 'He Is My Everything', 'I, John', 'Put Your Hand In The Hand', 'Reach Out To Jesus', 'There Is No God But God'

This session completed those begun the previous month. Two titles were recorded, 'I'll Be Home On Christmas Day' and 'Until It's Time For You To Go', in an attempt to improve on the May takes, but were not considered good enough to release. In the event, the earlier takes were issued. 'Bosom Of Abraham' was a disaster. It is ludicrously short – ninety seconds. Furthermore, when the song was released during Easter 1972, it was cut and pressed at 33.3 rpm, although labelled 45! It never stood a chance. 'He Is My Everything' marries new lyrics to the earlier double-hit tune 'There Goes My Everything'. 'I, John' is a fast gospel number, with rousing female vocals. Presley sings with conviction, and the result is one of the best numbers in this style from him for some time. A revival feel is also prevalent in 'Put Your Hand In The Hand', a fine performance tingling with life.

'Reach Out To Jesus' and 'There Is No God But God' are both insistent religious numbers. The first rises to a blitzkrieg finish, but the second is more straightforward – even simple. Neither shows Presley at his greatest, but his sincerity is not in doubt.

16/17 February, 1972
Venue: Hilton Hotel, Las Vegas
Titles issued: 'American Trilogy', 'It's Impossible', 'The Impossible Dream'

This version of 'American Trilogy', one of at least four Presley recordings, was used for his single release. It is a fine performance of this successful fusion of three great songs: 'I Wish I Were In Dixie', 'The Battle Hymn Of The Republic', and 'All My Trials'. It is done with tremendous conviction by Presley, and the single became a big hit for him in the UK in July 1972. 'It's Impossible', the surprising Perry Como hit of 1971 (his first for many years), is well performed, but the live recording suffers from poor backing sound. Other songs were recorded during Presley's shows at the Las Vegas Hilton, but are duplicated by alternative versions, most notable being 'The Impossible Dream' omitted from the comments in the first edition of this book, which was eventually issued on the posthumous album *He Walks Beside Me* in 1978. This Hilton performance remains the best of the several recorded at various stages of his career.

27–29 March, 1972
Venue: RCA Studios, Nashville
Titles recorded: 'Always On My Mind', 'Burning Love', 'Fool', 'It's A Matter Of Time', 'Separate Ways', 'Where Do I Go From Here?'

Generally a fine collection of songs. 'Always On My Mind' is well sung, with an appeal that suits this excellent song, but it is eclipsed by 'Burning Love'. This superb rocker is sung in tremendous style, powerful and rich. There is magnificent drumming from Ronnie Tutt. Neither 'Fool' nor 'It's A Matter Of Time' are in the same class, good as they are, especially 'Fool', where the arrangement is intriguing. 'Separate Ways' possibly reflects the state of Presley's marriage at this time, for he sings it with brooding sadness; but the arrangement is poor. 'Where Do I Go From Here?' is a fine performance of a mediocre song, with Ronnie Tutt saving the day instrumentally.

10 June, 1972
Venue: Madison Square Garden, New York
Titles recorded: 'All Shook Up', 'Also Sprach Zarathustra', 'American Trilogy', 'Can't Help Fallin' In Love', 'For The Good Times', 'Funny How Time Slips Away', 'Heartbreak Hotel', 'Hound Dog', 'I Can't Stop Loving You', 'Love Me', 'Love Me Tender', 'Never Been To Spain', 'Polk Salad Annie', 'Proud Mary', 'Suspicious Minds', 'Teddy Bear'/'Don't Be Cruel', 'That's All Right', 'The Impossible Dream', 'You Don't Have To Say You Love Me', 'You've Lost That Loving Feeling'

These recordings were possibly made as a trial for the project which was to take place the following January in Hawaii and were issued on one album, *Elvis As Recorded At Madison Square Garden*. When confronted with a number of similar live recordings it is not always useful to compare them. The different situations during each live performance mean that the individual gig is only a record of that particular time and place.

Although the titles are listed alphabetically above, they will be discussed in the order in which they appear. Apart from this being a recording of a live performance, there seems no point for Presley to have re-recorded old material.

The album is not one of Presley's most memorable. With many of these titles, Presley made his reputation in studio recordings that became classics. With the problems of, there was no musical reason for this album, and in no instance is the performance as good as the best of Presley's earlier versions.

As the album begins, the sound is harsh and constricted; but Presley is in excellent voice in 'That's All Right'. 'Proud Mary' is ragged at first and Presley is indistinct. 'Never Been To Spain' receives an outstanding performance. The Dusty Springfield hit 'You Don't Have To Say You Love Me' is straightforward, but overpowering. This segues into 'You've Lost That Loving Feeling', which receives a scrappy introduction from Presley. The voices overload the high frequencies, and although this is not flawless (Presley repeats the 'suit too tight' gag) it still exerts a tremendous feeling of passion. Feedback tends to trouble 'Polk Salad Annie' intermittently, and the old songs that end side one are variable. 'Love Me' is a simple performance, but 'All Shook Up', driven by superb drumming from Ronnie Tutt, is very fast. 'Heartbreak Hotel' lacks the quality of the original, and the final three, 'Teddy Bear'/'Don't Be Cruel' and 'Love Me Tender' are good, but add nothing to what we already have.

Next is 'The Impossible Dream'. This would have benefited from a studio recording, for Presley is not well balanced, and he takes time to get into his stride. There are also mistakes, which annoy on repetition. Presley gets a good top A at the end, but this is not one of his best performances. 'Hound Dog' begins humorously, and then we hear a very different version from the classic recording of 1956. The vocal line is completely altered, with funky flicks form James Burton's lead guitar, before the 'real' 'Hound Dog' returns. An unusual performance – but not to be taken seriously. 'Suspicious Minds' is not a good performance, though it improves after a poor start. 'For The Good Times' makes up for this: this is a performance without gimmicks. 'American Trilogy', is unfortunately, not serious enough. It begins as a send-up, but the cumulative power is overwhelming. 'Funny How Time Slips Away' is a throw-away performance until the final joke ending. Presley's now familiar closing numbers 'I Can't Stop Loving You' and 'Can't Help Fallin' In Love' are good enough, but, like the earlier songs, do not tell us anything new about the songs or the singer.

14 January, 1973
Venue: Honolulu International Centre Arena, Hawaii
Titles recorded: 'Big Hunk O' Love', 'Also Sprach Zarathustra', 'American Trilogy', 'Blue Hawaii', 'Blue Suede Shoes', 'Burning Love', 'Can't Help Falling In Love', 'Early Morning Rain', 'Fever', 'Hawaiian Wedding Song',

'Hound Dog', 'I Can't Stop Loving You', 'I'll Remember You', 'I'm So Lonesome I Could Cry', 'It's Over', 'Johnny B. Goode', 'Ipo', 'Long Tall Sally', 'Whole Lotta Shakin' Goin' On', 'Love Me', 'My Way', 'No More', 'See See Rider', 'Something', 'Steamroller Blues', 'Suspicious Minds', 'What Now My Love?', 'You Gave Me A Mountain', 'Welcome To My World'
N B 'Early Morning Rain', 'Hawaiian Wedding Song', 'Ipo' and 'No More' were not released

This session, recorded live in Hawaii, was a satellite show, beamed directly throughout the world. Within a few days a double album was released in JVC's CD-4 quadraphonic system, which became the first million-selling quadraphonic record. The songs are discussed in the order in which they appear on the album.

The show begins with the ubiquitous 'Also Sprach Zarathustra', the opening fanfare from Richard Strauss's symphonic poem of 1896, based on Friedrich Nietzsche's lengthy poem. This had been used by Stanley Kubrick for his film *2001* (1969) since when it had become the standard opening for almost every rock act in existence. The arrangement used here does not feature Presley, but the use of voices is effective. When Presley bursts on stage, the quadraphonic recording gives unbelievable realism and impact, the stereo mix being insignificant in comparison. Presley begins in great style, powerful but relaxed, and the band is brilliant. The drumming is magnificent, and the trumpets blaze through like a burst of sunlight. Presley's voice, however, lacks the last ounce of total command.

In 'Burning Love', which follows, Ronnie Tutt's solid drumming dominates the music. Presley rides the song and it is almost impossible to keep still while listening to this performance. As with all great rock bands, the band fractionally anticipates the beat. The George Harrison number 'Something' is finely sung, but the arrangement is too fussy for the first part of the song. This tends to affect Presley's performance, which is not outstanding. The next song, 'You Gave Me A Mountain', receives a performance of consummate power. It is impossible to overpraise either the orchestra or the piano playing of Glen Harding.

'Steamroller Blues' is very much in Presley's blood, but although he receives a fine accompaniment, it is too fast. For safety's sake, the previous day's rehearsal was also recorded. It would be interesting to compare this version with the version recorded the day before – the concert of 12 January, which has been made available, but only on video – in which Presley is preferable. He appears, in the earlier performance, to have been more relaxed, and comes across as being in much better voice. Showing his breadth of repertoire, Presley tackles the Sinatra hit of 1969 'My Way', and gives a performance certainly the equal of Sinatra's. Presley is in superb voice, and produces a thrilling top G, unforced, yet full of power right at the end. Mention must also be made of the beautiful solo violin in the second verse. Both 'Love Me' and 'Johnny B. Goode' show an understandable drop in voltage: the first is relaxed, and the second casual. But by any standards, especially with the fine harmony singing and magnificent guitar, these are excellent performances. In 'It's Over' (not the Roy Orbison song), the only performance Presley recorded of this, one can hear him turn from the microphone early on. It is too relaxed, but there is another fine top G here, too.

'Blue Suede Shoes', which Presley first recorded seventeen years before, is something of a self-parody, and in 'I'm So Lonesome I Could Cry' his voice lacks the finest sustained quality. It is a beautiful song, which would have benefited form a studio recording. 'I Can't Stop Loving You' is not to be compared to the 1969 Las Vegas version. What is noteworthy is the superb drumming, guitar and brass work. In 'Hound Dog' and 'Blue Suede Shoes', Presley mumbles words for effect – not for their musical impact.

The Gilbert Becaud song 'What Now My Love?' was a big hit for Shirley Bassey in 1962. This is the only recording by Presley of this fine number. He sings the first verse with great strength, but does not begin the second verse so well. The performance has a committed quality, but there are rough edges which would have been ironed out in a studio, although it is unlikely the fine ending would have been captured so well.

If the last few songs show a falling-away from the performances at the beginning of the show, 'Fever' is a superb performance. Although Presley had recorded it before, this is hypnotic, and there is an imaginative use of quadraphonic sound, as the tenor drum flicks across the rear images behind the listener. 'Welcome To My World' is another one-time only recording. Presley continues in fine voice, and the sole drawback is the eruption form the audience when they eventually recognise the song. 'Suspicious Minds' shows Presley at full stretch. The sudden drop to half speed, and the return to the *first* tempo is electrifying. 'I'll Remember You' continues this high standard. The gentle tempo (with a nice use of flutes in the orchestra) is beautifully phrased. The mixture of 'Long Tall Sally'/'Whole Lotta Shakin' Goin' On' has an infectious drive, and is better than the earlier 'reminiscence' of Presley's old rocking days. In 'American Trilogy' Presley is superb, and his final top A thoroughly deserves the ovation. In 'A Big Hunk O' Love' the driving rocker is a classic performance, with Glen Harding's thrilling pianism. After this, 'Can't Help Falling In Love' is a disappointment; words are either incoherent or missed out, and Presley is breathless. By this time it did not matter, for he had achieved the most extraordinary live recording of his career, and convincingly showed that he was still the undisputed master of popular music.

21–25 July, 1973
Venue: Stax Studios, Memphis
Titles recorded: 'Find Out What's Happening', 'For Old Times' Sake', 'Girl Of Mine', 'If You Don't Come Back', 'I've Got A Thing About You Baby', 'Just A Little Bit', 'Raised On Rock', 'Take Good Care Of Her', 'Three Corn Patches'

These were Presley's first studio recordings for sixteen months, and the first he had made at Stax. During the 1960s the Stax sound had been distinctive and influential, with a string of hits from such artists as William Bell, Judy Clay, and Booker T. and the MGs. Presley's last studio recording in Memphis was in February 1969, at the American Studios, but in 1973 they had closed their Memphis branch. 'Find Out What's Happening' is a good number, fast and bouncy and featuring a tight blend of female voices with Presley's fine vocal quality. Once again, we must mention James Burton's guitar as well as Bobby Eammon's excellent organ work. 'For Old Times' Sake' is a sentimental ballad, not out of the top drawer. Nor is Presley at his best.

Although the sessions were spread over five days, for the last two the personnel of the band were changed considerably, owing to previous commitments. This meant that Presley then had to work with unfamiliar musicians and it became clear on 24 July that the ensemble was not proving successful. Elvis left the studios to allow the musicians to lay down tracks for him to overdub later. While this is by no means unusual in pop sessions, it was almost unheard of for Presley. The only song completed in this way, 'Girl Of Mine', shows up this patchwork splicing. There is stiffness in the performance. 'If You Don't Come Back' is a superb 'dark' soul song by Lieber and Stoller. It has a wild choir in the right distance, and receives splendid performance, full of thick undertones and smouldering power, although the guitar solo at the end lets it down. 'I've Got A Thing About You Baby' shows the influence of the Stax Studios. This unpretentious song gets a suitably gentle performance. At first, it appears ordinary, but soon the magic begins to work. 'Just A Little Bit' is a faster number. This is another superb performance by Presley, with tight drumming from both Jerry Carrigan and Ronnie Tutt. The Stax influence is also noticeable in 'Raised On Rock': the bass line, brilliantly played by Tommy Cogbill, is worthy of special mention. The first three days' recordings were superior to those done later, but the pianist Bobby Wood played throughout the five days. He begins 'Take Good Care Of Her', on which strings (or possibly synthesiser) were overdubbed. Kathy Westmoreland sings a later verse well. Finally, 'Three Corn Patches' returns to rock 'n' roll, but in a curious way this song sums up these sessions. Presley seems in two minds and several voices throughout this number – from the hesitant opening to the raunchy middle section. But whereas in the best songs he was able to mould this variety into one experience, here he fails. One must, however, mention the dynamic chunky and boppy rock piano playing of Bobby Wood on this track.

This session is one of the most interesting Presley had undertaken for years, but the results are ultimately disappointing. First, the change in personnel was a serious mistake, but his did not affect the eight previously recorded songs. The material is variable, but contains enough good songs to have been successful; and the musicians, certainly those of the first three days at any rate, could hardly have been improved upon. However, this was the first time they had recorded in these studios. By the early 1970s, the importance of the sound engineer in rock music had grown enormously. Many rock musicians will testify that much of their success is due to the skill in balance and acoustic of those responsible for capturing the music on tape. In no way were the Stax Studios inferior – they had proved their merit by the important hits produced there. The problem for Presley was that they were the wrong type of studios. Used to producing the distinctive 'Stax' sound, the constricting effects of their methods of sound production have given these recordings a feeling that something is missing. This 'something' was the relaxed atmosphere which Presley needed to produce his best work.

24 September, 1973
Venue: Elvis Presley's home, Palm Springs, Los Angeles
Titles recorded: 'Are You Sincere?', 'I Miss You', 'Sweet Angeline'

The intention at these sessions, the first at one of Presley's homes, was to salvage something from the abortive last two days at Stax the previous July. At his home in Palm Springs, 'Sweet Angeline' was resurrected for vocal overdubbing. Presley and the other singers decided to record two other songs as well. 'Are You Sincere?' and 'I Miss You' are both slow ballads – but uninspired. They do not deserve commercial release, although they are well enough done. 'Sweet Angeline' is another slow ballad. It has parts of considerable interest and beauty, and given the circumstances can be counted as a success. But the flaws noted in the original Stax sessions are still apparent, and the song fails to catch fire.

10–16 December, 1973
Venue: Stax Studios, Memphis
Titles recorded: 'Good Time Charlie's Got The Blues', 'Help Me', 'I Got A Feeling In My Body', 'If That Isn't Love', 'If You Talk In Your Sleep', 'It's Midnight', 'Love Song Of The Year', 'Loving Arms', 'Mr Song Man', 'My Boy', 'Promised Land', 'She Wears My Ring', 'Spanish Eyes', 'Talk About The Good Times', 'There's A Honky-Tonk Angel', 'Thinking About You', 'You Asked Me To', 'Your Love's Been A Long Time Coming'

This was the second series of sessions recorded at Stax Studios in Memphis, and this time a smaller band played throughout the seven days. The varied material contains some remarkable performances. The problems with the Stax sound appear to have been overcome, perhaps by the use of a smaller band. In 'Good Time Charlie's Got The Blues' additional instruments were overdubbed. This is an unusual song; it is a slow, blues-influenced number, without being a blues. Presley sings this very well, with a sensitive and restrained feel, and is helped by fine vocal backing work from J.D. Sumner and The Stamps. But the character of this number only reveals itself after several hearings. 'Help Me' is again enhanced by the male backing group, and this religious medium up-tempo song shows Presley's ability to blend with harmony singers.

140

'I Got A Feeling In My body' has a distinctive Stax sound. Presley's voice is placed in the rear middle image. It has a strange quality, and the use of echo also detracts. In spite of all this, the performance is urgently infectious, and the result an unusual example of Presley being 'produced' to great effect. His repeated 'I-got-a, I-got-a, I-got-a' is sensational. 'If That Isn't Love' is a slow waltz, with a honky-tonk piano wandering in and out. There is more than a hint of Tom Jones in this performance, but Presley suffers from production drawbacks. 'If You Talk In Your Sleep', a song partly written by Red West, is a tremendous recording. It begins arrestingly, full of menace and flickering speed, and the orchestra arrangement is startlingly good, the interest occasionally passing from Presley to the orchestra. But there is no doubt who is in charge, and this little-known number has to be counted as one of Presley's greatest recordings of this period. A fine orchestral arrangement also appears on 'It's Midnight', but this is very different. From the humid opening, with a gentle acoustic guitar, harmonica and a soft yet solid bass, the song builds dramatically. This is a serious song, and Presley's performance is full of foreboding and horror. This constitutes another remarkable performance, which can plunge the listener into depression.

In 'Love Song Of The Year' solo violin and piano trace a delicate embroidery around Presley, but the overall effect is not of the best. The Stax sound is gain in evidence in 'Loving Arms', which begins in slow moody fashion. Presley is relaxed in 'Mr Song Man' but the drawback is the song. 'My Boy' proved a major hit in Britain; it is a sentimental ballad, similar in message to Tammy Wynette's 'D.I.V.O.R.C.E', but more dramatic. Presley is well suited to this strong meat, and surely his own divorce two months before added poignancy to the lyrics. The Chuck Berry number 'Promised Land' blows away the gloom with its fast-burning power. As in 'I Got A Feeling In My Body', in 'Promised Land' Presley sounds constricted, but the effect is appropriate and the tight performance is good. In 'She Wears My Ring' Presley revives a Solomon King hit of six years before. This is a simple and effective song but demands a clear, unfettered sound, and the echo distorts Presley's natural voice.

In 1973, Capitol Records re-issued the Al Martino song 'Spanish Eyes', which became a major hit. Presley revives it here, but although his performance is professional, and the recording good, the result hardly justifies the effort. Presley counts into 'Talk About The Good Times', a fun revival number with box piano; the backing of Voice is a great asset.

In spite of the outrageous title and the church organ introduction, 'There's A Honky-Tonk Angel' is another astonishing performance from Presley. The song is surprisingly good. In slow waltz tempo, the words have personal significance for Presley, who turns in a very moving performance. 'Thinking About You' is equally good, but is more obviously a pop song, a medium tempo number with a fluent bass line. The arrangement is good, and it is clearly recorded. Presley is in excellent voice, but the performance lacks the involvement, which is a feature of the best of these sessions. 'You Asked Me To' begins like 'The Jimmy Brown Song':

141

it is a simple arrangement, sung in straightforward style. The fine guitar work towards the end is possibly by Johnny Christopher. The final song, 'Your Love's Been A Long Time Coming', is best forgotten – it is a slow number without distinction.

20 March, 1974
Venue: Midsouth Coliseum, Memphis
Titles recorded and released: (in order on album) 'See See Rider', 'I Got A Woman', 'Love Me', 'Trying To Get To You', 'Long Tall Sally', 'Whole Lotta Shakin' Goin' On', 'Mama Don't Dance', 'Flip Flop And Fly', 'Jailhouse Rock', 'Hound Dog', 'Why Me Lord?', 'How Great Thou Art', 'Blueberry Hill'/'I Can't Stop Loving You' (medley), 'Help Me', 'American Trilogy', 'Let Me Be There', 'My Baby Left Me', 'Lawdy, Miss Clawdy', 'Can't Help Falling In Love'

This album, *Live In Memphis* is the most superfluous of Presley's career. Every title had been recorded by him at least once before, in performances which are invariably better. Those here are often below Presley's best, the band is not 'tight', many words are slurred, with scant regard for sense or atmosphere, and the audience constantly interrupts. The performances say nothing new. As if this was not bad enough, the record was packaged with the most inept sleeve in a succession of generally mediocre packagings. The sales for this album, by all accounts, flopped badly, and caused – perhaps for the first time – some hard thinking concerning the wisdom of churning out similar 'live' albums by Presley.

Chapter Fourteen

The final years, 1975–77

9–12 March, 1975
Venue: RCA Studios, Hollywood
Titles recorded: 'And I Love You So', 'Bringin' It Back', 'Fairytale', 'Green, Green Grass Of Home', 'I Can Help', 'Pieces Of My Life', 'Shake A Hand', 'Susan When She Tried', 'T-R-O-U-B-L-E', 'Woman Without Love'

This session was Presley's first studio visit for sixteen months. Following the failure of the *Live In Memphis* album, new material, recorded under the best conditions, was becoming urgently needed. The result was good, but only after substantial overdubbing in Nashville. With one or two exceptions, Presley seemed content to record songs that had already been hits for other singers. While this may be interesting, musically it did nothing for his career.

'And I Love You So', the Don Maclean song, was a hit on RCA for Perry Como in 1973. Presley's performance is not outstanding. 'Bringin' It Back' is even less memorable. The same is true of 'Fairytale', a good example of Nashville in the 1970s – although much of it was done in Hollywood! With 'Green, Green Grass Of Home', Presley revived a smash hit for Tom Jones, released in 1966. Presley's performance is tremendous but adds nothing to what Jones did with it. However, with Billy Swan's 'I Can Help', Presley seems out of touch. The song was a hit for Swan in 1974, but Presley's hectoring style is completely out of place. The electric piano and guitar are obtrusive. 'Pieces Of My Life' is a superlative performance:

Presley is right in tune, and every word is clear and given its due. 'Shake A Hand' is very slow, in old rocker style, updated by modern recording. This is a fine performance, showing that Presley had no peer in songs of this type. The quality of the musicians is remarkable but the song, which they try to bring to life, remains rooted to the spot.

'Susan When She Tried' is excellent; this toe-tapping number was a hit for the Statler Brothers in the USA. It is enhanced here by fabulous guitar work, but driving the song, over Ronnie Tutt's solid drumming, is Presley's voice. 'T-R-O-U-B-L-E' is also outstanding. This is a fine rocker, with Presley urging it along with terrific verve. The piano (either Glen Harding or David Briggs) is marvellous, and the only criticism is the restricted sound image – it should have been spread wider. Finally, 'Woman Without Love' is a good performance of a non-descript song.

2–8 February, 1976
Venue: Graceland, Memphis
Titles recorded: 'Bitter They Are, Harder They Fall', 'Blue Eyes Cry In The Rain', 'Danny Boy', 'For The Heart', 'Hurt', 'I'll Never Fall In Love Again', 'Love Comin' Down', 'Moody Blue', 'Never Again', 'She Thinks I Still Care', 'Solitaire', 'The Last Farewell'

These sessions were the first to be held at Graceland. It is unclear why it was necessary to move engineers and equipment to Presley's home, but whatever the reason, these recordings (like most of his work at the time) were extensively overdubbed, with variable results. The material lacks contrast, and it is impossible to avoid the feeling that this is a morbid collection, possibly affected by Presley's spells in hospital the previous year, and his father's heart attack a few months before.

The first song, 'Bitter They Are, Harder They Fall', is a slow, dramatic ballad, which receives a deeply moving performance. This song will never become popular, but it could hardly be better performed. It is clear that Presley's divorce affected his singing. In 'Blue Eyes Cry In The Rain', Presley was possibly experimenting with different recording techniques. The song is no great shakes, being a slow ballad.

'Danny Boy' is quite different. This famous setting of the 'Londonderry Air' inspires Presley to one of his finest performances. He begins alone, to be joined by solo piano (Glen Harding), and later by J.D. Sumner and The Stamps, to produce a sincere and restrained recording. 'For The Heart' is one of the few fast numbers in this session. In style it is typical of the mid-1970s, having a solid beat and a piano trying to update Floyd Cramer. This, plus the powerful instrumental backing and the optimistic nature of the song, makes a welcome change. Presley's singing was consistent at these sessions, and in 'Hurt' his voice is heard at its most startling. But the song is dated, and the accompaniment crude. This is not true of 'I'll Never Fall In Love Again', which was a major hit for Tom Jones. The influence of the Welsh singer is obvious. Occasionally Presley's voice falters as though overcome by emotion. This is great singing, and the effect is shattering. 'Love Comin' Down' is another slow ballad. But although Presley sings this well enough, the song lacks distinction.

In 'Moody blue', we hear a fine arrangement of a mediocre song. It has an up-tempo beat, but Presley sounds less than totally committed. The song does not suit his voice, but the arrangement almost compensates for the continuous sense of strain.

'Never Again' is another ballad with heavily overdubbed strings, which make a sickly sounding background. Presley sounds unusual, and this probably reveals his voice showing signs of wear and tear.

'She Thinks I Still Care' is good Nashville-influenced material, but Presley's voice lacks something. Perhaps he is set too far back. But the vocal quality fades and breaks as if he is suffering from breathing or throat troubles.

'Solitaire', a famous Neil Sedaka song, proved a great hit for Andy Williams. Again the words have personal significance for Presley, and his performance is outstanding, although he does not eclipse Williams. Presley chose the songs for these sessions and the material displays his discrimination. The final song, 'The Last Farewell', the international hit for Roger Whittaker (who wrote it), receives a very fine performance. The tempo is measured, and this fine song is given by Presley with due regard for the excellent lyrics.

29–31 October, 1976
Venue: Graceland, Memphis
Titles recorded: 'He'll Have To Go', 'It's Easy For You', 'Pledging My Love',
'There's A Fire Down Below', 'Way Down'
N B 'There's A Fire Down Below' was unissued, and probably not completed

Once more, Presley's inability to achieve consistent studio work forced these sessions to be held at his home. Although these were spread over three days, only four songs were recorded (the fifth was apparently unfinished, without Presley recording the vocal track). The songs could only be released after much additional work, in some cases in January 1977 in Nashville. This cosmetic work is generally successful.

'He'll Have To Go', the first hit for Jim Reeves in the UK (1960), was a surprising choice. The song is well known, and had long passed the peak of its popularity. Presley's performance is very slow and very long, at four minutes twenty-eight seconds. Although he is in good voice, the quality is not as good as in the past, apart for a deep G on the word 'low'. 'It's Easy For You' is another slow ballad, by Tim Rice and Andrew Lloyd Webber. As recorded, Presley's voice is placed very far back, almost constricted at first. The performance seems good enough, but the backing musicians are so outstanding (especially Ronnie Tutt) that they tend to detract from Presley.

'Pledging My Love' is another curiosity: at least twenty years out of date, this slow, rocking ballad, with its heavy dragging triplets, is musically nothing.

The session is redeemed by 'Way Down'. This was Presley's last original hit, and shows him at the height of his powers. In spite of the troubles that beset the session, this magnificent rock number brought out the best in this great artist. The throbbing bass line at the beginning catches the spirit of its bluesy coarseness, echoed by the flaying piano line. 'Way Down' was one of the most unusual hits for Presley, because a large part of its appeal is in the backing vocals and instrumental colour. However, he was the only singer who could have handled the lead vocal line with such aplomb.

25 April, 1977
Venue: Civic Centre, Saginaw
Titles recorded: 'If You Love Me', 'Little Darlin'', 'Unchained Melody'

Three live numbers, which were subjected to considerable overdubbing and other cosmetic treatment in the studio to make them acceptable for album release. 'If You Love Me' is well performed by Presley. The arrangements and dubbings are added with skill, but the result is mediocre. 'Little Darlin'' makes a change form the morbid material on which Presley had concentrated for some time. It is a good-humoured performance of a song with tongue-in-cheek reminiscences of late 1950s soft rock. This 'red-blue-jeans-and-a-ponytail' atmosphere is a breath of clean air, and British listeners who recall the palmy days of the Vernon Girls will know what to expect. 'Unchained Melody' is remarkable. The live recording featured Presley accompanying himself on the piano. For an album release, the idea to overdub a better backing track was right. In the live performance, Presley was carried away and his singing takes on a freedom not heard on disc for many years. The additions are in keeping with the spirit of his performance. This is an outstanding example of Presley in his last years, and thanks are due to those who brought about this realisation of what at first might have seemed poor material.

146

19–21 June, 1977

Venue: Omaha, Rapid City

Titles recorded: 'Also Sprach Zarathustra', 'See See Rider', 'That's All Right', 'Are You Lonesome Tonight?', 'Teddy Bear'/'Don't Be Cruel', 'You Gave Me A Mountain', 'Jailhouse Rock', 'How Great Thou Art', 'I Really Don't Want To Know', 'Hurt', 'Hound Dog', 'My Way', 'Can't Help Falling In Love', 'I Got A Woman'/'Amen', 'Love Me', 'If You Love Me', 'O Sole Mio'/'It's Now Or Never', 'Trying To Get To You', 'Hawaiian Song', 'Fairytale', 'Little Sister', 'Early Morning Rain', 'What'd I Say?', 'Johnny B. Goode', 'And I Love You So'

These were Presley's last recordings, taken live at concerts on the above dates. The concerts were filmed for a CBS television spectacular, and the recordings were issued after his death as a two-record set, *Elvis In Concert*. The strictures that applied to his earlier live recordings are not so relevant here, for the recording quality is amongst the best of Presley's live recordings. Nevertheless, the issue is largely a sentimental exercise. None of the material is new, and some songs – 'Love Me', for example – had been recorded as many as five times before.

Presley's comments between songs show him still a shy person; although he was a magisterial performer of charismatic quality, his half-apologetic comments, his slight stammering, the nervous laughs and sometimes garbled speech all reveal, as they did similarly in his 1968 television special, the shy boy from Tupelo, Mississippi. But Presley is in superb voice. Not for a long time had the ringing power and tenderness, the range of expression and the certainty of feeling been so clearly displayed. These performances needed no cosmetic surgery before release. In 'How Great Thou Art', for example, Presley's top As are amazing: they would be a credit to any singer. Some performances are given with great care: 'My Way', especially, a better performance than on the *Aloha From Hawaii* double album, suffers nothing from comparison with Frank Sinatra. The appearance of Sherrill Nielsen in the Italian verse of 'O Sole Mio' is a nice touch; it is a pity it was cut form the television show. 'Are You Lonesome Tonight?' begins magnificently, but unfortunately Presley messes up the words in the middle section. Although he recovers well by making a joke of it, the sincerity of the opening verses show that he did not mean this to be a send-up. However, one cannot escape the suspicion that some of the earlier rockers are put in – in very abbreviated form – for old times' sake; the performances are little more than sketches, with hectic, garbled words.

Comments from some of Presley's fans add to the memorial nature of the first album release. Although they were recorded at the time, nobody could have realised how significant they would shortly become. The most poignant comment is by Presley's father, recorded after his son's death. But Vernon is incorrect when he says the recordings were of Presley's last appearance. Elvis Presley's *last* concert was in Indianapolis, five days later on 26 June.

Chapter Fifteen

The best of the bootlegs

The reader may recall that in chapter eight we discussed the provenance of what, for the sake of convenience, we shall call by the generic term 'bootleg' in this chapter – unofficial releases of Presley material. These take the form of out-takes of studio work, unreleased masters or private recordings of live performances. Presley's name on a record has long been sufficient to sell the album, without it necessarily being heard, in large quantities all over the world to his millions of fans. Some people have felt that his name alone is all that is needed – if the material is there, then it merely has to be issued for large sales to be chalked up. But as anyone who has ever worked for a large multinational record company will tell you, the first important job of the record company is to get the product into the store. In this regard, RCA (later, BMG) were past masters at achieving this, what might at first appear comparatively simple, task.

RCA had a world-wide set-up, directed from the company's headquarters in Manhattan by a succession of brilliantly gifted presidents of the record division, and, down to the rookiest salesman in the smallest world territory, the company was able to supply any store in the western hemisphere within a few days. The first problem bootleggers have is that they do not possess such a world-wide sales force. Quite apart from anything else, once the record is in the store, its arrival should coincide with the fruits of the efforts of the promotion men. Reviews, air-play, television exposure and advertising, point-of-sale merchandising – all of these things, and more, have to be in place to inform the public that the record is now released and that it can be bought from their nearest record store.

It should be clear that, without such a world-wide set-up, the bootleggers' dreams of massive sales remain dreams. In addition, most record store owners are not fools, and it has to be said that the release of some of this unofficial material may be contractually suspect: by stocking it, the store owners may run the risk of legal action or the withdrawal of regular supply of official RCA product. But, equally, it has to be said that RCA has, without seeming to condone the practice, been aware that the numbers pressed of these bootleg albums are very small indeed – often measured in hundreds of copies, rather than in tens of thousands. The amount of money involved is not great, and the albums in question would seem to be bought solely by Presley devotees, to whom RCA, over many years, owes a debt of gratitude for their artist and to his memory. There is hardly an album in the many bootleg releases of unofficial Presley product that contains material not otherwise available commercially from RCA, the official recording in many ways being technically superior to that of the bootleg.

Nonetheless, the dyed-in-the-wool Presley enthusiast will want to hear as much of the master's work as possible and even the most casual reader will be aware of the existence of these unofficial albums.

It must be pointed out that no one can be certain as to precisely how many of these albums are available, and while it would be absurd in a book such as this not to mention them, or not to include a representative selection of these releases, what follows has to be seen as a largely personal choice from very many bootlegs. The individual reader may not therefore agree with the choice set out in this chapter, or may feel that a particularly important album has been overlooked. One can only state again that we are dealing with a volatile and unofficial market, and an album that the reader might prize highly could be one that has long been out of print, and may never see the light of day again. Such albums are largely, by their nature, compilations, and take their product from different recording sessions, in some cases spread over many years. Consequently, it has not proved possible to list the tracks entirely chronologically, for in some cases the recording dates themselves are unknown. Nevertheless, in so far as is practicable, the albums are listed in chronological order of performance.

12/13 and 19 January, 1957
Venue: Radio Recorders Studios, Hollywood
Bilko CD 1600: *The Best Of The Lost Binaural Takes*

Titles include: 'Peace In The Valley' (take 1); 'I Beg Of You' (takes 5, 10 and 11); 'That's When Your Heartaches Begin' (take 1); 'It Is No Secret' (take 12); 'Blueberry Hill' (take 8); 'Have I Told You Lately That I Love You?' (takes 1 and 7); 'Is It So Strange?' (takes 10 and 11)

RCA was the first major record company to experiment in making stereo recordings in the post-war era. In the early 1930s Bell Laboratories had demonstrated a form of binaural recording, at around the same time that RCA had also demonstrated a $33^1/_3$ rpm long-playing record, but both developments meant nothing at the height of the Great Depression. The post-war advent of tape recording, and its adoption virtually throughout the recording world from about 1949 onwards, meant that stereo was now a distinct possibility. But the long-playing record, clearly the best sound carrier for this recording system, was not then available world-wide, being launched in the USA in 1948 by Columbia and not taken up by RCA until several years later – and not until after RCA's answer to the long-playing record, the seven-inch 45 rpm disc, had also been launched. And so it was not until the early 1950s that what was termed in the USA as 'the battle of the speeds' seemed to be resolved. Only then could stereo recording be considered, and it was in 1954 that RCA first made stereo (binaural) recordings, although they could not then be issued.

A year or so was to pass before the binaural system was applied to popular artists – it had previously been used only for classical recordings – and, as the impact of a popular artist was still only through the single (the seven-inch 45 rpm disc), and such music was heard in the vast majority of cases on very small speakers, radios (which could not then broadcast in stereo) or on juke-boxes, the commercial needs for stereo releases of popular product were not great. Nonetheless, it was a prudent move on RCA's part to take some Presley sessions in stereo, as well as in mono, even if the results by the standards of only a few years later were comparatively crude. It is fascinating to note that a year after beginning his RCA career, Presley was being recorded by the company in genuine, if rather restricted, binaural form. This Bilko purports to be the 'best of the lost binaural takes' – although as they exist on this record they are hardly 'lost'.

Aside from the semantics, this is a very worthwhile adjunct to the Presley discography. The first take of 'Have I Told You Lately That I Love You?' breaks down, with Presley laughingly muttering 'Oh, shit!' before we hear the complete take 7 (at the very end of which, in the silence, Elvis mutters the same exclamation – much quieter). It should be noted that official stereo releases of these sessions were issued in 1988 by RCA/BMG, but there is something quite appealing in hearing Presley's studio work 'as it happened'. Here is a professional at work.

1958–68

Venue: RCA Studios, Nashville

'Angel Records' [not Angel Records, part of EMI] EP 10005: *Wings of an Angel*

Titles include: 'I Need Your Love Tonight' (takes 1–15, 10 June, 1958); 'Milky White Way' (takes 1–5, 30 October, 1960); 'His Hand In Mine' (takes 1–5, 30 October, 1960); 'Echoes Of Love' (takes 2–7 and 9, 26 May, 1963); 'Please Don't Drag That String Around' (takes 1–4, 26 May, 1963); 'US Male' (takes 1–4, 17 January, 1968); 'Wings Of An Angel' (jam version, 17 January, 1968)

In spite of the 'record company' name on the label, the 'Angel Records' in question here is emphatically not the label that is part of EMI. The CD here is particularly valuable for the Presley student, for it begins, as can be seen, with extant takes of 'I Need Your Love Tonight' – all fifteen of them. (Not all are complete performances, for occasionally there is a breakdown.) What is particularly interesting here is the constant standard of performance maintained throughout these takes. It is little short of amazing and is an object lesson to later artists as to how to approach the business of recording in a studio. Of great interest also is what is termed the 'jam version' of 'Wings Of An Angel' – not great music-making in this instance, but a rare glimpse of a great artist just relaxing amongst friends.

1960–71

Venues: Graceland; RCA Studios Nashville; American Studios Memphis

Lucky Records CDLR716: *Loose Ends* (vol I)

Titles include: 'I'm Beginning To Forget You', 'Mona Lisa', 'My Heart Cries For You', 'Dark Moon', 'Write To Me From Naples', 'Suppose' (all Graceland, recording dates unknown); 'Fame And Fortune' (21 March, 1960), 'Anything That's Part Of You' (15 October, 1961), 'You'll Be Gone', 'Easy Question' (both 18 March, 1962), 'Long Lonely Highway' (27 May, 1963), 'Beyond The Reef' (27 May, 1966), 'Come What May', 'Fools Fall In Love' (both 28 May, 1966), 'Mine', 'Singing Tree' (both 11 September, 1967) (all RCA Studios, Nashville); 'My Little Friend' (16 January, 1969), 'I'll Be There' (23 January, 1969), 'Kentucky Rain' (19 February, 1969), 'If I'm A Feel For Loving You' (21 February, 1969) (all American Studios, Memphis); 'The Sound Of Your Cry' (4 June, 1970), 'I'll Take You Home Again, Kathleen' (19 May, 1971), 'Silver Bells' (15 May, 1971) (both RCA Studios, Nashville)

This album begins with six tracks, all recorded at Graceland around about the mid-1960s – and which came to light after Elvis's death – which were clearly never meant for commercial release as they are of poor technical quality and balance. The result is a picture of a great singer trying out a set of numbers, not necessarily practising – for he hardly falters during each number, demonstrating that he knew them all very well – but singing, perhaps just for his own amusement, simply because his genius demanded it. It is a very touching picture indeed that emerges here, for the venue suggests that these might have been made purely for his own interest and use. The inclusion of 'You'll Be Gone', a complete take for the original 45 rpm version, makes this additionally valuable, and 'I Feel That I've Known You Forever' is taken from the sound-track of the film *Blue Hawaii* – with a great ending, as Elvis is brought up short by the girl. There are may gems here, including an alternative complete take of the Bobby Darin song, 'I'll Be There', which was a big hit in the UK for Gerry and the Pacemakers in the early part of 1965.

1960–77
Venues: Frankfurt, Germany; Nashville; ?Graceland; Montgomery, Alabama
MAC: MAC-RY 24.162: *Elvis Presley – The Colonel's Collection*
Titles include: 'Soldier Boy' (20 March, 1960, RCA Studios Nashville); AFN radio interview (? 1/2 March, Frankfurt); 'Are You Lonesome Tonight?' (take 2); 'Puppet On A String' (takes 7 and 10); 'You'll Never Walk Alone' (without Jordanaires overdub); 'If Every Day Was Like Christmas' (lead vocal by Red West, Elvis singing backing vocals); 'Anything That's Part of You'; 'Moonlight Swim' (home recording – venue and date unknown); 'Where No One Stands Alone' (16 February, 1977, Improved Sound Montgomery Alabama); 'Spanish Eyes' (home recording – duet with Sherrill Nielsen)

This album is a fascinating compilation of various odds and ends. For many people, the most revealing aspect will be the complete AFN Radio interview with Presley, made just a day or so before his return to the USA prior to his demobilisation from the US Army. In few other such interviews do Presley's inherent good manners, reserve and simple human appeal come across with anything like the combination of genuine qualities as they do here. What is also revealed in this extended interview is Presley's common sense when he discusses aspects of his career, and how the material he performs is actually chosen. Three other notables are the track in which Elvis takes backing vocals to Red West's very good rendition of 'If Every Day Was Like Christmas', and the home recordings –

particularly that with Sherrill Nielsen in 'Spanish Eyes'. The title of the album should be discounted.

(?early) August, 1969
Venue: International Hotel, Las Vegas
Fort Baxter ASCD 731-69: *Nevada All Star Shows*
Titles include: 'Blue Suede Shoes', 'I Got A Woman', 'All Shook Up', 'Love Me Tender', 'Jailhouse Rock'/'Don't Be Cruel', 'Heartbreak Hotel', 'Hound Dog', 'Memories', 'Mystery Train'/'Tiger Man', 'Baby, What'd You Want Me To Do?', 'Are You Lonesome Tonight?', 'Yesterday', 'Hey Jude', 'In The Ghetto', 'Suspicious Minds', 'What'd I Say?', 'Can't Help Falling In Love'

This CD says the tapes are of the opening night – but they are not. The opening night (31 July, 1969) of Elvis's engagement was given before a star-studded audience: the complete concert as recorded here is most likely that of his first night before a fee-paying, public audience. It is made endearing by his dialogue with the audience, which shows his attractive sense of humour. Here is virtually a complete concert, as it happened, the occasional warts and all, but the sense of atmosphere and the quality of Elvis's performance are clear for all to hear.

1968–70
Venues: Western Recorders, Los Angeles; American Sound Studios, Memphis
Groovy Records MAC-CD, Groovy 2068: *Edge Of Reality*
Titles include: 'Edge Of Reality' (takes 6 and 8), 'Wonderful World' (takes 5, 15, 17), 'A Little Less Conversation' (takes 10 and 16), 'Almost In Love' (all 7 March, 1968 – Western Recorders); 'Gentle On My Mind', 'You'll Think Of Me' (both 14 January, 1969), 'Suspicious Minds' (23 January, 1969), 'Rubberneckin'' (21 January, 1969) (all American Sound); 'Cryin' Time' (? July, 1970); 'Blue Suede Shoes'/'Whole Lotta Shakin'' (? live 19 August, 1970); 'Suzie Q' (details unknown, 'live on the road')

There are some unique recordings here, most notably the earliest-known version of the medley 'Blue Suede Shoes'/'Whole Lotta Shakin' from 1970, and the puzzling track 'Suzie Q', which is almost impossible to decipher but is undoubtedly Elvis somewhere in the middle distance. We hear the announcements by the producer and engineer, and little studio comments by Elvis and others, and an additional feature is the inclusion of undubbed versions (that is, the basic, unretouched studio recording) of four songs, together with the backing track – without Elvis singing – of 'Almost In Love'.

19 August, 1974
Venue: Las Vegas Hilton
Fort Baxter CD 2094: *If You Talk In Your Sleep*
Titles include: 'Big Boss Man', 'Proud Mary', 'Down In The Alley', 'Good Time Charlie's Got The Blues', 'Never Been To Spain', 'It's Midnight', 'If You Talk In Your Sleep', 'I'm Leavin'', 'Let Me Be There', 'Softly As I Leave You', 'If You Love Me (Let Me Know)', 'Love Me Tender', 'Polk Salad Annie', 'Promised Land', 'My Baby Left Me', 'Bridge Over Troubled Water', 'Fever', 'Hound Dog', 'Can't Help Falling In Love' (incomplete)

This is a tremendous concert. Those who maintain that Elvis was in some way less than at his best in his later years are completely routed by this unofficial taping of the show; he is clearly in command throughout and in excellent voice. It also demonstrates an aspect of Presley's music-making in a way not mentioned elsewhere. This is that at the outset of his career, and until about 1968, the record-buying public only had studio recordings by him to go on; that he was an outstanding studio artist is demonstrated again and again – the more so in many of these bootleg albums, where the public can hear his utter professionalism and consistency in take after take. But after about 1968, most of his recordings are of live performances: and in these we can hear what an outstanding live performer he was – time and again. Of very few artists can such a consistency in these two very different performing disciplines be found. The making of records and the giving of live concerts are at opposite ends of the performing spectrum. Elvis was undoubtedly a master of both, because he was, above all, a natural born singer who just loved to sing. One slightly sad aspect of this album is that the final track is not complete: either the engineer underestimated the amount of tape left, or Elvis took too much time introducing either the band or Telly Savalas (as he does on one occasion here), or that the song has been faded out to make some kind of ending, but the fact remains that the performance here does not come to an end.

30 August, 1976
Venue: University of Alabama Memorial Coliseum, Tuscaloosa, Alabama
Diamond Anniversary Editions, CD DAE 3595-1: *Old Times They Are Not Forgotten*

Titles include: 'Also Sprach Zarathustra', 'See See Rider', 'I Got A Woman'/'Amen', 'Love Me', 'If You Love Me (Let Me Know)', 'You Gave Me A Mountain', 'All Shook Up', 'Teddy Bear'/'Don't Be Cruel', 'And I Love You So', 'Jailhouse Rock', 'Fever', 'America The Beautiful', 'Early Mornin' Rain', 'What'd I Say?', 'Johnny B. Goode', 'Love Letters', 'Hail, Hail Rock 'n' Roll', 'Hurt', 'Hound Dog', 'Heavenly Father' (this track sung by Kathy Westmoreland), 'Mystery Train'/'Tiger Man', 'Can't Help Falling In Love'

This is a fascinating document. It was a hot night in Alabama, even though this concert began at 8.30 pm, and the heat seems to have had some effect of Elvis: he complains about it, and while his performance never falls below a very high standard, right from the beginning one can sense that he is not entirely at ease – at times, he sounds fractionally on edge, exemplified by constantly sliding from one note to another on just about every song in the first part of the concert. Also, the balance as recorded, while very good for what it is, reveals a flawed microphone placing – not with regard to Elvis himself, but in juxtaposition with the backing singers. This is improved upon later in the concert, as though the engineer was aware that something was not quite right.

There are some very fine performances here, and some highly recreative ones, too – notably 'Hound Dog' where Elvis hardly bothers with the words, sliding them one into another in a constant elision before moulding the vocal line into a thrilling, but all-too-short, jam session. The track 'Heavenly Father' is sung with much dramatic fervour, and no little purity of style, by Kathy Westermoreland. In all, this is one of the most valuable of the bootleg CDs, the digital restoration being very well done.

1970s
Venues: Various
Bilko Enterprises, BILKO CD 1595: *More Pure Elvis – The Lost Album*
Titles include: 'Moody Blue', 'When I'm Over You', 'It's A Matter Of Time', 'Sweet Angeline', 'Hurt', 'Shake A Hand', 'Promised Land', 'Heart Of Rome', 'If You Don't Come Back', 'Mr Songman', 'For Old Times' Sake', 'Love Coming Down'

Although tantalisingly entitled *The Lost Album*, this collection would seem to be made up almost entirely of 70s studio out-takes – and, occasionally, it sounds like it, with Elvis not always in the best of voice, notably at the of 'Mr Songman', where his voice loses its customary strength of line, and in the succeeding track, 'For Old Times' Sake', where he is occasionally out of tune and seems to be also out of breath – two faults which would normally debar such takes from release, and probably did so in the first place. What cannot be denied is the singer's obvious sincerity, and in spite of the vocal flaws Presley delivers some very moving performances here. We should also note the very good job that has been done with the original recordings in this instance.

Various recording dates
Venues: Unknown, but all studio recordings
Bilko Enterprises, BILKO 1598/99 [double CD]: *There's Always Me*
Titles include: CD 1 – 'Shake, Rattle And Roll' (takes 1, 2, 3, 5, 7); 'Lawdy, Miss Clawdy' (takes 7, 8, 9, 12); 'I Want You, I Need You, I Love You' (take 3); 'I Need Your Love Tonight' (take 7); 'I Got Stung' (takes 18–20); 'Ain't That Loving You Baby' (takes 9, 10); 'Fever' (take 1); 'Like A Baby' (takes 3, 4); 'Stuck On You'*; 'I Feel So Bad'*; 'Dirty Feeling'*; 'Thrill Of Your Love'*; 'Such A Night'*; 'Are You Lonesome Tonight?'*; 'Girl Next Door'*; 'A Mess Of Blues'*; 'It Feels So Right'*; 'Fame And Fortune'*; 'Surrender'*; 'Working On The Building' (take 2); 'I'm Coming Home'*; 'It's A Sin' (takes 1, 2); 'I Want You With Me' (take 1)*. CD 2 – 'There's Always Me' (takes 2, 6); 'Starting Today' (take 1); 'Sentimental Me' (take 1); 'Judy' (false start, then take 1); 'Put The Blame On Me' (false start, then take 1); 'For The Millionth And Last Time' (takes 2, 6, 10); 'Good Luck Charm' (takes 1, 2, 3); 'Anything That's Part Of You' (take 2); 'I Met Her Today' (takes 1, 7); 'I Feel That I've Known You Forever' (takes 1, 2); 'Just Tell Her Jim Said Hello' (takes 2, 5, 6); 'Suspicion' (takes 1, 2); 'She's Not You' (takes 1, 2); 'Echoes Of Love' (takes 2, 3); 'Please Don't Drag That String Around' (takes 1, 4, 5); 'Devil In Disguise' (takes 1, 2, 3); 'Never Ending' (takes 1, 2)
N B * unknown take numbers

This is absolutely fantastic. This double CD set contains sixty-seven complete or part complete performances of forty-two songs, recorded in outstanding sound quality and digitally remastered to the highest standards currently available. The result is one of the most complete pictures of Elvis in the recording studio that can ever have been assembled, and a picture that reinforces – if ever such reinforcement were needed – his claim to be one of the greatest recording artists of all time. The double set is subtitled 'Essential unreleased studio out-takes' and, for once, this blurb is nothing less than the plain truth. Not one of these performances or fragments falls below the highest vocal standards ever achieved by Elvis Presley at any time in his career, and the tingling excitement that always comes across from his performances never falters throughout the two hours, twenty minutes playing time of this incomparable set. Bilko Enterprises promise volume 2 'soon'; at this level, one can hardly wait.

One of the more remarkable things to emerge from listening to these various bootleg albums is the 'timelessness' of Elvis's performances – obviously, these are not new songs, nor is the style of performance new – but the inherent musicianship they show, quite apart from the quality of Elvis's voice, will ensure that they will never date, will never grow stale and will always exert a fascination for the attentive listener.

Part III

The Musician

Chapter Sixteen

Presley as performer

It may seem strange to some readers to see attention being devoted in this book to Elvis Presley as a performing musician, for such impact as he had in this regard first came to the attention of southern America well over thirty years ago, and his impact there, although great, was concentrated within too small a geographical area to have any more than local significance. His television appearances at the time also were not so numerous as to be instantly recalled. In addition, these early television appearances were in black and white, and rarely preserved on film in acceptable modern video quality. After his release from the US Army in 1960, Presley's live appearances virtually ceased for a decade. Eventually, when he did return to the stage it was not in what had – at the time – become regarded as classic rock venues but in the showbiz-hotel-ballroom circuit largely centred upon Las Vegas.

At first sight, therefore, it would seem somewhat irrelevant to attempt such a study. But even if we possess comparatively little precious visual evidence of Elvis Presley as a performer, in front of an audience (far less than we have of other rock stars or bands), we nevertheless do have enough, in my opinion, to attempt such an evaluation. Why should we attempt such an evaluation where our concentration has been upon Presley as a singer, attempting to show his importance in purely musical, and not in visual terms? In the first edition of this book, there would clearly have been little reason to attempt such a chapter, but since that time we have been fortunate in there having been made available to us a number of commercially-issued videos, enabling us to recall at will – as with his recordings – aspects of this remarkable musician's career.

In any event, the reader today will naturally wish to see some such undertaking made, for he will likely possess, or have access to, a home video machine, and will have seen one or other televised broadcasts of Presley's live appearances. But there remains another important consideration which has become more significant as time has elapsed. This is the visual presentation of popular music.

For a decade or more, it has been thought vital for a pop or rock act to have a video made of the singles which it hopes will succeed in the pop charts. It never used to be the case, and whilst there can be no argument that Presley's records sold all over the world to millions of people who never saw him even on film, and did so entirely through the quality of his voice by way of the recorded performances he gave, the singer – any singer, come to that – in addition to possessing a natural talent, also has (or ought to have) a driving ambition to sing in public. A recital of art songs, given in a small concert-hall, by a classically trained singer accompanied by a grand-piano, will contain elements of physical projection which are not available to the artist through the blind medium of recorded sound. A gesture here, a glance there, a sudden movement of the head, eyes or hands, might not of themselves seem of great consequence, but almost instinctively (and possibly also through rigorous training and coaching) they can add an extra dimension to the performance being witnessed by the audience. It is important to realise this characteristic even in so-called 'classical' music, for in essence it is exactly the same as in popular performances. It is quite clearly called for in opera, where the singer ought to be able to act a bit as well, and such things indicate that all vocal music has, in some way or another, to be projected. The projection cannot make a good singer out of someone who has no qualities to the voice, but it most certainly can enhance the performance itself, and thereby the music, if the singer is talented.

In Presley's case, we encounter a singer who was more than talented: in my view, he was a genius, transcendentally naturally-gifted, and the possessor of that unique quality of 'recognisability' possessed by very few recording artists which means that only a few seconds of their performances have to be heard before the performer can be recognised.

We often hear the phrase 'Star Quality', but when pressed to explain exactly what it means, more often than not those who use it cannot; the kind of answer we get runs along the lines of: 'You cannot explain it, but you recognise it when you hear it and see it.' If we can hear this unusual quality, and see it as well, then we ought to attempt to explain the phenomenon.

Assuming, for the sake of this argument, that Elvis Presley possessed this quality, what particular aspects of his performance can we identify which set him apart from other artists? It is important to remember that such an analysis will not be concerned with every minuscule detail of Presley's performances; it will be sufficient to concentrate on specific aspects. Nor should it be forgotten that we are dealing with the finished, filmed result; there are bootleg video tapes which show Presley in less than commanding control of rehearsals for his performance. Frankly, I consider such unauthorised films to be of no value. They are no more than the counterparts of recording outtakes which form no part of the finished product. Just as there is little more than curiosity value in seeing those bits of film in which an actor makes a mistake, after which everyone on the set breaks down in laughter, or of seeing a theatrical performance in which someone forgets their lines or makes a wrong entry, they cannot by any stretch of the imagination be considered suitable examples by which to judge the artistry of the performer in question, and I do not propose to consider them here.

The first thing that has to be said is that for a singer to make any kind of impact, the song being sung has to be put over' – it has to be 'performed'. It is no longer good enough for a singer merely to stand in front of a microphone before an audience and sing. For us to observe that today immediately tends to make us think that the singer in question is inexperienced: we no longer settle for that, and when we see it, we feel that there is something missing.

But there was a time when such a manner of singing was acceptable, and was indeed considered the only way in which a song should be sung. A crooner such as Frank Sinatra was a past master at this, using small facial and physical gestures to enhance the character of the song in question. What then, has changed in the performance of popular songs; why has it happened?

In this regard, there can be no question that Elvis Presley was the single and most important influence in this change. I would go further to say that he brought it about almost singlehandedly, yet – because coincidence can often help a natural force (in his case the natural force being his own natural musicianship) – his own physical response to the music he sang coincided with a growing advance in technology.

The main reason that singers of an older generation stood before a microphone was that the microphone was such a big and heavy instrument that it could not be moved: once it was in place on the stage, there it stood. For many years, therefore, singers simply had to stand (reasonably) still in order for the microphone to catch their voice.

But to look at the early Presley shots of him singing we can see quite clearly his eruptive, almost frustrated attempts to break out of this confining performing straitjacket; his adaptation to the limits of the old bulky microphone was that whilst his mouth remained close to the microphone, the rest of his body did not. The gyrations of his legs, the balls of his feet often static, the circular movement of his pelvis and legs (not for nothing was he earlier dubbed 'Elvis the Pelvis'), the

163

forward and backward movement of his trunk – all of these could happen whilst his head remained not too far from the microphone. And when the physical movement made his head move away from the microphone – well, move the microphone. This he did, and in the process virtually made the microphone an extension of his body; sideways, at an angle, sometimes almost horizontally touching the floor. In truth, nothing – or very little – like this in the performance of popular songs had ever been seen before. To some, such movements were physically suggestive of simulated sex, but this view is too simplistic. Occasionally, some of Presley's movements probably were such simulation, but not – surely – in a calculating manner; if they happened, they were entirely spontaneous and naturally unforced. After all, such a physical response to the natural beat of the music as Presley made – and we should not forget that the music he was creating in those early years was utterly unlike anything which had been heard before, certainly far removed from the repertoire of a Frank Sinatra – is in essence very similar to that of primitive man in village tribal dances, the kind of thing familiar to us from film travelogues. African rhythms can be highly complex; and the natural rhythms of other primitive societies can, on the other hand, be highly predictable, in which case the cumulative impact of constant repetition produces a hypnotic, trance-like state wherein the physical response of the dancer appears beyond control. Now, it may be that some will claim that such movements are also akin to simulated sex, but just as a street-dancer will move to the music he hears – whether it be that of a mechanically-wound organ (the kind of thing that was common at the beginning of the century in our big cities), or the ghetto-blaster of more recent times – for most people the result is nothing more or less than dancing, pure and simple. Natural musicianship – which at this stage surely needs no further proof – with his spontaneous reaction to the music itself, produced this extraordinary performance. A contemporary of Presley's, the crooner Johnnie Ray, was equally noted for his very physical responses – in effect not unlike Presley's – to the music he sang. It would, therefore, be wrong to claim that Presley started it; he did not; but it would be equally wrong to deny that he brought this style of performance to a far greater degree of stylisation, and even theatricality, than ever before.

This theatricality was to introduce another element into his stage appearance: he would directly (encipher as he could) involve the audience – or, rather, those people sitting in the first few rows. Elvis would often pick out at random one girl in the second or third row and sing directly to her for a few moments, often pointing directly to her at some appropriate moment in the song. The effect was electrifying; here was immediate eye-contact, the demonstrable rapport between singer and audience, and the hapless (but often thrilled) member of the audience singled out in this way became the personification of the dreams of her contemporaries.

Of course any singer could do this: we have not yet arrived at the single most important ingredient in his star mix. But when one thinks that it was in those songs, by that singer, that such theatricality was shown, one can the more easily imagine the kind of impact he must have had in his early years.

And he did this because of the nature of the music he performed. The hand-gesture, pointing out a member of the audience, is enormously effective in slow ballads, or in a slower, bluesy, number, but in fast rock music a different approach is called for. We have seen that early rock is musically quite primitive: in its simple chords and basic and simple rhythm, and so on – the essence of such music is as primitive as that of uncivilised societies. Its importance is twofold: in the response this music generated in millions of people throughout the world, and in the actual quality (the originality, the musical nature, the directness and simplicity, and so on) of the music itself as exemplified in the recorded performance. Nor should it be forgotten that in the mid-1950s millions of record-buyers all over the world responded immediately to Elvis's records without ever having seen him.

Elvis's movements in response to the beat and nature of the song are one thing, but his physical appearance is another. This, also, must be considered in discussions of his 'star quality'. Few would deny that Presley, although not necessarily qualifying for Mr Adonis finals, was physically attractive; whatever may have happened to his body in the closing months of his life, there is no doubt that as a teenager his physical appearance made him attractive to many. He was slim and the lower half of his trunk and legs moved well, lithely and with great freedom: nothing prevented a smooth, almost balletic, dance-like response to the music. As he had been singing for years, the upper part of his torso was well-developed, the result of breathing deeper and more regularly than non-singers, and as can be seen in his pre-Army films, overall he had a physical movement that was entirely free from encumbrance.

His face whilst not being 'beautiful' in the 'pretty-boy' manner, was distinctive and certainly not unappealing. Whatever rumours and suggestions many have been put about concerning his life-style, no-one has ever suggested that Presley resorted to, or had need of, plastic surgery. The shape of his face was oval, verging on the long when he was slim, but full; the jawline was firm, the mouth perfectly proportioned with a slight hint of thinness in the upper lip, accentuated by the lines to either side of his nostrils, which gave hint of sullenness, of smouldering resentment, yet somehow without aggression. His teeth, carefully prepared by modern dentistry, were on the large side, which actually contributed to his manly appearance, and his forehead, high and wide – but not excessively so – betokened a natural intelligence, which was also softened by his full head of hair (he never wore a wig) which tended to reassure those who otherwise might initially have been alarmed by the sound of his singing. This hint of sullenness, of course, was confirmed by the straight nose, and the single most important physical feature, his ideally-spaced blue-grey eyes. There was a constant all-seeing quality about Presley's gaze which could become hypnotic, and could have been absurd were it not for the full, slightly hooded eyelids which softened such commanding vision directing his gaze straight at the observer in an intimate manner, and for his constant – and appealing – habit of slightly bending his head forward, as if in deference. There was never, in Presley's appearance on stage, the slightest hint of arrogance or of superiority. This, in many ways, was the nature of his 'star quality', his inherent 'niceness', which at all times softened the eruptive, revolutionary nature of the music he sang and any threat it might have seemed to contain, aided by his natural polite manner, ensured that his image remained one with which people felt secure.

Such were Presley's physical characteristics; we should now consider what use he made of them, and how they contributed to his overall stage-presence. As was implied earlier, the coincidence of advances in technology – development of the transistor and microchip – actually helped Presley to realise and refine his own performing skills. The breakthrough afforded to communication in the modern world by these spin-offs from the American space programme led, among other things, to more sensitive but infinitely smaller microphones: in particular, the hand-held instrument freed the performer from the confines of the statically-placed microphone. We should not forget that such developments came about towards the end of Elvis's performing career; but nevertheless the range and freedom of his stage movements in the late 1960s and early 1970s were considerably extended by the use of such less-confining microphones. Equally, no longer a rough-and-ready teenager, he was unable to exhibit such physical gyrations as previously, but the die had been cast. Apart from his singing – the single most important aspect of his skill as a performer – his fame as a physically-powerful mover on stage was already so well established by the time of his return to live performing that he only had to suggest such movements for the response to be invoked in the audience.

This meant also that by then he knew perfectly well what he was doing; there is, in the later stage shows, an element of calculation which is entirely absent from his earlier appearances. In those snips of footage from the 1950s, there is no doubt that he almost literally threw himself into what he was doing; after all, why should he not do that – what had he to lose? The Colonel could see that such publicity as was thus generated might be turned to Elvis's advantage; but the central point is that no matter what impact Elvis's physical response to his performing had, his movements were spontaneous and unforced, the physical manifestation of the rhythmic heart of the music he performed. In this way, and in this way only, was Elvis Presley a profound and utterly original innovator whose impact on his contemporaries and on subsequent generations has still not been fully appreciated.

Physical movement is one thing; singing is another. And this leads us to what is infinitely the most important aspect of Presley as a performer: his voice. recent scientific discoveries have led to the identification of 'voice-patterns', which are very similar to finger-printing. The voice is unique to the individual, and cannot be duplicated (at least not naturally) despite the skills of imitators or impersonators. It is often the case that over the telephone a son's voice will be mistaken for that of his father: without the visual aspect, confusion can arise. But it is very different where singing is involved. We are often surprised at the difference between a man's speaking and singing voice; equally, the singing voice is unique to the individual, as unique a thing as the person's facial appearance or basic character traits. It can only be, therefore, a natural gift, over which possession the person has no control.

What can it have been about Elvis Presley's voice which caused so many millions of people, all over the world, to be moved to buy his records? The same question can be asked about every other singer of the past: Caruso, John MacCormack and Mario Lanza are three very different random examples of greatly-gifted individuals who made an enormous impact through the quality of their voice. The answer, in part, is that the emotion conveyed by singing strikes a responsive chord: as Presley recorded over seven hundred songs, of a very wide range and character, this emotion runs every gamut – so it is never the same emotion. As it is never the same emotion, but the impact is the same, he must have possessed a unique ability to perform a wide range of material equally well. And equally, his voice remained entirely recognisable over such a range.

Here we come to the heart of the matter. Presley's vocal range was exceptional – amazingly so for an untrained singer. It ranged from low F in the bass register to top B flat and B in the tenor range. This is over two octaves: most people can only manage just over one octave. Quite apart from the range of Presley's voice (and this range remained with him throughout his life, a fact proved by his recordings) the equally surprising thing was that its quality and distinctive timbre remained constant throughout this range. This is also exceptional and quite the most conclusive proof – if any were needed – that Elvis Presley possessed a natural gift for singing which was completely and utterly rare. For if it were not – where are all the other Elvis Presleys?

Finally, the voice itself: naturally gravitating downwards, its depth, founded upon finely resonating vocal chords, is the epitome of masculine vocal quality. There is no falseness here, no falsetto, no acquired accent – in short, nothing was added and nothing was taken away. The result is, again, wholly unique: in Elvis Presley's recorded voice, we can hear a natural force devoid of artificiality. That

167

is, we can feel a force of nature, something awe-inspiring which simply had to be; Elvis Presley had no choice but to become a singer – no man could have successfully resisted the demands of such a creative gift. In every respect, therefore, our observations show this man was born to sing. No wonder he made such an impact as a performer. After him, the singing of popular songs was changed for ever.

Chapter Seventeen

Today, tomorrow and forever

It is important to remember that Elvis Presley was of the first rock 'n' roll generation. He was its greatest practitioner, the supreme genius of rock, the fountainhead from which virtually all other rock stars (and bands) throughout the world have sprung. Therefore, at the time of his death, he was also among the oldest. Today, we think little or nothing of rock stars undertaking world tours in their forties, or of being fatter or balder or whatever than when they first appeared before us. Indeed, we are so used to stars using expensive cosmetic surgery in a frequently futile attempt to appear young looking that we tend either to look down on or ignore their vanity.

It was one thing for famous ballad singers such as Frank Sinatra or Perry Como to continue singing in public in their fifties and sixties, for they largely appealed to an older generation and their art could be heard in very much smaller venues and in more intimate surroundings than those in which rock stars are obliged to appear. But it was quite another matter for Elvis Presley, the major force of the music of energy, movement and aggression, to go on stage clearly quite a bit heavier than in his teens, and proceed to belt out the songs that made him famous twenty years or so earlier. To be fair, Presley had always sung ballads, and had done much to adapt and tailor his live appearances to an older generation, but, as this book has attempted to show, his greatness is almost always revealed in his more up-tempo performances than in his slower ones. Even so, this is a generalisation, and is meant as no more than that.

The point is that in the mid-1970s the world had simply not seen rock stars performing in their forties: no one knew quite what to expect from them, and in

Presley's case his triumphant return in 1968 was such an astonishing achievement that the public was not ready for a change of emphasis. The myriad characters that a later star such as David Bowie had employed to demonstrate his own range of creativity were largely unknown. Once a singer had established himself, and carefully created (or had created for him) an 'image' (to use a frequently misunderstood and too easily applied term) it wasn't considered feasible in those days to set about altering the latter – at least, not radically. In any case, Elvis Presley was a singer, not a composer. The merest glance at his early life demonstrates that he was a born singer; he had to sing in the way that other great musicians have to play the piano or conduct symphony orchestras. They do not necessarily have to write songs.

Another point which should be borne in mind is that when Presley came to prominence the singer-songwriter as such simply did not exist – or if he did, he was regarded as completely out of the ordinary. The breakthrough of the singer-songwriter came in the early 1960s, and did so simultaneously in a number of countries. We could spend much time discussing why this phenomenon came about when it did, but such a discussion would be largely irrelevant to the main point of Elvis Presley's individuality and how he – mistakenly as it turned out, and probably tragically – fought a never-ending battle with his body to shed the pounds he quickly put on, either as a reaction to a previous crash diet or as a result of pigging out over some inner sensitivity and hurt.

Consequently, Elvis felt he had to preserve his (or his advisors?) perception of his image, and there is some evidence to suggest that his death was hastened, and probably even brought on, by the strains he put upon is body in this way. Doctors strongly advise against subjecting the body to severe diets when the patient is suffering from arrhythmia (the actual cause of Presley's death), but it would appear that even if Presley had been given this advice (which is unlikely, as there was no evidence to show that he had suffered from irregular heartbeats before – perhaps he thought them natural, and not worth mentioning to his doctor), he would not have taken it: he was too anxious to preserve the all-important image. Today, of course, most people would not give a damn about their own or their idol's appearance, especially if it were a matter of life and death. But in the mid-1970s, it was quite another matter.

If times have changed with regard to what is publicly acceptable in rock musician's images, we should not forget the impact that Elvis Presley's death had upon the world in general. If he had merely been a 'once great has-been' his death would have merited little more than an item or two in the world's news, as the deaths of so many other rock stars had done. But in England, for example, the news of his death broke into scheduled television and radio programmes, and for many days afterwards the national news was dominated by the repercussions of the death of one singer. It is important to get this into perspective. By no stretch of the imagination could Elvis Presley's death be seen to merit such coverage: the news domination was not the mere fact of his death – sudden and utterly unexpected though it had been – but the world-wide public reaction to his death. We shall return to this later and examine it in some detail, but this universal reaction showed beyond all possible doubt that the then-current opinion of most writers on rock music – that Presley was a pathetically out-dated washed-up has been – was hopelessly out of touch with what the overwhelming majority of people actually thought. Not for the first time, and certainly not for the last, were the opinions of music critics shown to be arrant nonsense. It is instructive to read what some commentators were saying about Presley in the months preceding his death, airily writing him off, and contrast it with what they have said about him since. The international reaction to his death showed him to have had a staggering impact on generations of music lovers, obliging, even forcing, those writers to revise far upwards their opinions of his greatness.

And yet, one of the more remarkable aspects about the Elvis Presley phenomenon is that in the years since his death his stature has increased immensely. To commemorate the tenth anniversary of his demise, national television stations ran seasons of Elvis Presley films; documentaries on his life were shown; and tributes from singers, including those who were mere children at the time of his death, were fulsome in their praise of the man who still exerted the most profound influence. It became no longer regarded as undignified to admit to admiring Elvis Presley, even in the highest social circles (for he had never enjoyed the chic fashion of later bands and singers during his lifetime), and such admissions were the direct result of this constant stream of books, recordings and commemorative events.

Not for one moment should we imagine that this was the result of some highly successful record company 'hype', for RCA (or BMG as the company is now often known, since its acquisition by the Bertelsman Music Group in 1986) had never been the kind of corporation to capitalise on an artist's death, frequently though the opportunity in their case arose. The demand for Presley's recordings in the months following his death took RCA by surprise, and subsequently the company rightly tended to leave to specialist repackaging houses the task of putting together suitable material for their particular customers and market requirements. In this regard, they were helped considerably by the sheer scope and extent of Elvis Presley's recorded legacy – over seven hundred different songs. The greater respect which is now accorded Elvis Presley, and which has arisen since his death, is – I am convinced – a genuinely spontaneous popular movement, unforced and growing naturally.

Why should this be so? Are there any reasons, other than that of the public's recognition of Presley's unique genius, as to why a dead singer's influence should appear stronger ten years after his death than it had been in, say, the five years

171

before it, especially in the field of popular music, where fashion and the ability to appear either live or on video are generally accepted as being crucial to success? Some might argue that we are, thanks to the books on Presley, which have appeared during recent years, more able to understand the impulses and forces that shaped his career; it is unfortunate that the view that he was influenced by sex and drugs has been given far more credence than it deserves. Mistaken and irrelevant as I believe this view to be, it has gained such great currency that I feel it has to be considered here.

Let us take the question of drugs first. If the generally accepted version of events is to be believed, then during the fifteen years or so prior to his death Presley gradually became a hopeless pill-popping drug addict, imposing his addictive needs upon those closest to him to feed his growing appetite (in more ways than one!) for drugs. The main source for these allegations is the book *Elvis – What Happened?* by three of his closest confidants, a publication which has formed the basis for several posthumous claims regarding Presley's private life. However, as we have noted earlier, several contradictions have to be set against the claims of the joint authors – three men, who, since they had been brusquely dismissed from Presley's service, may be thought by some not to be entirely disinterested in attacking their previous employer's character.

Among these are books by other members of his staff, equally close to him, that utterly refute the allegations of drug-taking. It may be that Presley was indeed a drug addict, who successfully kept his addiction secret from some members of his staff for years, while openly admitting to others and encouraging them to supply him with the 'medication' his condition demanded. This is unlikely, however; what possible good could it have done him to lead this double life within his own home? And – if indeed he kept this matter a secret – why would those unaware of his addiction only be women?

We should consider his upbringing in this regard. His mother's influence was all-pervasive: she was an honest, God-fearing, hard-working, regular church-goer. This influence cannot be ignored or discounted. Gladys Presley adored her son. She almost literally worshipped the ground upon which he walked, and throughout his life Elvis Presley, even to those who cordially detested everything he did and all he stood for, remained a polite, decent, honest, generous and essentially shy human being. Would such a man, who was coincidentally one of the wealthiest in the USA, need drugs? Of course, it was perfectly possible, for events have shown all too tragically that the curse of drug-taking in the western world is not confined to any one race, age group or social class: but with Presley we have documentary records far in excess of those available for most other people, and he was not of the universally accepted drug-taking generation or its successors. Frankly, my own feelings are that I believe Presley probably did more than experiment with pill-popping, and equally that his drug-taking has been sensationally over-stated. But by far the most compelling reason for giving him the benefit of the doubt is the result of his autopsy – which poses for those who maintain he was drug-riddled at the time of his demise a big, unanswered and unanswerable question.

We have seen that within an hour of his body being found at Graceland, it had been taken to Memphis hospital, whereupon he had been pronounced dead on arrival. Almost immediately, an autopsy began to be carried out – a legal requirement in all such cases of DOA. Because of Presley's eminence, it is important to restate that this autopsy was finally performed by the head of the hospital's pathology department, in the presence of eight other pathologists. Therefore, no fewer than nine doctors presided at Elvis Presley's autopsy, a case of medical attention which must be unparalleled in the field of popular entertainment. What did these nine doctors find in the body of this great singer who had died suddenly? Clearly, we have to take their word. But did they find drugs in his body, did they ascribe the cause of his death to over-indulgence in some banned substances, or the fatal effects the prolonged usage of such would have caused, on a vital organ? No – unfortunately for those who would like to believe the drugs theory, these nine doctors found no traces of any harmful substances at all. The cause of his death, as we have mentioned before, was (and I quote from their findings) 'in plain English, an irregular heartbeat'. In other words, at the time of his death, Elvis Presley was clean.

Or are we to believe in the theory of some mass cover-up by these professional men? Are we seriously supposed to think that in some way they conspired to hide the true cause of death? And, if so, for what reasons? The man was dead; he could be harmed no further. Drug-related deaths of rock musicians are by no means unknown. No one would have thought that much of it in Elvis Presley's case, had it been true, and if there had been a cover-up, is it not extraordinary that in the years since the event, not one of these nine doctors has broken ranks and told the truth? Quite apart from the breathtaking scope of such unimaginably unethical behaviour by these professional men, the facts, so far as we know them today, are much less sensational than many would have us believe: whatever led to Presley's death that day, it would seem that drug-taking was not a part of it.

Or so it would seem. There is unconfirmed, circumstantial evidence which implies that a cover-up was, indeed, engineered – but not by the pathologists. The evidence consists of a confidential report by a respected laboratory on samples allegedly taken from Presley's body during the autopsy. A number of independent forensic scientists have unanimously agreed that the samples show a potentially lethal combination of drugs. The implications are, however, unsavoury – not least for the medical profession and those who performed the autopsy. It may be that the fifty-year embargo placed on certain of the autopsy's findings (itself by no means uncommon: such a course is used to protect the family of the deceased –

but when it is used, the question is often raised, 'protect the family from what?') will, when finally released, show evidence of drug-taking. But, even if it does, it will matter little, and has less bearing on our views than some would insist it should.

Nevertheless, mud sticks. And if, by some perverted logic, it would appear that we now accept Presley more readily because we believe him to have been a drug addict, then that says more about us than anything else, and certainly nothing about his music-making. It would seem that undoubtedly the drug question is a massive red herring, and has now to be discounted.

The other matter we should consider is Presley's sexuality. In this regard, revelations about his early years that have come to light since his death do have a bearing. We now know that his father spent some time in jail for theft, at the crucial period in Elvis's life between the ages of four and five when the adult male's sexuality is then immutably fixed. The absence of a father figure, but more importantly the sharing of the mother's bed by the four year old boy (a foregone conclusion in Presley's case, given this mother's otherwise obsessive care of him), gave rise to a classic Oedipus complex condition. This manifests itself in a variety of ways, but all are characterised by a far greater than normal fondness for the mother figure in adult life, amounting to reverence. In many instances, this leads to a complete inability to relate sexually to a mature woman once a boy has reached manhood. A woman, either venerated as a mother figure, or chosen because of her likeness to the mother, cannot be approached sexually without extreme difficulty.

One logical and obvious consequence of such a difficulty is the complete rejection of female sexuality; homosexuality, in fact. Another is the veneration of the mother figure carried to such extremes that the adult man adores only the virgin, and cannot make love either to a woman who is pregnant or who has given birth. Once the woman has conceived, once her womanhood has been breached, she is therefore no longer a virgin, and is no longer to be admired as a pure figure. This often leads to fantasies centred upon virginal pubescent girls. A passing reference to this in *Elvis – What Happened?* confirms the factors leading to the breakdown of Presley's marriage, and tells us more about his relationship with his mother, and his desire to have Priscilla stay at Graceland from an age that few parents would permit today (even though there is no suggestion of any fully developed sexual liaison between them), than the authors imagined.

It is quite clear that Presley's increasing reluctance to relate to his wife sexually after the birth of their daughter confirms his Oedipal tendencies. It is equally clear, however, that his subsequent life (after his divorce) shows a massive attempt to effect a reversal of this tendency, although Priscilla could not now be part of his life. A man in Presley's position would regard his behaviour as perfectly natural, as indeed for him it was – it was not his 'fault'. As must be obvious, he was deeply in love with Priscilla, no matter what fantasy pedestal he placed her on, and the divorce, when it came, was a traumatic experience for him. The adult trauma, the divorce from his ideal mother figure, was probably as severe as the death of his own mother, and it says a great deal for his inner strength of character that, instead of sinking into a self-indulgent well of depression (in which, in his position of wealth, a massive sex and drugs binge would have seemed an understandable, if ultimately self-destructive course to have taken), he gradually began to relate in a more balanced manner to woman, most notably in his later life to Ginger Alden, whom he was expected to marry. It is true that she was virtually twenty years younger than he was, so the fascinating for the much younger woman was still very much present.

However much we may speculate upon the problems Presley experienced in attempting to come to terms with this aspect of his adult sex life, such behaviour as he showed is very common. Indeed, it is more common than most people imagine. In this regard, therefore, we have a double-edged situation: on the one hand, Presley was acting no differently, in essence, from millions of other men; yet, on the other, as a greatly gifted singer, it is more than probable that he found a sublimated outlet for his natural sex drive, thwarted from otherwise achieving its fullest expression, in his singing. It is a further matter for conjecture whether his singing career would have been vastly different from what it became had his father never gone to prison. My own opinion is that it would not, or at least not by very much, because, before he became separated from his father at that crucial age in his development, he had already shown the clearest signs of his natural musicianship and, more importantly, his gifts as a singer. In other words, as a singer he was born, not made. And again, however interesting it may be for some to speculate on his sex life, this part of his life has no bearing on his genius, and on the expression of that genius – his recorded performances. For we will never know how his early maturity, his sense of being a loner, his shyness and his consequent sexual frustrations at not being able to find the virgin figure until after he joined the Army had any bearings on his singing.

Is the power and passion he imparts in those classic early rock numbers nothing more than the outpouring in musical terms of his own inner frustrations? Maybe. But what does it mean to us even if we accept that that was the case? The short answer is, ultimately, nothing, for nothing can alter that power and passion and how we as individuals relate to it, although we may speculate that those born a few years after Presley were themselves subjected to precisely the same kind of father absence, as their fathers were called up to fight World War II, and that through their massive acceptance of Presley's recordings they collectively, spontaneously and unconsciously related to the very frustrated power and passion he showed in them.

Ultimately, and however we choose to come to it, we are confronted with the essence of the man's importance: his singing, and what it meant and continues to mean to many millions of people. This essence is of a complex nature: the memory of what it was and from whence it came, and its ability to recreate for us an era that has long since passed, are aspects that lead us on to a further realisation; that music is a living organism in time, and that through the medium of recordings a performance can be recreated for us at will and is this, essentially, indestructible.

Chapter Eighteen

A study in music

As Elvis Presley passed into history, his premature end left a grieving family and dejected friends. Millions of people all over the world who never met him, but heard him sing, shared in a sense of loss. But he also left a recorded legacy of around seven hundred songs – his life's work as a singer – which we have examined in the course of this book. As we have seen, by no means all of these are worthy of detailed attention. But as must be clear, even to the most casual reader, that with his death a remarkable singer had passed from the face of the earth. During his lifetime, Elvis Presley appeared before millions of people, and sales of his records numbered many tens of millions. At this level, when nobody can say – or really cares – exactly how many records he sold, the sheer weight of numbers is itself the strongest reason for examining his legacy.

If some disaster were to wipe out our books, tapes, film and records of historical and contemporary events, and a future generation found only a few clues as to Elvis Presley's identity, what would they make of him? If they knew merely that he was born the only son of very poor parents, and that when he died, aged forty-two, millions mourned him all over the world, that tens of thousands flocked to his home in a vain attempt to glimpse his body, and that countless others attended memorial services in many countries, buying all manner of objects connected with him, they would surely wonder what sort of man could have made such an impact. A religious leader? A politician? A general? A king? None of these: he was a man who sang songs.

The reactions to Elvis Presley's death constitute the most extraordinary demonstration for decades of the power of music to reach the hearts and minds of millions of people. When Beethoven died, in March 1827, many thousands followed his coffin through the streets of Vienna – at a time when modern communications did not exist, and when the population of Vienna itself was not much greater than the number of mourners. The number of people moved to attend Elvis Presley's burial was similar to those who flocked to Beethoven's; but what sets Presley apart is that modern communications enable millions to watch an event without leaving their homes. If tens of thousands felt impelled to go to Presley's home and camp for days and nights, how many more all over the world watched the events on television?

Yet premature deaths of popular singers are not unknown. Other figures in popular music have died in much more violent and degrading circumstances than Presley. Buddy Holly and Eddie Cochran were killed while travelling, and the list of later rock stars who took their own lives – Janis Joplin, Jimi Hendrix, Paul Kossoff, Jim Morrison, Keith Moon, Sid Vicious, among many others – is regrettably, longer. None of these made such an impact as Elvis Presley. It could be argued that they died when their lives were not even half-finished so far as their music-making was concerned, while at forty-two Presley's name was already of legendary proportions. In a sense this is true, but two things must be remembered. The first is that if Presley's career was unlikely to show much further development, the millions for whom and to whom Presley spoke through his performances regarded his as a vital force in popular music. The second is that Elvis Presley was to many the most important figure in world rock music – he was also the *first* rock performer of any consequence.

With some artists who have died prematurely, greater success occasionally comes after death. Buddy Holly is a case in point, and the country singer Jim Reeves, is possibly the most remarkable example. This posthumous success is partly explained by the amount of unreleased material available at the time of the singer's death. But soon after Presley's death the single 'Way Down' became a massive international hit, and although it is possible that the emotion generated by his death contributed to its success, the record is such an outstanding example of pop music, and one of Presley's best performances, that it would have been a hit at any time.

Presley's success as the most important figure in pop music from 1956 until his death has to be measured by its length and its international appeal. For more than twenty years Elvis Presley produced a string of major international hits which transcended language, culture and fashion. In Britain, for example, during these years Elvis Presley had an unprecedented total of ninety-four different singles enter the Top 50 charts. Wherever the music was heard, from the coffee bars of the 1950s to the discos of the late 1970s, the enjoyment, raw energy, good humour and sentimentality – in short, all of those things that go to make up the pleasure of being young and alive – are enshrined in hundreds of Presley's records. For several generations, the youth of many countries were set free by this man's music. Presley became synonymous with having a good time, and his string of hits, from 'Heartbreak Hotel' to 'Way Down', entered the subconscious of millions of people. To hear these songs again brings back the memory which itself meant so much. When people learned that Presley had died, the sympathy and sadness of all those to whom he meant so much was released.

Another reason for the sympathy goes beyond music. Ten years after Presley burst upon the musical world, the Beatles breathed new life into popular music. At first they marked a return to a basic, raw quality, which Presley himself had revealed. The mid-1960s, however, were notable for other things: political protest fed by the war in Vietnam; the increase in drug-taking by young people all over the world; a rise in the numbers of young people; a sexual freedom made easy by more liberal laws and the contraceptive pill. A collective culture shock ran counter to the established standards of older generations. Many singers found themselves caught up in one or more of these movements. Other sections of the public were alienated, and rock music became exclusive, reserved only for initiates who confirmed in dress, behaviour and mores.

Elvis Presley remained aloof from these changes. He preached no public sermons on politics, sex or drugs. He remained true to himself, and true to the one thing which for him really mattered – his music. This meant that when he died, no factions hated him. Acknowledged as the most important popular singer of his day, Presley remained above all an entertainer.

A large number of the mourners at the memorial services following Presley's death were teenagers. Where one might have expected such congregations to be made up of Presley's contemporaries for whom he personified their hopes and aspirations, many of those who did turn up were not even born when Presley had already established himself as the dominant force in rock music. Clearly Presley's greatest performances transcend those years and speak as vividly as when first released. Whereas most singers of his time have faded into obscurity, the compulsive quality of his best performances have lost none of their magic; indeed, they have actually taken on a more significant character.

Why should this be so? Is it a purely musical phenomenon? In many ways it is. But success in popular music has also to be viewed in a sociological light.

By the early 1950s a new generation – the first post-World War II generation – had begun to arise. Each generation tends to react against its immediate predecessor, in an attempt to establish its own identity. If the popular music of the early 1950s was based on that of the dance floor, dominated by dance styles, then it was clear that a different form of popular music was needed, to which the youth of the new generation could relate. The new generation had already begun to assert its individuality in dress and hair-style. In Britain, for example, the Teddy Boy fashion had begun to catch on; but the dance associated with it – the Creep, as opposed to the jive – was a lethargic stroll around the floor.

With Elvis Presley's 'Heartbreak Hotel', the dam was burst, and the floodgates opened. Here was a man who sang without any pretence at sophistication. The words – insofar as they could be understood at all – seemed to erupt from his body. The music was raw, basic, totally unsubtle. Stripped of all pretension, cut to the bone, lean, lithe, agile – this was the angry music of the revolution.

As time went by, Presley became a more varied singer, instilling his own distinctive character into all he sang. He possessed a rare gift: the recognisable voice. A few words from any of his songs, and it could *only* be Elvis Presley singing. Why did it mean so much to young people when he died? In some ways, the conditions were similar to those which existed when Presley first appeared. The West experienced severe economic recession during the early 1970s. Many young people found themselves less well-off than in the intervening period. The pop music establishment failed to note this sociological change, and at first rejected the grass-roots reaction against the sophisticated music of a handful of jet-setting millionaire stars. But there was a return to basic, raw music, which Presley first personified and which led, ten years later, to the emerging careers of a new generation of rock stars. When Bob Dylan hitched down the freeways in the early 1960s to visit the ailing Woody Guthrie in hospital, and wrote 'Lonesome Traveller', the post-beat generation could identify with the song. By the early 1970s, with Dylan travelling in his own jet, he was a lonesome traveller for very different reasons. Few of his original followers could identify with the millionaire and his trappings.

In addition, the 1960s saw the consolidation of soul music, a welcome black-based popular music, which by the early 1970s had become a dominant force. But what had not happened for a long time was a distinctive youth music – predominantly white – which marked a return to basic roots. As out-of-work teenagers have no money to spend, it was also clear that the conditions existed for music of a violent reaction. Presley's death coincided with this, and as music of the archetypal white working-class boy from a deprived background, the early Presley records took on a new lease of life. They spoke again to a young generation – and to an older one, too, for a general nostalgia for the 1950s – quickly capitalised upon by films – manifested itself.

Popular music, as understood today, is so often bound up with other things that it is difficult to remember it *is* still music. Advertising, promotion, films, television, concerts, articles and the hundred-and-one other things that a record company has to employ to bend the ear of the public towards a particular artist seem to take over. The details of Elvis Presley's early life appear to come from a bygone age: with six teachers in a high school of 1,700 pupils, what chance did he have of a good education? With a strict non-conformist upbringing and a mother who walked him to school until he was fifteen, to what independence could he aspire?

Presley's importance was achieved solely through music. He had nothing else to give, no sermon or political creed to preach. Nor, I suspect, did he seek the wealth that came his way. Obviously a truck driver would like extra money; but I do not believe that Elvis Presley actively set out to become a superstar. The child of two, barely able to talk, so fascinated by the sound of singing that he leaves his mother's arms to get nearer the choir – could there be more convincing proof that he was naturally musical? The boy who looked forward to going to church, because of the opportunity it gave him to sing? The shy, diffident youth, who confounded his friends by finding the courage to stand to sing in front of 1,500 fellow pupils? The stammering truck driver, who plucked up the courage to go into a recording studio, alone, 'just to hear what I sounded like'?. The man who broke down in tears when he was told to quit singing and go back to driving a truck – just when he had finished an appaling performance at the country's leading country music venue – and then go on to confound the critics at an illustrious venue a few weeks later?

By all rational standards, Elvis Presley's career should never have got started at all. Sam Phillips of Sun Records was not at first impressed, and neither were Bill Black or Scotty Moore. But Presley's persistence, strangely at odds with his non-musical behaviour, was deep-seated.

Presley's was the most important formative and influential singing voice in popular music of the last half-century – possibly of all time. There could have been no more opportune place for him to have been born than in the Deep South of the USA. For it was there that the two main streams of popular music – black and white – met.

Although many years were to pass before the blacks in the South achieved a measure of equality, when Presley was about ten years old – at about the time of the end of World War II – the early signs of a change in society were beginning to appear. In some ways, the war had promoted a measure of integration, with black soldiers enlisted alongside white.

Memphis had been a capital of both blues and country music for some time. The economic recession of the 1930s had opened up a wider market for both types of music. RCA and CBS, for example, discovered in the 1930s that records by black blues artists sold well in the big cities of the north-eastern USA and the far west. Country music too was exportable, although it later came to be called country and western, as the western part included instruments from the western states – drums, electric guitars and fuller use of piano. The upshot was that blues and country music found a bigger audience. It is significant that one of the most prolific of the black blues singers – Tampa Red (Hudson Whittaker) – devoted most of his recording time between 1935 and 1936 to 'popular' songs, especially for the white market. The growth of radio in the 1930s as the popular entertainment medium meant that these recordings reached the ears of those who would not previously have heard such music.

In this way, the young Elvis Presley heard the black blues singers who greatly influenced him. He would not have been allowed to attend the black clubs where

181

they performed. Tampa Red, Blind Willie McTell and James DeBerry and his Memphis Playboys, as well as Sonny Boy Williamson I, are all traceable influences on Presley's rare blues recordings.

White and black singers met more frequently in the field of gospel music; and this was clearly another major influence on Presley's life. In this regard, Memphis – and the state of Mississippi – was in the heart of gospel country. The old hymns with their four-square harmony, which had such an effect on the young boy, are not so very different in harmonic structure from the blues. The gospel songs stemmed from the white settlers, who brought with them the Lutheran chorales of western European protestantism. But while the blues is secular music, gospel songs are sacred, and this means that the revival meetings, for all their fire-and-brimstone sermons, found the congregation rooted to the spot. In other words, it is not possible to dance to church music, for a congregation in pews is physically prevented from dancing. Musically, the interest must fall not on the rhythm of the hymn, but on its harmony. As a result, the harmonic interest of gospel music is much more important than in the blues music. You never hear a choir sing the blues.

A second important influence is the other main musical stream in the South – country music. Again it is curious how Presley seemed to have been born just at the right time.

If one man put country music on the map, it was the legendary Hank Williams. Williams died in 1953, at the age of twenty-nine. Few who heard him will ever forget him. In the post–war years, Hank Williams greatly broadened the appeal of what came to be called country and western, largely through his appearances in the immensely popular Louisiana Hayride shows.

But it was also due to the efforts of earlier singers that this branch of music had developed outside of the farmsteading communities of the rural southern states. People such as Jimmie Rodgers, the Carter Family, Red Foley (who composed 'Old Shep' and was the first country artist to have his own networked radio show – *Avalon Time* – in 1939), and Ernest Tubbs, were household names to many – including the Presleys.

By the late 1940s and early 1950s this branch of music was developing further offshoots. The growth of radio and television, rising living standards, and the greater sophistication brought about in recordings by the advent of tape, all conspired to deal a mortal blow to the ethnic country and western music. Of course, it remained a specialist field, but tended to become subordinated to a new phenomenon – bluegrass music. This was at first almost the single-handed invention of Bill Monroe, whose haunting high tenor voice, occasionally in duet with other, lower, male singers and accompanied by a small group in which the banjo predominated, seemed to personify the music of the Appalachian Mountains. It became enormously successful, and was a clear influence on Elvis Presley. In his very first recording session for Sun in July 1954, Presley recorded

Bill Monroe's 'Blue Moon Of Kentucky', in a performance that reveals the bluegrass roots.

Nor were these the only influences which saturated the young Presley. His stint as a cinema usher in Loew's Theater brought him into contact with the musical film, and the mainstream popular music of the day. The 1952 movie, *With A Song In My Heart*, has an extended sequence featuring 'Blue Moon', and this may have been where Presley learned it. Apart from this 'standard' repertoire, white singers as diverse as Johnnie Ray (whose 'Such A Night' must have been a seminal influence), Red Ingle and his Natural Seven, and more urban singers such as Frankie Laine (who betrays a strong country lineage) are in the Presley mix.

There is little pure folk music in Presley's make-up. More significant is the close-harmony style of the barbershop quartets (the Jordanaires, founded in 1948 in Springfield, Missouri, specialised in this music for a time), and the patriotic fervour of much popular music during the decade 1935–45. This was not expressed so much in hit songs of the time as in 'popular cantatas' such as Earl Robinson's 'Ballad For Americans' – which became a sensational vehicle for Paul Robeson during the war. More important is George Kleinsinger's 'I Hear America Singing', which was a similar vehicle for John Charles Thomas, whose politics were as far to the right as Robeson's were to the left. The patriotism of these highly successful works, with their solo baritones commandingly calling America to action, was infectious, and again left deep marks on the young Presley's musical mind, surfacing decades later in his great recordings of the 'American Trilogy'.

Against this background of curiously interlinked musical influences runs the deep river of jazz. Apart from the blues, there was nothing of traditional, or modern, jazz in Presley's music-making except for the technical features of his singing, which are quite jazz-like.

A classically trained singer or instrumentalist will spend years perfecting a style in which purity of tone, consistency of timbre, clarity of expression and proper intonation all become second nature, to be used to interpret a wide variety of music, which must first adhere faithfully to the written instructions of the composer. In jazz, none of these things applies. There is no such thing as an inelegant jazz sound. No note is considered out of tune if it is sung or played flat. It is by no means necessary to pronounce every syllable correctly, as long as the character of the song is conveyed. All effects in jazz are acceptable, and may be used at the discretion of the performer – even though the realisation of a number may be almost unrecognisable to its composer.

Popular singers of the mid-1950s – that is, those who were not rock singers – frequently adopted elements of classical style. It was considered important to sing in tune, to pronounce words, and to breathe properly. What Presley brought to popular music was the deliberate 'dirtiness' of jazz – *not* a style in which anything goes, but a style in which anything was acceptable, if it worked. This is not to be found in any other rock singers of his time – or before. Up to a point, Johnnie Ray had done the same, but this was against the background of a big band sound. Why was it then that Sam Phillips wanted a white man who sounded like a black singer?

Was it because black singers had better voices? No. It was because the black singer had two priceless attributes largely denied the white singers: first, an instinctive feel for the blues; and second, a highly developed sense of rhythm. Nobody needs reminding that the negroes of the United States were carried to that country from Africa, and carried with them their own music. A characteristic free yet highly complex syncopation was carried to America by the early slaves, and transformed into the expressive lines of jazz and blues music. But a chordal structure of European origin was added to give an undercurrent of simple duple or triple beats. It was a small step from this to rock music, and in two of Presley's most famous numbers – 'Heartbreak Hotel' and 'Hound Dog' – these roots are revealed for all to hear.

If Presley's achievements in rock music are unassailable, then his ability as a blues singer is by no means so widely known. It is sad that he never recorded blues albums, for he was a natural blues singer, as Sam Phillips certainly knew. His reputation would have done much to make this branch of music more popular. His classic blues recordings 'Reconsider Baby' and 'Merry Christmas Baby', dating from 1960 and 1971 respectively, are both outstanding performances.

Since Presley's achievements as a blues singer are so little known, let us look at 'Merry Christmas Baby' in some detail. It is a basic 12-bar blues in G minor; but what is astonishing is that, for perhaps the only time in his career, Presley reveals the full range of his voice and his natural feel for the blues. He uses his voice as an instrument as he endeavours to match the amazing guitar work of James Burton (surely influenced by Johnny 'Guitar' Watson). Presley hums, moans and shouts. The piano is free and florid – the use of the high keyboard register is unusual and distinctive; but it is Presley's earthy, yet subtle and hypnotic singing in the opening verse that inspires the musicians. The gamut of his voice – from low, growly Gs to a staggering, thrilling top B flat – *sung*, not falsetto – is so surprising, and so unlike anything else Presley did, as to cause one to rethink entirely one's attitude to this singer. Even Presley's cry of 'Dig it, James, dig it!' become part of the musical fabric. Nothing is more remarkable than the complete understanding of these performers, and the way in which they slightly anticipate the beat. This is not only the essence of blues, but the essence of rock, and runs completely counter to European classical music. (This is clearly revealed in the several attempts during the last ten or fifteen years to get rock bands to play concerts with symphony orchestras.) On paper, the music looks the same; but the instinct of the rock musician is slightly to anticipate the beat, especially if it is not the first beat of a bar. This is precisely what is found in the work of the best blues performers. Hearing Presley's instinctive blues work on 'Merry Christmas Baby', one is easily able to picture the young boy, sitting close to the radio, enthralled by the blues coming from the loudspeaker.

We should not forget, however, that Presley was first a country singer. His fame did much to reawaken interest in this distinctive musical style. Running through his career, one can find many examples of excellent country material. However, the development of Nashville into one of the major popular recording centres of the world was not solely due to Presley: RCA must take much of the credit, as well as Chet Atkins and other major figures, such as Carl Perkins, Charlie Rich and Johnny Cash. But Elvis Presley never forgot his country roots. The album *Elvis Country* is an excellent example of how Nashville developed.

Presley's importance extends into other areas too. In gospel music and in modern popular songs by his younger contemporaries his achievement was considerable. But it was as a top rock singer that his effect was most widely felt. His influence on a wide range of singers was very marked. Naturally his influence was most potent at the time of his greatest early success, during 1956 and 1957. We have seen how singers such as Gene Vincent and Eddie Cochran were clearly influenced by him; but a whole host of other stars also acknowledge his dominance.

In many ways, the most interesting of these was Buddy Holly. Holly, who was killed on 3 February, 1959 was one of the few singers at the time who seemed able to challenge Presley's popularity.

Holly remains a fascinating figure, for he was a highly creative and individual rock star on his own. There is no doubt, however, that Presley influenced Holly to some degree; and it should be remembered that Holly's success came at a time (1958–59) when Presley was preoccupied by films, his Army call-up, and his mother's death. But this was two-way traffic. Holly also influenced Presley; the change of emphasis into 'soft rock' of 1959–62 stems in part from Holly's more subtle and less bludgeoning approach.

But one other American singer, even more wide-ranging in scope than Presley, also had a mutual influence with him. This was Bobby Darin, a great singer and composer who, since his death at Christmas 1973, has been largely forgotten. Darin's own rock numbers, especially the classic song 'Bullmoose', were eclipsed by his own versatility. Darin was one of Presley's favourite singers, and Elvis frequently attended Darin's performances.

However, Presley's achievement was so vast, and the scope of his singing so wide and long-lasting, that few singers in the last thirty-five years have remained untouched by one or other of his styles. Singers as different as Johnny Burnette, Chris Farlowe, Glen Campbell, Alice Cooper, Sam Cooke and Pat Boone, along with countless others, have all at one time or another acknowledged their debt to him.

Above all Presley reached many millions of ordinary men and women, who were moved by the manner of his singing. Presley's importance transcends the influences that moulded him, and those which he had on other people. His importance also transcends the nature of his originality. It finally resides in the hearts and minds of millions of people who, whether for one brief moment or for a lifetime, found in his music-making the expression of their own hopes and aspirations.

Part IV

Documentary

I

Presley and the cinema

From time to time in the main body of this book, the reader will have seen references to Elvis Presley's films. While no one could legitimately claim that these constitute a significant chapter in the history of the cinema, or even the major part of his life, the fact remains that over a period of thirteen years, form 1956 to 1969 – or eleven when one considers that for two of those years Presley was serving in the US Army – he made thirty-one feature films.

Thirty-one films over eleven years is, even by the standards of Hollywood in its heyday, a large number for a leading actor to have undertaken. This averages almost three a year, and is very many more than any other rock singer has made. For the majority of these films, Presley was earning $1,000,000 a picture, and as they almost invariably had a musical element, millions more records were sold as a consequence. Therefore although Presley's position as a popular music innovator would not have been altered had he not made these films, even if some of them hardly enhanced his career, they should naturally form part of a study of his work, as long as it is clearly understood that they at all times have to remain at one side of the main thrust of his musical life.

In 1956, following the phenomenal impact Elvis had had through his recordings and television appearances, Hal Wallis of Paramount Pictures offered the singer a screen test in Hollywood. This was seriously approached both by Elvis and by Colonel Parker: Elvis acted a scene from a planned forthcoming film *The Rainmaker* (which eventually starred Burt Lancaster – not in the part Elvis played!) with Frank Faylen; he also sang one or two songs, one of which was 'Blue

Suede Shoes'. As a result, Wallis offered the singer a seven-year non-exclusive contract; with this and the main contract in his pocket, Colonel Parker lost no time in using his leverage to get Elvis into another film by a rival studio – Twentieth-Century Fox.

The result was that Elvis Presley's screen debut occurred in 1956 in the film *Love Me Tender*. The original title was *The Reno Brothers* – of whom Elvis was one (Clint Reno). Set at the time of the American Civil War, the part that Elvis took was not really suitable for him: nor is this special pleading, for surely an unbiased opinion would conclude that given the comparatively feeble story-line and the somewhat indifferent script, Elvis acquitted himself rather well. There are scenes when his inexperience is apparent – his acting is a little wooden and unconvincing on occasions – but the final section of the film, in which he plays the dying Clint Reno, is surprisingly good, giving clear evidence of a genuine, if small, acting talent. What surely did not go unnoticed was that the film made a profit of almost $5 million – a very unexpected bonus, and undoubtedly due almost entirely to Elvis's appearance in it.

His next film, the first Paramount Pictures release, was the similarly titled *Loving You*, which came out eight months later. The original title was *Lonesome Cowboy*, and the film was clearly meant to be a thinly disguised dramatisation of Elvis's recent life. Therefore, there were few acting demands placed upon him. *Loving You*, a pleasant tale of popular music in the South in the mid-1950s, is a valuable document for the preservation of a style of concern-giving which has long since disappeared. In addition, Elvis now had about eight songs to perform, all germane to the story (as opposed to the mere handful in *Love Me Tender*), and did them very well indeed. This was the early Elvis 'love' – one can be sure of that. Finally, the film runs for twelve minutes longer than his first, and he is undoubtedly the star. The film also marked, with his debut in a major starring role, the first of his many films with distinguished co-stars – an aspect of the Presley filmography which has largely received no comment, but which gives some indication of the esteem in which he was held. Appearing with Elvis in *Loving You* were Lizabeth Scott and Wendell Corey; the film also marked the debut of Dolores Hart, and, in the concluding audience scene, Vernon and Gladys Presley can be clearly recognised.

Three months after the release of *Loving You* came his first MGM picture, *Jailhouse Rock*. Whatever impact his first two films had had, it was nothing compared to this. Very few films – if any – in the past had caused riots within the cinemas and on the streets: the effect of powerful early rock music was as much a social matter as it was musical. Once more, the film offered little challenge to Elvis's acting talent, but was spectacularly successful in affording him the showcase for some stunning musical performances. This was Presley up to date, not the veiled 'bio-pic' of *Loving You*; the excitement and electricity were superbly caught and still pack a hefty punch today. One sad footnote was the death of his talented co-star Judy Tyler, soon after the release of the film.

The impact of *Jailhouse Rock* meant that Presley could not be ignored. His next film, *King Creole*, was awaited with eager anticipation by some and with fear and dread by others. Eight months after *Jailhouse Rock* was released, *King Creole* hit the world's screens. This was clearly a step upwards in film-making: another Paramount Pictures film, Presley's co-stars were Carolyn Jones, Dolores Hart, Dean Jagger and Walter Matthau. The story was based on Harold Robbin's novel *A Stone For Danny Fisher*; the director was Michael Curtiz. At 115 minutes, this was to be Presley's longest film, and it was also the last film he made in black and white.

The attractions of *King Creole* are manifold: in the first place, the story is good, and the screenplay was the best he had had up to then. The musical ingredient is finely balanced, and the songs themselves are of a wide range and style, with something for everyone. In addition, *King Creole* clearly proves that Presley had a certain acting talent. Indeed, his participation in the fight scenes was such that the film was banned in Ireland and elsewhere.

With these four films, then, Elvis Presley began his movie acting career. Interrupted by his Army service, this period of twenty months which saw their release established him as a major box-office attraction. Certainly, this attraction was less for his acting ability than for his singing – or rather his 'performance image', but to those prepared to look below the musical surface in parts of his first films, most notably in *King Creole*, Presley showed himself to possess a marked talent for acting. There is no knowing what he could have gone on to achieve, had the military call-up not interrupted his developing cinema career.

When it was resumed two years later, the atmosphere had changed slightly. The success of the early Presley films was not lost on the managers of other rock stars: in the intervening period, a succession of mainly indifferent films had appeared, all geared around rock music. Presley, also, after the enforced lay-off, was obliged to reassert himself, and had to do so through the musical film. In addition, far from the teenage riots engendered by *Jailhouse Rock*, he had a new audience, not only a teenage one, but one now including their parents.

G.I. Blues was a perfect film for the period: national service was a fact of life for teenage men throughout the world, so the relevance of the background was universal. The music was entirely appropriate, and Norman Taurog's direction was admirable. There is a genuine sense of fun in this film, to which no one could take exception; entirely free from pretence, and with the talented Juliet Prowse at her most beguiling, *G.I. Blues* was an ideally successful movie which has not, in spite of the background, dated.

His next film, *Flaming Star*, has already been mentioned several times in the main body of this book; it is one that I rate highly in the Presley canon. Virtually devoid of music, the powerful story, with its racial undertones and fratricidal strife, is very well done indeed, and Presley – in the demanding role of a half-breed who eventually returns to his mother's Indian roots, at a time of immense social upheaval – plays an exceptional part exceptionally well. There can be no doubt that Presley almost literally threw himself into the part of Pacer, for he was physically called upon to do some wide-ranging things. The reasons for the comparative commercial failure of this film have already been discussed in chapter six; and such was the power of the studios that with this film Presley's serious acting development virtually came to an end.

However, a film once commenced can hardly be cancelled, especially if the star is Elvis Presley, and his next film, *Wild In The Country*, while not so dramatically powerful a vehicle as *Flaming Star*, nevertheless was not such a disappointment with regard to his acting ability as might be inferred. In addition, there was a reasonable amount of music. But the main difficulty with this film is the film itself, not the individual performances, which are generally excellent. Presley co-starred with Hope Lange, Tuesday Weld, Millie Perkins, Rafer Johnson and John Ireland, but the story-line does not permit anyone to dominate the movie and is too downbeat – murder, suicide, corruption, psychiatry. These are legitimate matters for a film to tackle, but they are not well handled by the director, Phillip Dunne, although he had an excellent script (by Clifford Odets) and cast with which to work.

With one or two exceptions, Presley's following films soon settled into a predictable routine, based upon that of his next, and eighth, *Blue Hawaii*. The model was excellent: *Blue Hawaii* is beautifully set, with tremendous colour and atmosphere, and contains fourteen songs, several of which are outstanding. The resultant sound-track album sold almost two million copies within six months, and the film did very good business indeed. This, clearly, was *it* for the movie investors and they wanted more of the same highly successful formula.

And so, for the following seven or eight years, Elvis Presley made twenty-two feature films of a similar nature, often on 'location' – *Viva Las Vegas*, *Fun In Acapulco*, *California Holiday* (original US title *Spinout*), *It Happened At The World's Fair*, *Paradise Hawaiian Style* (an unsuccessful attempt to recreate the impact of *Blue Hawaii*) – invariably playing an unmarried man in his twenties who has some kind of 'action' job, such as speedway rider, boxer, cowboy, 'underwater demolition man', sailor, yacht captain, airline pilot – and so on. He meets a girl and the rest is pure formula.

However, it must not be thought that every one of these films is entirely similar; often there is a surprising twist or two in the telling, and Elvis is never less than himself. It must also not be forgotten that a number of distinguished film actors and actresses appeared in some of these films: Angela Lansbury, Gig Young, Charles Bronson, Stella Stevens, Ursula Andress, Ann-Margaret, William Demarest, Barbara Stanwyck, Leif Erickson, Shelley Fabares, Jackie Coogan, Chips Rafferty, Norman Rossington, Bill Bixby, Burgess Meredith, Joan Blondell, Nancy Sinatra, Rudy Vallee, James Sikking, John Carradine, Vincent Price, Mary Tyler Moore, Elsa Lanchester, Edward Asner and Regis Toomey – the presence of stars of this quality certainly have ensured at least an acceptable standard, and there are some wonderful moments.

His last three feature films, *Charro*, *The Trouble With Girls* and *Change Of Habit*, make a curious trio. *Charro* is a definite attempt to make a more serious movie; in this western, Elvis sings just one song, and is bearded throughout. The story is not without merit – but it surely demanded a better treatment than director Charles X. Warren was able to summon on this occasion – and the supporting cast was undistinguished. Consequently, after years of not having had his acting ability stretched at all, Elvis was virtually called upon to save the movie, which was almost beyond him. *The Trouble With Girls* has claim to being his least worthwhile film; the story is not too innocuous, but the pace is slow, and Elvis does what he can with some comparatively poor material. The supporting cast includes Vincent Price, and their contribution is by no means worthless, but Elvis is the star and for much of the time he does little more than stand there.

Change Of Habit concluded Presley's acting career; it is not an unworthy film. In it, Elvis plays a doctor, for the one and only time, who received help from three nuns (out of costume) in keeping his surgery going in a run-down New York neighbourhood. With co-stars Mary Tyler Moore, Edward Asner and Regis Toomey, the film has a nice mixture, the musical element is not large (it is difficult to see how it could have been otherwise) and the story is well-crafted and directed. It would be wrong, however, to claim too much for the resultant picture, which remains pleasantly harmless and innocuous.

The two succeeding documentary films, *Elvis – That's The Way It Is* and *Elvis On Tour*, cannot claim to be other than eye-witness accounts of his professional life. Of their type, they are both excellent.

The films we have vary from the very good to the indifferent, and even the least worthy of them provides us – and future generations – with examples of his singing. Therefore, each one is valuable to some degree and cannot be ignored in the course of a discussion of his life and work. Taken overall, Elvis Presley's film career is a fascinating adjunct to his singing career, but ultimately it is frustrating to contemplate what might have been. That he possessed a genuine talent of acting cannot – on the evidence of *Jailhouse Rock*, *King Creole*, *G.I. Blues*, *Flaming Star*, *Wild in The Country*' and *Blue Hawaii* – be seriously doubted, although it would be wrong to assert that he was any way towards being a great actor, even in promise. Nevertheless, had he had the right vehicles, or been a more self-assertive character, or had those in positions of influence been persuaded to take a chance or two, there is no knowing what might have been achieved.

Filmography

Part 1 – Feature films

1956

LOVE ME TENDER
CinemaScope
Release date: 16 November, 1956
Studio: Twentieth-Century Fox
Running time: 89 minutes

Cast:

Clint	Elvis Presley
Vance	Richard Egan
Cathy	Debra Paget
Siringo	Robert Middleton
Brett Reno	William Campbell
Mike Gavin	Neville Brand
The Mother	Mildred Dunnock
Major Kincaid	Bruce Bennett
Ray Reno	James Drury
Ed Galt	Russ Conway
Kelso	Ken Clark
Davis	Barry Coe

Credits:

Producer	David Weisbart
Director	Robert D. Webb
Screenplay	Robert Buckner
Story	Maurice Geraghty
Photographer	Leo Tover
Music	Lionel Newman
Art Direction	Lyle R. Wheeler/ Maurice Ransford
Special Effects	Ray Kellogg
Technical Advisor	Col Tom Parker

Songs: 'Love Me Tender', 'Let Me', 'Poor Boy', 'We're Gonna Move'

1957

LOVING YOU
Vista Vision and Technicolor
Release date: 9 July, 1957
Studio: Paramount Pictures
Running time: 101 minutes

Cast:

Deke Rivers	Elvis Presley
Glenda	Lizabeth Scott

Tex Warner	Wendell Corey
Susan Jessup	Dolores Hart
Carl	James Gleason
Tallman	Ralph Dumke
Skeeter	Paul Smith
Wayne	Ken Becker
Daisy	Jana Lund

Credits:

Producer	Hal B. Wallis
Director	Hal Kanter
Screenplay	Herbert Baker/
	Hal Kanter
Story	Mary Agnes
	Thompson
Photographer	Charles Lang Jr
Editor	Howard Smith
Special Photographic	
Effects	John P. Fulton
Art Directors	Hal Pereira/
	Albert Nozaki
Assistant Director	James Rosenberger

Songs: 'Teddy Bear', 'Got A Lot O' Livin' To Do', 'Loving You', 'Lonesome Cowboy', 'Hot Dog', 'Mean Woman Blues', 'Let's Have A Party'

JAILHOUSE ROCK

CinemaScope
Release date: 21 October, 1957
Studio: Metro-Goldwyn-Mayer
Running time: 96 minutes

Cast:

Vince Everett	Elvis Presley
Peggy van Alden	Judy Tyler
Hunk Houghton	Mickey
	Shaughnessey
Sherry Wilson	Jennifer Holden
Eddy Talbot	Dean Jones
Laury Jackson	Anne Neyland
Warden	Hugh Sanders

Credits:

Producer	Pandro S. Berman
Director	Richard Thorpe
Screenplay	Guy Trosper
Story	Ned Young
Photographer	Robert Bronner
Editor	Ralph E. Winters
Assistant Producer	Kathryn Hereford
Music Supervisor	Jeff Alexander
Art Directors	William A. Horning
	/Randell Duell
Special Effects	A. Arnold Gillespie
Assistant Director	Robert E. Reylen
Technical Advisor	Col Tom Parker

Songs: 'Jailhouse Rock', 'Treat Me Nice', 'Young And Beautiful', 'I Wanna Be Free', 'Don't Leave Me Now', 'Baby, I Don't Care', 'One More Day'

1958

KING CREOLE

Release date: 4 June, 1958
Studio: Paramount Pictures
Running time: 115 minutes

Cast:

Danny Fisher	Elvis Presley
Ronnie	Carolyn Jones
Nellie	Dolores Hart
Mr Fisher	Dean Jagger
'Forty' Nina	Liliane
	Montevecchi
Maxie Fields	Walter Matthau
Mimi	Jan Shepard
Charlie LeGrand	Paul Stewart
Shark	Vic Morrow

Credits:

Producer	Hal B. Wallis

Director	Michael Curtiz
Associate Producer	Paul Nathan
Screenplay	Herbert Baker/
	Michael Vincente
	Gazzo
Story	Harold Robbins,
	A Stone For
	Danny Fisher
Photographer	Russell Harlan
Editor	Warren Low
Art Directors	Hal Pereira/Joseph
	MacMillan Johnson
Special Photographic	
Effects	John P. Fulton
Assistant Director	D. Michael Moore
Technical Advisor	Col Tom Parker

Songs: 'King Creole', 'As Long As I Have You', 'Hard Headed Woman', 'Trouble', 'Dixieland Rock', 'Don't Ask Me Why', 'Lover Doll', 'Crawfish', 'Young Dreams', 'Steadfast, Loyal And True', 'New Orleans', 'Turtles And Gumbo', 'Banana'

1960

G.I. BLUES
Technicolor
Release date: 20 October, 1960
Studio: Paramount Pictures
Running time: 104 minutes

Cast:

Tulsa MacCauley	Elvis Presley
Rick	James Douglas
Cooky	Robert Ivers
Lili	Juliet Prowse
Tina	Leticia Roman
Marla	Sigrid Maier
Sgt McGraw	Arch Johnson

Credits:

Producer	Hal B. Wallis
Director	Norman Taurog
Associate Producer	Paul Nathan
Screenplay	Edmund Beloin/
	Henry Garson
Photographer	Loyal Griggs
Editor	Warren Low
Music scored and	
conducted by	Joseph L. Lilley
Music numbers	
staged by	Charles O'Curran
Art Directors	Hal Pereira/
	Walter Tyler
Technical Advisor	Col Tom Parker

Songs: 'G.I. Blues', 'Tonight Is So Right For Love', 'Frankfurt Special', 'Wooden Heart', 'Pocketful Of Rainbows', 'Didya Ever?', 'What's She Really Like?', 'Shoppin' Around', 'Big Boots', 'Doin' The Best I Can'

FLAMING STAR
CinemaScope, De Luxe Color
Release date: 20 December, 1960
Studio: Twentieth-Century Fox
Running time: 101 minutes

Cast:

Pacer Burton	Elvis Presley
Clint Burton	Steve Forrest
Roslyn Pierce	Barbara Eden
Neddy Burton	Dolores Del Rio
Pa Burton	John McIntyre
Buffalo Horn	Rudolfo Acosta
Doc Phillips	Ford Rainey
Dred Phillips	Karl Swenson
Angus Pierce	Richard Jaeckel
Dorothy Howard	Anne Benton
Will Howard	L.O. Jones
Jute	Tom Reese

Credits:

Producer	David Weisbart
Director	Don Siegel
Screenplay	Clair Huffaker/
	Nunnally Johnson
Photographer	Charles G. Clarke
Editor	Hugh S. Fowler
Art Directors	Duncan Cramer/
	Walter M. Simonds
Music	Cyril Mockridge
Musical Director	Lionel Newman
Technical Advisor	Col Tom Parker

Songs: 'Flaming Star', 'A Cane And A High-Starched Collar'

1961

WILD IN THE COUNTRY
CinemaScope, De Luxe Color
Release date: 15 June, 1961
Studio: Twentieth-Century Fox
Running time: 114 minutes

Cast:

Glenn Tyler	Elvis Presley
Irene Sperry	Hope Lange
Noreen	Tuesday Weld
Betty Lee	Millie Perkins
Davis	Rafer Johnson
Phil Macy	John Ireland
Uncle Rolfe	William Mims
Dr Underwood	Raymond Greenleaf
Monica George	Christina Crawford
Flossie	Robin Raymond
Mrs Parsons	Doreen Lang
Mr Parsons	Charles Arnt

Credits:

Producer	Jerry Wald
Director	Philip Dunne
Screenplay	Clifford Odets
Story	J.R. Salamanca
Photographer	William C. Mellor
Editor	Dorothy Spencer
Music	Kenyon Hopkins
Art Directors	Jack Martin Shaw/
	Preston Ames
Technical Advisor	Col Tom Parker

Songs: 'Lonely Man', 'I Slipped, I Stumbled, I Fell', 'In My Way', 'Wild In The Country'

BLUE HAWAII
Panavision, Technicolor
Release date: 14 November, 1961
Studio: Paramount Pictures
Running time: 101 minutes

Cast:

Chad Gates	Elvis Presley
Maile Duval	Joan Blackman
Abigale Prentace	Nancy Walters
Fred Gates	Roland Winters
Sarah Lee Gates	Angela Lansbury
Jack Kelman	John Archer
Mr Chapman	Howard McNear
Mrs Manaka	Flora Hayes
Mr Duval	Gregory Gay
Mr Garvey	Steve Brodie
Mrs Garvey	Iris Adrian
Patsy	Darlene Tomkins
Sandy	Pamela Alkert
Beverly	Christian Kay

Credits:

Producer	Hal B. Wallis
Director	Norman Taurog
Associate Producer	Paul Nathan
Screenplay	Hal Kanter
Story	Allan Weiss
Photographer	Charles Lang

Editors — Warren Low/ Terry Morse

Special Photographic Effects — John P. Fulton

Music scored and conducted by — Joseph L. Lilley

Music numbers staged by — Charles O'Curran

Art Directors — Hal Pereira/ Walter Tyler

Technical Advisor — Col Tom Parker

Songs: 'Blue Hawaii', 'Almost Always', 'Aloha Oe', 'No More', 'Can't Help Falling In Love', 'Rock-a-Hula Baby', 'Moonlight Swim', 'Ku-u-ipo', 'Ito Eats', 'Slicin' Sand', 'Hawaiian Sunset', 'Beach Boy Blues', 'Island Of Love', 'Hawaiian Wedding Song', 'Steppin' Out Of Line'

1962

FOLLOW THAT DREAM
Panavision, De Luxe Color
Release date: 29 March, 1962
Studio: United Artists
Running time: 110 minutes

Cast:

Toby Kwimper	Elvis Presley
Pop Kwimper	Arthur O'Connell
Holly Jones	Anne Helm
Alicia Claypole	Joanna Moore
Carmine	Jack Kruschen
Nick	Simon Oakland
Eddy and Teddy	Gavin and Robert
Bascomb	Koon
Adriane	Pam Ogles

Credits:

Producer — David Weisbart

Director — Gordon Douglas

Screenplay — Charles Lederer

Story: based on the play, — *Pioneer, Go Home!* by Richard Powell

Photographer — Leo Tover

Editor — William B. Murphy

Music — Hans J. Salter

Music Editor — Robert Tracy

Technical Advisor — Col Tom Parker

Songs: 'What A Wonderful Life', 'I'm Not The Marrying Kind', 'Sound Advice', 'Follow That Dream'

KID GALAHAD
Color by De Luxe
Release date: 25 July, 1962
Studio: United Artists
Running time: 95 minutes

Cast:

Walter Gulick	Elvis Presley
Willie Grogan	Gig Young
Dolly Fletcher	Lola Albright
Rose Grogan	Joan Blackman
Lew Nyak	Charles Bronson
Leiberman	Ned Glass
Maynard	Robert Emhardt
Otto Danzig	David Lewis
Joie Shakes	Michael Dante
Zimmerman	Judson Pratt
Sperling	George Mitchell
Marvin	Richard Devon

Credits:

Producer	David Weisbart
Director	Phil Karlson
Screenplay	William Fay
Story	Francis Wallace
Photographer	Burnett Guffey
Editor	Stuart Gilmore
Art Director	Cary Odell

Music	Jeff Alexander
Technical Advisor	Col Tom Parker
Presentation	The Mirisch Company

Songs: 'King Of The Whole Wide World', 'This Is Living', 'Riding The Rainbow', 'Home Is Where The Heart Is', 'I Got Lucky', 'A Whistling Tune'

GIRLS! GIRLS! GIRLS!
Panavision, Technicolor
Release date: 2 November, 1962
Studio: Paramount Pictures
Running time: 106 minutes

Cast:

Ross Carpenter	Elvis Presley
Robin Ganter	Stella Stevens
Laurel Dodge	Laurel Goodwin
Wesley Johnson	Jeremy Slate
Chen Yung	Guy Lee
Kin Yung	Benson Fong
Madame Yung	Beulah Quo
Sam	Robert Strauss
Alexander Stavros	Frank Puglia
Madame Stavros	Lili Valenty
Leona and Linda Stavros	Barbara and Betty Beal
Arthur Morgan	Nestor Paiva
Mrs Morgan	Ann McCrea
Mai and Lai Ting	Ginny and Elizabeth Tiu

Credits:

Producer	Hal B. Wallis
Director	Norman Taurog
Associate Producer	Paul Nathan
Screenplay	Edward Anhalt/ Allan Weiss
Story	Allan Weiss
Photographer	Loyal Griggs

Art Directors	Hal Pereira/ Walter Tyler
Music	Joseph L. Lilley
Music staged by	Charles O'Curran
Assistant Director	Mickey Moore
Technical Advisor	Col Tom Parker

Songs: 'Girls! Girls! Girls!', 'I Don't Wanna Be Tied', 'Where Do You Come From?', 'I Don't Want To', 'We'll Be Together', 'A Boy Like Me, A Girl Like You', 'Earth Boy', 'Return To Sender', 'Thanks To The Rolling Sea', 'Song Of The Shrimp', 'The Walls Have Ears', 'We're Coming In Loaded'

1963

IT HAPPENED AT THE WORLD'S FAIR
Panavision, Metrocolor
Release date: 3 March, 1963
Studio: Metro-Goldwyn-Mayer
Running time: 105 minutes

Cast:

Mike Edwards	Elvis Presley
Diane Warren	Joan O'Brien
Danny Burke	Gary Lockwood
Sue-Lin	Vicky Tu
Vince Bradley	H.M. Wynant
Miss Steuben	Edith Atwater
Barney Thatcher	Guy Raymond
Miss Ettinger	Dorothy Green
Walter Ling	Kam Tong
Dorothy Johnson	Yvonne Craig

Credits:

Director	Norman Taurog
Screenplay	Si Rose/ Seaman Jacobs
Photographer	Joseph Ruttenburg

Editor — Frederic Steinkamp
Music — Leith Stevens
Art Directors — George W. Davis/ Preston Ames
Music staged by — Jack Baker
Assistant Director — Al Jennings
Technical Advisor — Col Tom Parker
A Ted Richmond Production

Songs: 'I'm Falling In Love Tonight', 'Relax', 'How Would You Like To Be', 'Beyond The Bend', 'One Broken Heart For Sale', 'Cotton Candy Land', 'A World Of Our Own', 'Take Me To The Fair', 'They Remind Me Too Much Of You', 'Happy Ending'

FUN IN ACAPULCO
Technicolor
Release date: 21 November, 1963
Studio: Paramount Pictures
Running time: 98 minutes

Cast:
Mike Windgren — Elvis Presley
Margarita
Dauphine — Ursula Andress
Dolores Gomez — Elsa Cardenas
Maximillian — Paul Lukas
Raoul Almeido — Larry Domasin
Moreno — Alejandro Rey
José — Robert Carricart
Jamie Harkins — Teri Hope

Credits:
Producer — Hal B. Wallis
Director — Richard Thorpe
Screenplay — Allan Weiss
Photographer — Daniel L. Fapp
Editor — Warren Low
Art Directors — Hal Pereira/ Walter Tyler
Technical Advisor — Col Tom Parker

Songs: 'Fun In Acapulco', 'Vino, Dinero Y Amor', 'Mexico', 'El Tora', 'Marguerita', 'The Bullfighter Was A Lady', 'There's No Room To Rhumba In A Sports Car', 'I Think I'm Gonna Like It Here', 'Bossa Nova Baby', 'You Can't Say No In Acapulco', 'Guadalajara'

1964

KISSIN' COUSINS
Panavision, Metrocolor
Release date: 6 March, 1964
Studio: Metro-Goldwyn-Mayer
Running time: 96 minutes

Cast:
Josh Morgan — Elvis Presley
Jodie Tatum — Elvis Presley
Pappy Tatum — Arthur O'Connell
Ma Tatum — Glenda Farrell
Capt Robert Salbo — Jack Albertson
Selena Tatum — Pam Austin
Midge — Cynthia Pepper
Azalea Tatum — Yvonne Craig
General Donford — Donald Woods
Sgt Bailey — Tommy Farrell
Trudy — Beverly Powers
Dixie — Hortense Petra
General's Aide — Robert Stone

Credits:
Producer — Sam Katzman
Director — Gene Nelson
Screenplay — Gerald Drayson Adams/Gene Nelson
Story — Gerald Drayson Adams
Photographer — Ellis W. Carter

Editor Ben Lewis
Music supervised and
conducted by Fred Karger
Art Directors George W. Davis/
Eddie Imazu
Assistant Director Eli Dunn
Technical Advisor Col Tom Parker

Songs: 'Kissin Cousins' (Nos 1 and 2),
'One Boy, Two Little Girls', 'There's
Gold In The Mountains', 'Catchin' On
Fast', 'Barefoot Ballad', 'Once Is
Enough', 'Smoky Mountain Boy',
'Tender Feeling'

VIVA LAS VEGAS
Panavision, Metrocolor
Release date: 20 April, 1964
Studio: Metro-Goldwyn-Mayer
Running time: 86 minutes

Cast:
Lucky Jordan Elvis Presley
Rusty Martin Ann-Margaret
Count Elmo
Mancini Cesare Danova
Mr Martin William Demarest
Shorty Fransworth Nicky Blair

Credits:
Producers Jack Cummings/
George Sidney
Director George Sidney
Screenplay Sally Benton
Photographer Joseph Biroc
Editor John McSweeney Jr
Music George Stoll
Assistant Director Milton Feldman
Technical Advisor Col Tom Parker

Songs: 'Viva Las Vegas', 'If You Think I
Don't Need You', 'The Lady Loves

Me', 'I Need Somebody To Lean On',
'C'mon Everybody', 'Today, Tomorrow
And Forever', 'Santa Lucia'

ROUSTABOUT
Techniscope, Technicolor
Release date: 12 November, 1964
Studio: Paramount Pictures
Running time: 101 minutes

Cast:
Charlie Rogers Elvis Presley
Maggie Morgan Barbara Stanwyck
Cathy Lean Joan Freeman
Joe Lean Leif Erickson
Madame Mijanou Sue Ann Langdon
Harry Carver Pat Buttram
Marge Joan Stanley
Arthur Nielson Dabs Greer
Fred Steve Brodie
Sam Norman Grabowski
Lou Jack Albertson
Cody Marsh Joel Fluellen
Hazel Jane Dulo
Little Egypt Wilda Taylor

Credits:
Producer Hal B. Wallis
Associate Producer Paul Nathan
Director John Rich
Screenplay Anthony Lawrence/
Allan Weiss
Story Allan Weiss
Photographer Lucien Ballard
Music Joseph L. Lilley
Assistant Director D. Michael Moore
Technical Advisor Col Tom Parker

Songs: 'Roustabout', 'Poison Ivy
League', 'Wheels On My Heels', 'It's A
Wonderful World', 'It's Carnival Time',
'Carny Town', 'One Track Heart',
'Hard Knocks', 'Little Egypt', 'Big

Love, Big Heartache', 'There's A
Brand New Day On The Horizon'

1965

GIRL HAPPY
Panavision, Metrocolor
Release date: 22 January, 1965
Studio: Metro-Goldwyn-Mayer
Running time: 96 minutes

Cast:

Rusty Wells	Elvis Presley
Valerie	Shelley Fabares
Big Frank	Harold J. Stone
Andy	Gary Crosby
Wilbur	Jody Baker
Sunny Daze	Nita Talbot
Deena	MaryAnn Mobley
Romana	Fabrizio Mioni
Doc	Jimmy Hawkins
Sgt Benson	Jackie Coogan
Brentwood Von	
Durgenfeld	Peter Brooks
Mr Penchill	John Fielder
Betsy	Chris Noel
Laurie	Lyn Edington
Nancy	Gale Gilmore
Bobbie	Pamela Curran
Linda	Rusty Allen

Credits:

Producer	Joe Pasternak
Director	Boris Sagal
Screenplay	Harvey Bullock/ R.S. Allen
Photographer	Philip H. Lathrop
Editor	Rita Roland
Music	George Stoll
Assistant Director	Jack Aldworth
Technical Advisor	Col Tom Parker

Songs: 'Girl Happy', 'Spring Fever', 'Fort Lauderdale Chamber Of Commerce', 'Startin' Tonight', 'Wolf Call', 'Do Not Disturb', 'Cross My Heart And Hope To Die', 'The Meanest Girl In Town', 'Do The Clam', 'Puppet On A String', 'I've Got To Find My Baby'

TICKLE ME
Panavision, DeLuxe Color
Release date: 15 June, 1965
Studio: United Artists
Running time: 90 minutes

Cast:

Lonnie Beale	Elvis Presley
Pam Merritt	Jocelyn Lane
Vera Radford	Julie Adams
Stanley Potter	Jack Mullaney
Estelle Penfield	Merry Anders
Hilda	Connie Gilchrist
Brad Bentley	Edward Faulkner
Deputy Sturdivent	Bill Williams
Henry	Louis Elias
Adolph	John Dennis
Janet	Laurie Burton
Clair Kinnamon	Linda Rogers
Sibyl	Ann Morel
Ronnie	Lilyan Chauvin

Credits:

Producer	Ben Schwalb
Director	Norman Taurog
Story and Screenplay	Elwood Ullman/ Edward Bernds
Photographer	Loyal Griggs
Editor	Archie Marshek
Music Director	Walter Scharf
Art Director	Arthur Lonergan
Assistant Director	Artie Jacobson
Technical Advisor	Col Tom Parker

Songs: 'Tickle Me', 'I'm Yours', 'I Feel That I've Known You Forever', 'Dirty, Dirty Feeling', 'Put The Blame On Me', 'Easy Question', 'Slowly But Surely'

HARUM SCARUM
Metrocolor
Release date: 15 December, 1965
Studio: Metro-Goldwyn-Mayer
Running time: 95 minutes

Cast:

Johnny Tyronne	Elvis Presley
Princess Shalimar	Mary Ann Mobley
Aishah	Fran Jeffries
Prince Dara	Michael Ansara
Zacha	Jay Novello
King Toranshad	Philip Reed
Sinan	Theo Marcuse
Baba	Billy Barty
Mohar	Dirk Harvey
Juina	Jack Castanzo
Captain Heret	Larry Chance
Leilah	Barbara Werle
Emerald	Brenda Benet
Sapphire	Gail Gilmore
Amethyst	Wilda Taylor
Sari	Vicki Malkin

Credits:

Producer	Sam Katzman
Director	Gene Nelson
Screenplay	Gerald Drayson Adams
Photographer	Fred H. Jackman
Editor	Ben Levin
Music supervised and conducted by	Fred Karger
Art Directors	George W. Davis/ H. McClure Capps
Technical Advisor	Col Tom Parker

Songs: 'Harem Holiday', 'My Desert Serenade', 'Go East, Young Man', 'Mirage', 'Kismet', 'Shake That Tambourine', 'Hey Little Girl', 'Golden Coins', 'So Close Yet So Far'

1966

FRANKIE AND JOHNNY
Technicolor
Release date: 20 July, 1966
Studio: United Artists
Running time: 87 minutes

Cast:

Johnny	Elvis Presley
Frankie	Donna Douglas
Nellie Bly	Nancy Kovak
Mitzi	Sue Ann Langdon
Braden	Anthony Eisley
Cully	Harry Morgan
Pog	Audrey Christie
Blackie	Robert Strauss
Wilbur	Jerome Cowan
Earl Barton	Wilda Taylor,
Dancers	Larri Thomas, Dee Jay Mattis, Judy Chapman

Credits:

Producer	Edward Small
Director	Fred de Cordova
Screenplay	Alex Gottlieb
Story	Nat Perrin
Photographer	Jacques Marquette
Editor	Grant Whytock
Music Director	Fred Karger
Technical Advisor	Col Tom Parker

Songs: 'Frankie And Johnny', 'Come Along', 'Petunia, The Gardener's

Daughter', 'Chesay', 'What Every Woman Lives For', 'Look Out, Broadway', 'Beginner's Luck', 'Down By The Riverside', 'When The Saints Go Marching In', 'Shout It Out', 'Hard Luck', 'Please Don't Stop Loving Me', 'Everybody Come Aboard'

PARADISE, HAWAIIAN STYLE
Technicolor
Release date: 8 August, 1966
Studio: Paramount Pictures
Running time: 91 minutes

Cast:

Rick Richards	Elvis Presley
Judy Hudson	Suzanne Leigh
Danny Kohana	James Shigeta
Jan Kohana	Donna Butterworth
Lani	Marianna Hill
Pua	Irene Tsu
Lehua	Linda Wong
Joanna	Julie Parrish
Betty Kohana	Jan Shepard
Donald Belden	John Doucette
Moki	Philip Ahn
Mr Cubberson	Grady Sutton
Andy Lowell	Don Collier
Mrs Barrington	Doris Packer
Mrs Belden	Mary Treen
Peggy Holdren	Gigi Verone

Credits:

Producer	Hal B. Wallis
Associate Producer	Paul Nathan
Director	Michael Moore
Screenplay	Allan Weiss/ Anthony Lawrence
Story	Allan Weiss
Photographer	W. Wallace Kelley
Editor	Warren Low
Music	Joseph L. Lilley

Art Directors	Hal Pereira/ Walter Tyler
Technical Advisor	Col Tom Parker

Songs: 'Paradise, Hawaiian Style', 'House Of Sand', 'Queenie Wahine's Papaya', 'Scratch My Back', 'Drums Of The Islands', 'Dog's Life', 'Datin'', 'Stop Where You Are', 'This Is My Heaven'

SPINOUT
Panavision, Metrocolor
Release date: 14 December, 1966
Studio: Metro-Goldwyn-Mayer
Running time: 95 minutes

Cast:

Mike McCoy	Elvis Presley
Cynthia Foxhugh	Shelley Fabares
Diane St Clair	Diane McBain
Les	Deborah Walley
Susan	Dodie Marshall
Curly	Jack Mullaney
Lieut Tracy Richards	Will Hutchins
Philip Short	Warren Berlinger
Larry	Jimmy Hawkins
Howard Foxhugh	Carl Betz
Bernard Ranley	Cecil Kellaway
Violet Ranley	Una Merkel
Blodgett	Frederic Warlock
Harry	Dave Barry

Credits:

Producer	Joe Pasternak
Director	Norman Taurog
Screenplay	Theodore J. Flicker /George Kirgo
Photographer	Daniel L. Fapp
Editor	Rita Roland
Music	George Stoll

Associate Producer Hank Moonjean
Technical Advisor   Col Tom Parker

Songs: 'Spinout', 'I'll Be Back', 'All That I Am', 'Am I Ready', 'Stop, Look, Listen'

1967

EASY COME, EASY GO
Technicolor
Release date: 14 June, 1967
Studio: Paramount Pictures
Running time: 95 minutes

Cast:

Ted Jackson	Elvis Presley
Jo Symington	Dodie Marshall
Diana Bishop	Pat Priest
Judd Whitman	Pat Harrington
Gil Carey	Skip Ward
Schwartz	Sandy Kenyon
Captain Jack	Frank McHugh
Cooper	Ed Griffith
Ship's Officers	Reed Morgan,
	Mickey Elley
Vicki	Elaine Beckett
Mary	Shari Nims
Zoltan	Diki Lawrence
Artist	Robert Lawrence
Madame Neherina	Elsa Lanchester

Credits:

Producer	Hal B. Wallis
Associate Producer	Paul Nathan
Director	John Rich
Screenplay	Allan Weiss/
	Anthony Lawrence
Photographer	William Margulies
Editor	Archie Marshek

Music	Joseph L. Lilley
Art Directors	Hal Pereira/
	Walter Tyler
Technical Advisor	Col Tom Parker

Songs: 'Easy Come, Easy Go', 'The Love Machine', 'Yoga Is As Yoga Does', 'You Gotta Stop', 'Sing, You Children', 'I'll Take Love'

DOUBLE TROUBLE
Panavision, Metrocolor
Release date: 24 May, 1967
Studio: Metro-Goldwyn-Mayer
Running time: 90 minutes

Cast:

Guy Lambert	Elvis Presley
Jill Conway	Annette Day
Gerald Waverly	John Williams
Claire Dunham	Yvonne Romain
The Wiere	
Brothers	Themselves
Archie Brown	Chips Rafferty
Arthur Babcock	Norman Rossington
Georgie	Monty Landis
Morley	Michael Murphy
Inspector	
DeGrotte	Leon Askin
Iceman	John Alderson
Captain Roach	Stanley Adams
The G Men	Themselves

Credits:

Producers	Judd Bernard/
	Irwin Winkler
Director	Norman Taurog
Screenplay	Jo Heims
Story	Marc Brandel
Photographer	Daniel L. Fapp
Editor	John McSweeney
Music	Jeff Alexander

Art Directors   George W. Davis/
                 Merrill Pye
Assistant Director   Claude Binyon Jr
Technical Advisor   Col Tom Parker

Songs: 'Double Trouble', 'Baby, If You'll Give Me All Your Love', 'Could I Fall In Love', 'Long-Legged Girls With Short Dresses On', 'City Of Night', 'Old MacDonald', 'I Love Only One Girl', 'There's So Much World To See', 'It Won't Be Long'

CLAMBAKE

Techniscope, Technicolor
Release date: 4 December, 1967
Studio: United Artists
Running time: 99 minutes

Cast:

Scott Heywood	Elvis Presley
Diane Carter	Shelley Fabares
Tom Wilson	Will Hutchins
James Jamison III	Bill Bixby
Sam Burton	Gary Merrill
Duster Heywood	James Gregorys
Ellie	Amanda Harley
Sally	Suzy Kaye
Gloria	Angelique Pettyjohn

Credits:

Producers	J. Levy/A. Gardner/ A. Laven
Director	Arthur Navel
Screenplay	Arthur Brown Jr
Story	Arthur Brown Jr
Photographer	William Margulies
Editor	Tom Rolf
Music	Jeff Alexander
Technical Advisor	Col Tom Parker

Songs: 'Clambake', 'Who Needs Money', 'A House That Has

Everything', 'Confidence', 'Hey, Hey, Hey', 'You Don't Know Me', 'The Girl I Never Loved'

1968

STAY AWAY, JOE

Panavision, Metrocolor
Release date: 14 March, 1968
Studio: Metro-Goldwyn-Mayer
Running time: 98 minutes

Cast:

Joe Lightcloud	Elvis Presley
Charlie Lightcloud	Burgess Meredith
Glenda Callahan	Joan Blondell
Annie Lightcloud	Katy Jurado
Grandpa	Thomas Gomez
Hy Slager	Henry Jones
Bronc Hoverty	L.Q. Jones
Mamie Callahan	Quentin Dean
Mrs Hawkins	Anne Seymour
Congressman Morrissey	Douglas Henderson
Lorne Hawkins	Angus Duncan
Frank Hawk	Michael Lane
Mary Lightcloud	Susan Trustman
Hike Bowers	Warren Vanders
Bull Shortgun	Buck Kartalian
Marlene Standing Rattle	Caitlin Wyles

Credits:

Producer	Douglas Laurence
Director	Peter Tewksbury
Screenplay	Michael H.A. Hoey
Story	Dan Cushman
Photographer	Fred Koenekamp
Editor	George W. Brooks
Music Score	Jack Marshall
Assistant Director	Dale Hutchinson
Technical Advisor	Col Tom Parker

Songs: 'Stay Away', 'All I Needed Was The Rain', 'Stay Away, Joe', 'Dominic'
NB Presley also sings a few bars of a song called 'Lovely Mamie' during the course of the film

Songs: 'Speedway', 'Let Yourself Go', 'Your Time Hasn't Come Yet, Baby', 'He's Your Uncle, Not Your Dad', 'Your Groovy Self', 'There Ain't Nothing Like A Song'

SPEEDWAY
Panavision, Metrocolor
Release date: 13 June, 1968
Studio: Metro-Goldwyn-Mayer
Running time: 90 minutes

Cast:

Steve Grayson	Elvis Presley
Susan Jacks	Nancy Sinatra
Kenny Donford	Bill Bixby
R.W. Hepworth	Gale Gordon
Abel Esterlake	William Schallert
Ellie Esterlake	Victoria Meyerink
Paul Dado	Ross Hagen
Birdie Kebner	Carl Ballantine
Juan Medala	Ponice Ponce
The Cook	Harry Hickox
Billie Jo	Christopher West
Mary Ann	Miss Beverly Hills
Ted Simmons	Harper Carter
Lloyd Meadows	Bob Harris
Carrie	Courtney Brown
Billie	Dana Brown

Credits:

Producer	Douglas Lawrence
Director	Norman Taurog
Screenplay	Philip Shuken
Photographer	Joseph Ruttenberg
Editor	Russell Farrell
Music	Jeff Alexander
Art Directors	George W. Davis/ Leroy Coleman
Assistant Director	Dale Hutchinson
Technical Advisor	Col Tom Parker

LIVE A LITTLE, LOVE A LITTLE
Panavision, Metrocolor
Release date: 9 October, 1968
Studio: Metro-Goldwyn-Mayer
Running time: 89 minutes

Cast:

Greg	Elvis Presley
Bernice	Michele Carey
Mike Landsdown	Don Porter
Penlow	Rudy Vallee
Harry	Dick Sargent
Milkman	Sterling Holloway
Ellen	Celeste Yarnall
Delivery Boy	Eddie Hodges
Robbie's Mother	Joan Shawlee
Miss Selfridge	Mary Grover
Receptionist	Emily Banks

Credits:

Producer	Douglas Lawrence
Director	Norman Taurog
Screenplay	Michael A. Hoey/ Dan Greenburg
Story	Dan Greenburg
Photographer	Fred Koenekamp
Editor	John McSweeney
Music	Billy Strange
Art Directors	George W. Davis/ Preston Ames
Assistant Director	Al Shenberg
Technical Advisor	Col Tom Parker

Songs: 'Almost In Love', 'A Little Less Conversation', 'Edge Of Reality', 'Wonderful World'

1969

CHARRO
Panavision, Metrocolor
Release date: 3 September, 1969
Studio: National General Pictures
Running time: 98 minutes

Cast:

Jesse Wade	Elvis Prelsey
Tracey	Ina Balin
Vince	Victor French
Sara	Barbara Werle
Billy Roy	Solomon Sturges
Marcie	Lynn Kellogg
Gunner	James Sikking
Opie Keetch	Paul Brinegar
Heff	Harry Landers
Lt Rivera	Tony Young
Sheriff Ramsey	James Almanzar
Moody	Charles H. Gray
Jerome Selby	John Pickard
Martin Tilford	Garry Walberg
Gabe	Duana Grey
Lige	Rodd Redwing
Henry Carter	J. Edward McKinley

Credits:

Executive Producer	Harry A. Caplan
Producer/ Director	Charles Marquis Warren
Screenplay	Charles Marquis Warren
Story	Frederic Louis Fox
Photographer	Ellsworth Fredericks
Editor	Al Clark
Art Director	James Sullivan
Music	Hugo Montenegro
Music Editor	John Mick
Assistant Director	Dink Templeton

Technical Advisor   Col Tom Parker

Song: 'Charro'

THE TROUBLE WITH GIRLS
Panavision, Metrocolor
Release date: 10 December, 1969
Studio: Metro-Goldwyn-Mayer
Running time: 99 minutes

Cast:

Walter Hale	Elvis Presley
Charlene	Marlyn Mason
Betty	Nicole Jaffe
Nita Nix	Sheree North
Johnny	Edward Andrews
Mr Drewcolt	John Carradine
Caril	Anissa Jones
Mr Morality	Vincent Price
Maude	Joyce Van Polten
Willy	Pepe Brown
Harrison Wilby	Dabney Coleman
Mayor Gilchrist	Bill Zuchert
Mr Perper	Pitt Herbet
Clarance	Anthony Teague
Constable	Med Flory

Credits:

Producer	Lester Welch
Director	Peter Tewksbury
Screenplay	Arnold Peyser/ Lois Peyser
Story	Day Keene/ Dwight Babcock
Photographer	Jacques Marguette
Editor	George W. Brooks
Music	Billy Strange
Art Directors	George W. Davis/ Edward Carfagno
Technical Advisor	Col Tom Parker

Songs: 'Almost', 'Clean Up Your Own Backyard'

1970

CHANGE OF HABIT
Technicolor
Release date: 21 January, 1970
Studio: NBC-Universal
Running time: 93 minutes

Cast:

Dr John Carpenter	Elvis Presley
Sister Michelle	Mary Tyler Moore
Sister Irene	Barbara MacNair
Sister Barbara	Jane Elliot
Mother Joseph	Leorna Dana
Lieut Moretti	Edward Asner
The Banker	Robert Emhart
Father Gibbons	Regis Toomey
Rose	Doro Merande
Lily	Ruth McDevitt
Bishop Finley	Richard Karlson
Julio Hernandez	Nefti Millet
Desiree	Laura Figuerosa
Amanda	Lorena Rich

Credits:

Producer	Joe Connelly
Director	William Graham
Associate Producer	Irving Paley
Screenplay	James Lee/
	S.S. Schweitzer/
	Eric Bercovici
Story	John Joseph/
	Richard Morris
Photographer	Russell Metty
Editor	Douglas Stewart
Music	William Goldenberg
Technical Advisor	Col Tom Parker

Songs: 'Change Of Habit',
'Rubberneckin'', 'Let Us Pray', 'Have A
Happy'

Filmography

Part 2 – Documentary films

1970

ELVIS – THAT'S THE WAY IT IS
Panavision, Metrocolor
Release date: 15 December, 1970
Studio: Metro-Goldwyn-Mayer
Running time: 107 minutes

Credits:
Director	Denis Sanders
Assistant Director	John Wilson
Photographer	Lucien Ballard
Technical Advisor	Col Tom Parker
Editors	Henry Berman/
	George Folsey

Songs: Extracts, rehearsal sequences and live performances of over twenty-seven songs

1973

ELVIS ON TOUR
Metrocolor
Release date: 6 June, 1973
Studio: Metro-Goldwyn-Mayer
Running time: 93 minutes

Credits:
Producer/Director	Pierre Adidge
Associate Producers	Sidney Levin/
	Robert Abel
Photographer	Robert Thomas
Technical Advisor	Col Tom Parker

Songs: Extracts and live performances of twenty-four songs

Filmography

Part 3 – Live performances on video and laser disc

The following official video and laser disc releases are especially recommended; while there are in existence rough 'bootleg' videos of Elvis's performances, their availability is questionable and technically they are in no way to be preferred to the following titles.

1950s
ELVIS IN HOLLYWOOD
Colour footage from 1950s movies, with screen out-takes and home movies
BMG-RCA 74321 13988-3/6

1960s
ELVIS – ONE NIGHT WITH YOU
Colour
BMG-RCA 74321 10660-3/6
Lightyear Entertainment
72259-72196-3

1968
ELVIS '68 COMEBACK SPECIAL
Colour
BMG-RCA 74321 10662-3/6
Lightyear Entertainment
72259-72198-3

1973
ELVIS – ALOHA FROM HAWAII
Colour, 'Thirty Of Elvis' Greatest Hits'
BMG-RCA 74321 10661-3/6
Lightyear Entertainment
72259-75197-3

Various dates
ELVIS – THE LOST PERFORMANCES
MGM-United Artists M 202759

Various dates
THIS IS ELVIS
Warner Bros 11173

Various dates

**ELVIS THE GREAT
PERFORMANCES – Vol I CENTER
STAGE**
Buena Vista 1032

Various dates
**ELVIS THE GREAT
PERFORMANCES – Vol II THE
MAN AND THE MUSIC**
Buena Vista 1033

II

Select discography

With the considerable amount of recouplings, reissues and custom packages of many of the Presley recordings, it is not possible to provide a fully detailed discography. Those who wish to pursue this subject are referred initially to *Elvis Sessions: The Recorded Music Of Elvis Aron Presley (1953–1977)* by Joseph A. Tunzi, published in Chicago by JAT Productions in 1993, which is by far the most complete and reliable listing of every recording Presley is known to have made.

The selected discography that follows lists only long-playing records and compact discs. Singles, EPs and tape formats are not included. Broadly speaking, the albums are listed in chronological order of issue, not necessarily of recording. Because they first saw the light of day on vinyl, and many were recorded with the long-playing record format in mind, the discography is led by the long-playing (LP) issue. There are many instances where the compact disc (CD) equivalent is identical in content to the LP, but a compact disc can play for up to eighty minutes, significantly longer than an LP. As the discography reaches recent issues, we find more titles contained on CDs than on LPs. There are many Presley enthusiasts who still treasure their original LPs, and some who maintain that in the CD transfer something of the original is lost. For these reasons, also, the numbers after each album are as follows: first, the US LP number; second, the UK LP number; and last the CD number.

Such is the universal availability of product today that one CD number will be the same for each album throughout the world. At the beginning of Elvis Presley's RCA career, these recordings were issued in the UK by EMI on the HMV label; these early LP releases are not shown, as every one of the songs is now available in other forms on different albums. Although the albums are mainly listed in chronological order, I have not hesitated to adopt a different order where it proved more sensible to do so. Thus the album of virtually all of the Sun recordings is listed not in the year when it first appeared – 1976 – but at the head of the list.

Finally, there is a rough guide to the worth of each album: a record is awarded stars (maximum of three) according to its importance. Detailed comment can be found in the description of the sessions involved. When an album is listed without stars it is considered to be below the best standards although it may have the occasional good track.

Elvis Presley has been dead for almost twenty years as these words are written; there are few unreleased tracks that would add anything to our perception of his artistry, yet, as we have shown, his importance remains as great as ever: it is only right that his material should be made available to today's buyers in the formats of today. As a result, this means an ever-proliferating series of recouplings and reissues from RCA. We should welcome this, although such proliferation plays havoc with a discography; at all times, the intention here is to make it relatively easy for the interested listener to locate both the recording he or she wishes and the comments on it contained within Part II. It is to be hoped that by the judicious use of the Documentary Part IV, the reader will be clearly guided.

1   1954/55
THE SUN SESSIONS
That's All Right/Blue Moon Of Kentucky/I Don't Care If The Sun Don't Shine/Good Rockin' Tonight/Milkcow Blues Boogie/You're A Heartbreaker/I'm Left, You're Right, She's Gone/Baby, Let's Play House/Mystery Train/I Forgot To Remember To Forget/I'll Never Let You Go/I Love You Because/Trying To Get To You/Blue Moon/Just Because
     APM1-1675   HY 1001   CD: ND 89107   ★★★★★★★

2   1956
ROCK 'N' ROLL (original title: ELVIS PRESLEY)
Blue Suede Shoes/I'm Counting On You/I Got A Woman/One-Sided Love Affair/I Love You Because/Tutti Frutti/Trying To Get to You/I'm Gonna Sit Right Down And Cry/I'll Never Let You Go/Blue Moon/Money Honey
     LPM 1254   SF 8233   CD: ND 89046   ★★★★★★★

3   1956
ROCK 'N' ROLL No 2 (US title: ELVIS)
Rip It Up/Love Me/When My Blue Moon Turns To Gold Again/Long Tall Sally/First In Line/Paralyzed/So Glad You're Mine/Old Shep/Ready Teddy/Anyplace Is Paradise/How's The World Treating You/How Do You Think I Feel
     LPM 1283   SF 7528   CD: ND 81382   ***

4   1957
LOVING YOU
Mean Woman Blues/Teddy Bear/Loving You/Got A Lot O' Livin' To Do/Lonesome
Cowboy/Hot Dog/Party/Blueberry Hill/True Love/Don't Leave Me Now/Have I
Told You Lately That I Love You/I Need You So
    LPM 1515   PL 42358   CD: ND 81515   **

5   1957
ELVIS' CHRISTMAS ALBUM
Santa Claus Is Back In Town/White Christmas/Here Comes Santa Claus/I'll Be
Home For Christmas/Blue Christmas/Santa Bring My Baby Back To Me/O Little
Town of Bethlehem/Silent Night/Peace In The Valley/I Believe/Take My Hand,
Precious Lord/It's No Secret
    LOC 1035   RD 27052   CD: ND 90300   ***

6   **ELVIS' GOLDEN RECORDS (vol I)**
Hound Dog/Loving You/All Shook Up/Heartbreak Hotel/Jailhouse Rock/Love
Me/Too Much/Don't Be Cruel/That's When Your Heartaches Begin/Teddy
Bear/Love Me Tender/Treat Me Nice/Any Way You Want Me/I Want You, I Need
You, I Love You
    LPM 1707   RB 16069   CD: ND 81707   ***

7   1958
KING CREOLE
King Creole/As Long As I Have You/Hard Headed Woman/Dixieland Rock/Don't
Ask Me Why/Lover Doll/Young Dreams/Crawfish/Steadfast, Loyal And True/New
Orleans
    LPM 1884   RD 27088   CD: ND 83733   **

8   1959
FOR LP FANS ONLY/ELVIS
That's All Right/Lawdy, Miss Clawdy/Mystery Train/Playing For Keeps/Poor Boy/My
Baby Left Me/I Was The One/Shake, Rattle And Roll/I'm Left, You're Right, She's
Gone/You're A Heartbreaker
    LPM 1990   RD 27120   CD: ND 90359   ***

9   1959
A DATE WITH ELVIS
Blue Moon Of Kentucky/Young And Beautiful/Baby I Don't Care/Milkcow Blues
Boogie/Baby, Let's Play House/Good Rockin' Tonight/It Is So Strange/We're
Gonna Move/I Want To Be Free/I Forgot To Remember To Forget
    LPM 2011   RD 27128   CD: ND 90360   **

10 1959
ELVIS' GOLDEN RECORDS (vol II)
50,000,000 ELVIS FANS CAN'T BE WRONG
I Need Your Love Tonight/Don't/Wear My Ring Around Your Neck/My Wish Came
True/I Got Stung/One Night/A Big Hunk O' Love/I Beg Of You/A Fool Such As
I/Doncha Think it's Time

    LPM 2075   RD 27159   CD: ND 89429   ***

11 1960
ELVIS IS BACK
Make Me Know It/The Girl Of My Best Friend/I Will Be Home Again/Dirty, Dirty
Feeling/The Thrill Of Your Love/Soldier Boy/Such A Night/It Feels So Right/The
Girl Next Door/Like A Baby/Reconsider Baby

    LSP 2231   SF 5060   CD: ND 89013   ***

12 1960
G.I. BLUES
Tonight Is So Right for Love/What's She Really Like/Frankfurt Special/Wooden
Heart/G.I. Blues/Pocketful Of Rainbows/Shoppin' Around/Big Boots/Didja
Ever/Blue Suede Shoes/Doin' The Best I Can

    LSP 2256   SF 5078   CD: ND 83735   **

13 1961
HIS HAND IN MINE
His Hand In Mine/I'm Gonna Walk Dem Golden Stairs/In My Father's House/Milky
White Way/Known Only To Him/I Believe In The Man In The Sky/Joshua Fit The
Battle/Jesus Knows Just What I Need/Swing Down Sweet Chariot/Mansion Over
The Hilltop/If We Never Meet Again/Working On The Building

    LSP 2328   SF 5094   CD: ND 83935   ***

14 1961
SOMETHING FOR EVERYBODY
There's Always Me/Give Me The Right/It's A Sin/Sentimental Me/Starting
Today/Gently/I'm Comin' Home/In Your Arms/Put The Blame On Me/Judy/I Want
You With Me/I Slipped, I Stumbled, I Fell

    LSP 2370   SF 5106   CD: ND 84116

15 1961
BLUE HAWAII
Blue Hawaii/Slicin' Sand/Almost Always True/Aloha Oc/Can't Help Fallin' In
Love/Rock-A-Hula-Baby/Moonlight Swim/Ku-u-i-po/Ito Eats/Hawaiian
Sunset/Beach Boy Blues/Island Of Love/Hawaiian Wedding Song

    LSP 2426   SF 8145   CD: ND 83683   *

16 1962

POT LUCK

Kiss Me Quick/For Old Times' Sake/Gonna Get Back Home Somehow/Easy
Question/Steppin' Out Of Line/I'm Yours/Something Blue/Suspicion/I Feel That
I've Known You Forever/Night Rider/Fountain Of Love/That's Someone You
Never Forget

    LSP 2523   SF 5135   CD: ND 89098   **

17 1962

GIRLS! GIRLS! GIRLS!

Girls! Girls! Girls!/I Don't Wanna Be Tied/Where Do You Come From/I Don't
Want To/We'll Be Together/A Boy Like Me, A Girl Like You/Return To
Sender/Because Of Love/Thanks To The Rolling Sea/Song Of The Shrimp/The
Walls Have Ears/We're Coming In Loaded

    LSP 2621   SF 7534   CD: 74321 134302   *
                                            [Part: with three extra songs]

18 1963

IT HAPPENED AT THE WORLD'S FAIR

Beyond The Bend/Relax/Take Me To The Fair/They Remind Me Too Much Of
You/One Broken Heart For Sale/I'm Falling In Love Tonight/Cotton Candy Land/A
World Of Our Own/How Would You Like To Be/Happy Ending

    LSP 2697   SF 7675   CD: 74321 13412 [Part]

19 1963

ELVIS' GOLDEN RECORDS (vol III)

It's Now Or Never/Stuck On You/Fame And Fortune/I Gotta Know/Surrender/I
Feel So Bad/Are You Lonesome Tonight?/His Latest Flame/Little Sister/Good Luck
Charm/Anything That's Part Of You/She's Not You

    LSP 2765   SF 7630   CD: ND 82765   ***

20 1963

FUN IN ACAPULCO

Fun In Acapulco/Vino Dinero Y Amor/Mexico/El Toro/Marguerita/The Bullfighter
Was A Lady/No Room To Rhumba In A Sports Car/I Think I'm Gonna Like It
Here/Bossa Nova Baby/You Can't Say No In Acapulco/Guadalajara/Love Me
Tonight/Slowly But Surely

    LSP 2756   PL 42357   CD: 74321 13412 [Part]

21 1964

KISSIN' COUSINS

Kissin' Cousins No 2/Smokey Mountain Boy/There's Gold In The Mountains/One
Boy, Two Little Girls/Catchin' On Fast/Tender Feeling/Anyone/Barefoot

Ballad/Once Is Enough/Kissin' Cousins/Echoes Of Love/Long Lonely Highway
    LSP 2894   PL 42355   CD: 0788366362 [Part]

22 1964
ROUSTABOUT
Roustabout/Little Egypt/Poison Ivy League/Hard Knocks/It's A Wonderful
World/Big Love, Big Heartache/One Track Heart/It's Carnival Time/Carny
Town/There's A Brand New Day On The Horizon/Wheels On My Heels
    LSP 2999   PL 42356   CD: 74321 134322 [Part]

23 1965
GIRL HAPPY
Girl Happy/Spring Fever/Fort Lauderdale Chamber Of Commerce/Starting'
Tonight/Wolf Call/Do Not Disturb/Cross My Heart And Hope To Die/The Meanest
Girl In Town/Do The Clam/Puppet On A String/I've Got To Find My Baby/You'll
Be Gone
    LSP 3338   SF 7714   CD 74321 134332 [Part]

24 1965
ELVIS FOR EVERYONE
Your Cheatin' Heart/Summer Kisses, Winter Tears/Finders Keepers Losers
Weepers/In My Way/Tomorrow Night/Memphis Tennessee/For The Millionth And
Last Time/Forget Me Never/Sound Advice/Santa Lucia/I Met Her Today/When It
Rains It Really Pours
    LSP 3450   SF 7752   CD [NYA]

25 1965
HARUM SCARUM/HAREM HOLIDAY
Harem Holiday/My Desert Serenade/Go East Young Man/Mirage/Kismet/Shake
That Tambourine/Hey Little Girl/Golden Coins/So Close Yet So Far/Animal
Instinct/Wisdom Of The Ages
    LSP 2468   SF 7767   CD: 74321 134332

26 1966
FRANKIE AND JOHNNY
Frankie And Johnny/Come Along/Petunia The Gardener's Daughter/Chesay/What
Every Woman Lives For/Look Out Broadway/Beginner's Luck/Down By The
Riverside/When The Saints Go Marching In/Shout It Out/Hard Luck/Please Don't
Stop Loving Me/Everybody Come Aboard
    LSP 3553   SF 7793   CD: 07863 663602 [Part]

27 1966
PARADISE HAWAIIAN STYLE
Paradise Hawaiian Style/Queenie Wahine's Papaya/Scratch My Back/Drums Of
The Island/Darin'/A Dog's Life/House Of Sand/Stop Where You Are/This Is My
Heaven/Sand Castles

    LSP 3643   SF 7810   CD: 07863 663602 [Part]

28 1966
SPINOUT (UK title: CALIFORNIA HOLIDAY)
Stop Look And Listen/Adam And Evil/All That I Am/Never Say Yes/Am I
Ready/Beach Shack/Spinout/Smorgasbord/I'll Be Back/Down In The
Alley/Tomorrow Is A Long Time

    LSP 3702   SF 7820   CD: 07863 663612

29 **HOW GREAT THOU ART**
How Great Thou Art/In The Garden/Somebody Bigger Than You Or I/Farther
Along/Stand By Me/Without Him/So High/Where Could I Go But To The
Lord?/By And By/If The Lord Wasn't Walking By My Side/Run On/Where No One
Stands Alone/Crying In The Chapel

    LSP 3758   SF 8206   CD: ND 83758   ***

30 1967
DOUBLE TROUBLE
Double Trouble/Baby If You'll Give Me All Your Love/Could I Fall In Love/Long
Legged Girl/City By Night/Old MacDonald/I Love Only One Girl/There's So Much
World To See/It Won't Be Long/Never Ending/Blue River/What Now, Where Next,
Where To?

    LSP 3787   SF 7892   CD: 07863 663612

31 1967
CLAMBAKE
Guitar Man/Clambake/Who Needs Money/A House That Has
Everything/Confidence/Hey, Hey, Hey/You Don't Know Me/The Girl I Never
Loved/How Can You Lose What You Never Had/Big Boss Man/Singing Tree/Just
Call Me Lonesome

    LSP 3893   SF 7917   CD: 07863 663622 [Part]

32 1968
ELVIS GOLD RECORDS (vol IV)
Love Letters/Witchcraft/It Hurts Me/What'd I Say/Please Don't Drag That String
Around/Indescribably Blue/Devil In Disguise/Lonely Man/A Mess Of Blues/Ask
Me/Ain't That Loving You Baby/Just Tell Her Jim Said Hello

    LSP 3921   SF 7924   CD: ND 83921   **

221

33 1968
SPEEDWAY
Speedway/There Ain't Nothing Like A Song/Your Time Hasn't Come Yet
Baby/Who Are You/He's Your Uncle, Not Your Dad/Let Yourself Go/Your Groovy
Self (Sung by Nancy Sinatra/Five Sleepy Heads/Western Union/Mine/Goin'
Home/Suppose

    LSP 3989   SF 7957   CD: 07863 [NYA, Part]

34 1968
ELVIS SINGS FLAMING STAR
Flaming Star/Wonderful World/Night Life/All I Needed Was The Rain/Too Much
Monkey Business/Yellow Rose Of Texas/The Eyes Of Texas/She's A Machine/Do
The Vega/Tiger Man

    CAS 2304   INTS 1021   CD: 07863 [NYA, Part]   *

35 1968
ELVIS NBC TV SPECIAL
Trouble/Guitar Man/Lawdy, Miss Clawdy/Baby What Do You Want Me To
Do/Heartbreak Hotel/Hound Dog/All Shook Up/Can't Help Falling In
Love/Jailhouse Rock/Love Me Tender/Where Could I Go But To The Lord?/Up
Above My Head/Saved/Blue Christmas/One Night/Memories/Nothingville/Big
Boss Man/Guitar Man/Little Egypt/Trouble/If I Can Dream

    LPM 4088   RD 8011   CD: ND 83894

36 1969
FROM ELVIS IN MEMPHIS
Wearing That Loved On Look/Only The Strong Survive/I'll Hold You In My
Heart/Long Black Limousine/It Keeps Right on A-Hurtin'/I'm Moving On/Power
Of My Love/Gentle On My Mind/After Loving You/True Love Travels On A Gravel
Road/Any Day Now/In The Ghetto

    LSP 4155   SF 8029   CD: ND 90548   ***

37 1969
FROM MEMPHIS TO VEGAS – FROM VEGAS TO MEMPHIS
Record 1: Blue Suede Shoes/Johnny B. Goode/All Shook Up/Are You Lonesome
Tonight?/Hound Dog/I Can't Stop Loving You/My Babe/Mystery Train/Tiger
Man/Words/In The Ghetto/Suspicious Minds/Can't Help Falling In Love
Record 2: Inherit The Wind/This Is The Story/Stranger In My Own Home Town/A
Little Bit Of Green/And The Grass Won't Pay No Mind/Do You Know Who I
Am?/From A Jack to A King/The Fair's Moving On/You'll Think Of Me/Without
Love

    LSP 6020   SF 8080/1   CD: Record 2 only,   **
                                                  Back In Memphis, ND 90599

38 1970
LET'S BE FRIENDS
Stay Away Joe/If I'm A Fool/Let's Be Friends/Let's Forget About The
Stars/Mama/I'll Be There/Almost/Change Of Habit/Have A Happy
    CAS 2408   INTS 1103   *

39 1970
ON STAGE
See See Rider/Release Me/Sweet Caroline/Runaway/The Wonder Of You/Polk
Salad Annie/Yesterday/Proud Mary/Walk A Mile In My Shoes/Let It Be Me
    LSP 4362   SF 8128   CD: ND 90549   *

40 1970
ALMOST IN LOVE
Almost In Love/Long Legged Girl/Edge Of Reality/My Little Friend/A Little Less
Conversation/Rubberneckin'/Clean Up Your Own Backyard/US Male/Charro/Stay
Away Joe
    CAS 2440   INTS 1206   *

41 1970
ELVIS' CHRISTMAS ALBUM
Blue Christmas/Silent Night/White Christmas/Santa Claus Is Back In Town/I'll Be
Home For Christmas/If Every Day Was Like Christmas/Here Comes Santa
Claus/O Little Town Of Bethlehem/Santa Bring My Baby Back/Mama Liked The
Roses
    CAL 2428   INTS 1126   **

42 1970
THAT'S THE WAY IT IS
I Just Can't Help Believing/Twenty Days And Twenty Nights/How The Web Was
Woven/Patch It Up/Mary In The Morning/You Don't Have To Say You Love
Me/You've Lost That Loving Feeling/I've Lost You/Just Pretend/Stranger In The
Crowd/The Next Step Is Love/Bridge Over Troubled Water
    LSP 4445   SF 8162   *

43 1971
ELVIS COUNTRY
Snowbird/Tomorrow Never Comes/Little Cabin On The Hill/Whole Lotta Shakin'
Goin' On/Funny How Time Slips Away/I Really Don't Want To Know/There Goes
My Everything/It's Your Baby, You Rock It/The Fool/Faded Love/I Washed My
Hands In Muddy Water/Make The World Go Away
    LSP 4460   SF 8172   CD: 74321 146922   **

44 1971
YOU'LL NEVER WALK ALONE
You'll Never Walk Alone/Who Am I/Let Us Pray/Peace In The Valley/We Call On
Him/I Believe/It Is No Secret/Sing You Children/Take My Hand Precious Lord
> CAL 2472   INTS 1286   *

45 1971
LOVE LETTERS FROM ELVIS
Love Letters/When I'm Over You/If I Were You/Got My Mojo Working/Heart Of
Rome/Only Believe/This Is Our Dance/Cindy Cindy/I'll Never Know/It Ain't No
Big Thing (But It's Growing)/Life
> LSP 4530   SF 8202   CD: ND 89011   **

46 1971
C'MON EVERYBODY
C'mon Everybody/Angel/Easy Come, Easy Go/A Whistling Tune/Follow That
Dream/King Of The Whole Wide World/I'll Take Love/I'm Not The Marrying
Kind/This Is Living/Today, Tomorrow And Forever
> CAL 2518   INTS 1286   *

47 1971
ELVIS SINGS THE WONDERFUL WORLD OF CHRISTMAS
O Come All Ye Faithful/The First Noel/On A Snowy Christmas Night/Winter
Wonderland/The Wonderful World Of Christmas/It Won't Seem Like
Christmas/I'll Be Home On Christmas Day/If I Get Home On Christmas
Day/Holly Leaves And Christmas Trees/Merry Christmas Baby/Silver Bells
> LSP 4579   SF 8221   CD: ND 81936   **

48 1972
ELVIS NOW
Help Me Make It Through The Night/Miracle Of The Rosary/Hey Jude/Put Your
Hand In The Hand/Until It's Time For You To Go/We Can Make The
Morning/Early Morning Rain/Sylvia/Fools Rush In/I Was Born About 10,000 Years
Ago
> SLP 4671   SF 8266   CD: 74321 14831   **

49 1972
HE TOUCHED ME
He Touched Me/I've Got Confidence/Amazing Grace/Seeing Is Believing/He Is
My Everything/Bosom Of Abraham/An Evening Prayer/Lead Me, Guide Me/There
Is No God But God/A Thing Called Love/I John/Reach Out To Jesus
> LSP 4690   SF 8275   CD: ND 90611   **

50 1972
ELVIS AS RECORDED AT MADISON SQUARE GARDEN
Also Sprach Zarathustra/That's All Right/Proud Mary/Never Been To Spain/You
Don't Have To Say You Love Me/You've Lost That Loving Feeling/Polk Salad
Annie/Love Me/All Shook Up/Heartbreak Hotel/Teddy Bear/Don't Be Cruel/Love
Me Tender/The Impossible Dream/Hound Dog/Suspicious Minds/For The Good
Times/American Trilogy/Funny How Time Slips Away/Can't Stop Loving You/Can't
Help Falling In Love

    LSP 4776   SF 8296   CD: ND 90633   *

51 1972
BURNING LOVE AND HITS FROM HIS MOVIES
Burning Love/Tender Feeling/Am I Ready?/Tonight Is So Right For
Love/Guadalajara/It's A Matter Of Time/No More/Santa Lucia/We'll Be Together/I
Love Only One Girl

    CAS 2595   INTS 1414   *

52 1973
ALOHA FROM HAWAII VIA SATELLITE
Also Sprach Zarathustra/See See Rider/Burning Love/Something/You Gave Me A
Mountain/Steamroller Blues/My Way/Love Me/Johnny B. Goode/It's Over/Blue
Suede Shoes/I'm So Lonesome I Could Cry/I Can't Stop Loving You/Hound
Dog/What Now My Love?/Fever/Welcome To My World/Suspicious Minds/I'll
Remember You/Long Tall Sally/Whole Lotta Shakin' Goin' On/American Trilogy/A
Big Hunk O' Love/Can't Help Falling In Love

    VPSX 6089   DPS 2040   CD: PD 82642   *

53 1973
ELVIS
Fool/Where Do I Go From Here/Love Me Love/The Life I Lead/It's Still Here/It's
Impossible/For Loving' Me/Padre/I'll Take You Home Again Kathleen/I Will Be
True/Don't Think Twice, It's All Right

    APL1 0283   SF 8378   CD: 07863 502832   *

54 1973
RAISED ON ROCK
Raised On Rock/Are You Sincere?/Find Out What's Happening/I Miss You/Girl Of
Mine/For Old Times' Sake/If You Don't Come Back/Just A Little Bit/Sweet
Angeline/Three Corn Patches

    APL1 0388   APL1 0388   CD: 07863 503882   **

55 1974
ELVIS A LEGENDARY PERFORMER (vol 1)
That's All Right/I Love You Because/Heartbreak Hotel/Love Me/Trying To Get To
You/Love Me Tender/Peace In The Valley/A Fool Such As I/Tonight's All Right for
Love/Are You Lonesome Tonight?/Can't Help Falling In Love
    CPL1 0341   CPL 0341   **

56 1974
GOOD TIMES
Take Good Care Of Her/Loving Arms/I Got A Feeling In My Body/If That Isn't
Love/She Wears My Ring/I've Got A Thing About You Baby/My Boy/Spanish
Eyes/Talk About The Good Times/Good Time Charlie's Got The Blues
    CPL 0475   APL1 0475   CD: 07863 504752   *

57 1974
ELVIS AS RECORDED LIVE ON STAGE IN MEMPHIS
See See Rider/I Got A Woman/Love Me/Trying To Get To You/Long Tall
Sally/Whole Lotta Shakin' Goin' On/Mama Don't Dance/Flip Flop And
Fly/Jailhouse Rock/Hound Dog/Why Me Lord?/How Great Thou Art/Blueberry
Hill/I Can't Stop Loving You/Help Me/American Trilogy/Let Me Be There/My Baby
Left Me/Lawdy, Miss Clawdy/Can't Help Falling In Love
    APL1 0606   APL1 0606   CD: 07863 506062

58 1974
PROMISED LAND
There's A Honky-Tonk Angel/Help Me/Mr Songman/Love Song Of The Year/It's
Midnight/Your Love's Been A Long Time Coming/If You Talk In Your
Sleep/Thinking About You/You Ask Me To
    APL1 0873   APL1 0873   CD: ND 90598   **

59 1975
TODAY T-R-O-U-B-L-E
And I Love You So/Susan When She Tried/Woman Without Love/Shake A
Hand/Pieces Of My Life/Fairytale/I Can Help/Bringin' It Back/Green, Green Grass
Of Home
    APL1 1039   APL1 1039   CD: 90660   **

60 1976
ELVIS A LEGENDARY PERFORMER (vol 2)
Harbor Lights/I Want You, I Need You, I Love You/Blue Suede Shoes/Blue
Christmas/Jailhouse Rock/It's Now Or Never/A Cane And A High-Starched
Collar/Blue Hawaii/Such A Night/Baby What You Want Me To Do/How Great
Thou Art/If I Can Dream

CPL1 1349   CPL1 1349   ***

61 1976
FROM ELVIS PRESLEY BOULEVARD, MEMPHIS, TENNESSEE
Hurt/Never Again/Blue Eyes Crying In The Rain/Danny Boy/The Last Farewell/For
The Heart/Bitter They Are, Harder They Fall/Solitaire/Love Coming Down/I'll
Never Fall In Love Again
APL1 1506   APL1 1506   CD: 74321 146912   **

62 1977
WELCOME TO MY WORLD
Welcome To My World/Help Me Make It Through The Night/Release Me/I Really
Don't Want To Know/For The Good Times/Make The World Go Away/Gentle On My
Mind/I'm So Lonesome I Could Cry/Your Cheatin' Heart/I Can't Stop Loving You
APL1 2274   PL 12774   *

63 1977
ELVIS IN DEMAND
Suspicion/High Heel Sneakers/Got A Lot O' Livin' To Do/Have I Told You Lately
That I Love You?/Please Don't Drag That String Around/It's Only Love/The
Sound Of Your Cry/Viva Las Vegas/Do Not Disturb/Tomorrow Is A Long Time/It's
A Long Lonely Highway/Puppet On A String/The First Time Ever I Saw Your
Face/Summer Kisses, Winter Tears/It Hurts Me (without Jordanaires)/Let It Be
Me
PL 42003   ***

64 1977
MOODY BLUE
Unchained Melody/If You Love Me (Let Me Know)/Little Darlin'/He'll Have To
Go/Let Me Be There/Way Down/Pledging My Love/Moody Blue/She Thinks I Still
Care
APL1 3021   PL 13021   CD: ND 90252   **

65 1977
ELVIS IN CONCERT
Also Sprach Zarathustra/See See Rider/That's All Right/Are You Lonesome
Tonight?/Teddy Bear/Don't Be Cruel/You Gave Me A Mountain/Jailhouse
Rock/How Great Thou Art/I Really Don't Want To Know/Hurt/Hound Dog/My
Way/Cant Help Falling In Love/I Got A Woman/Amen/Love Me/If You Love Me/O
Sole Mio (sung by Sherill Nielsen)/It's Now Or Never/Trying To Get To
You/Hawaiian Wedding Song/Fairytale/Little Sister/Early Morning Rain/What'd I
Say/Johnny B. Goode/And I Love You So
APL2 2587   PL 02587 (23)   CD: 74321 146932   **

66 1978
ELVIS A LEGENDARY PERFORMER (vol 3)
Hound Dog/Interview With Elvis And Col Parker/Danny/Fame And
Fortune/Frankfort Special/Britches/Crying In The Chapel/Surrender/Guadalajara/
It Hurts Me/Let Yourself Go/In The Ghetto/Let It Be Me
    CPL 1-3078 [Picture disc]/CPL 1-3082 PL 13082   **

67 1978
HE WALKS BESIDE ME
He Is My Everything/Miracle Of The Rosary/Where Did They Go,
Lord?/Somebody Bigger Than You Or I/An Evening Prayer/The Impossible Dream
(The Quest) [unreleased live version[/If I Can Dream [unreleased
version]/Padre/Known Only To Him/Who Am I?/How Great Thou Art
    AFL1 2772   PL 12772   **

68 1979
OUR MEMORIES OF ELVIS
Are You Sincere?/It's Midnight/My Boy/Girl Of Mine/Take Good Care Of Her/I'll
Never Fall In Love Again/Your Love's Been A Long Time Coming/Spanish
Eyes/Never Again/She Thinks I Still Care/Solitaire
NB These performances are without later overdubbings by backing vocalists
    AQL1 3279   PL 13279   **

69 1979
OUR MEMORIES OF ELVIS (vol 2)
Got A Feeling In My Body/Green, Green Grass Of Home/For The Heart/She
Wears My Ring/I Can Help/Way Down/There's A Honky-Tonk Angel/Find Out
What's Happening/Thinking About You/Don't Think Twice, It's All Right
    AQL 1-3448   PL 13448   **

Following Elvis's death, RCA's releases of his recordings were almost invariably
made up of recouplings of existing product, sometimes grouped generically to
make a more coherent album. The remaining listings in the select discography
are concerned with the more important of such issues, especially those
containing previously unavailable material.

70 1980
ELVIS ARON PRESLEY
Eight-record box set, containing almost 90 tracks, grouped generically as follows:
An Early Live Performance/Elvis Monologue/An Early Benefit Performance/
Collectors' Gold From The Movie Years/The TV Specials/The Las Vegas Years/Lost
Singles/Elvis At The Piano/The Concert Years [Part 1 and Concluded]
    CPL8-3699   PL 83699   ***

71 1981
THIS IS ELVIS – ORIGINAL SOUNDTRACK
His Latest Flame/Moody Blue/That's All Right/Shake, Rattle And Roll/Flip, Flop
And Fly/Heartbreak Hotel/Hound Dog/Hy Gardner Interview/My Baby Left
Me/Merry Christmas Baby/Mean Woman Blues/Don't Be Cruel/(Let Me Be Your)
Teddy Bear/Jailhouse Rock/Army Swearing-in/G.I. Blues/Departure For Germany
And Return Home – Press Conferences/Too Much Monkey Business/Love Me
Tender/I Got A Thing About You Baby/I Need Your Love Tonight/Blue Suede
Shoes/Viva Las Vegas/Suspicious Minds/JC's Award To Elvis/Promised
Land/Madison Square Garden Press Conference/Are You Lonesome Tonight?/My
Way/An American Trilogy/Memories
    CPL2 5029   PL 25829   ***
[NYA] indicates that the CD release has been announced but the catalogue
number is not yet available

72 1983
ELVIS A LEGENDARY PERFORMER (vol 4)
When It Rains, It Really Pours/Interview From Tampa 1956/One Night/I'm
Beginning To Forget You/Mona Lisa/Wooden Heart/Plantation Rock/The Lady
Loves Me/Swing Down Sweet Chariot/That's All Right/Are You Lonesome
Tonight?/Reconsider Baby/I'll Remember You
    CPL1-4848   PL 14848   **

73 1983
ELVIS: THE FIRST LIVE RECORDINGS
Introductions, Elvis And Horace Logan/Baby Let's Play House/Maybelline/
Tweedle Dee/That's All Right/Recollections By Frank Page/Hound Dog
    JEM Records PB-3601   *

74 1983
ELVIS: THE HILLBILLY CAT
Introduction/Elvis With Horace Logan/That's All Right/Elvis Talks About His
Musical Style/Blue Moon Of Kentucky/Recollections By Frank Page/Good Rockin'
Tonight/I Got A Woman
    JEM PB-3602   *

75 1984
A GOLDEN CELEBRATION
Six-record box set: The Sun Sessions Out-takes/The Dorsey Brothers Stage
Show/The Milton Berle Show/The Steve Allen Show/The Mississippi–Alabama
Farm And Dairy Show/The Ed Sullivan Show/Elvis At Home/Collectors'
Treasures/Elvis
    CPM6-5172   ***

76 1987
THE COMPLETE SUN SESSIONS
Containing all of The Master Takes (see album 1 in this listing) together with extant out-takes and other alternate takes of the songs

    6414-1-R [Double LP set]   CD: PD 86414   ***

77 1988
ESSENTIAL ELVIS, THE FIRST MOVIES
Containing more than one performance of most of the following:
Love Me Tender/Let Me/Poor Boy/We're Gonna Move/Loving You/Party/Hot Dog/Teddy Bear/Mean Woman Blues/Got A Lot O' Livin' To Do/Lonesome Cowboy/Jailhouse Rock/Treat Me Nice/Young And Beautiful/Don't Leave Me Now/I Want To Be Free/Baby I Don't Care

    6738-1-R   CD: PD 89980   **

78 1988
STEREO '57 ESSENTIAL ELVIS (vol 2)
Containing more than one performance of most of the following:
I Beg Of You/Is It So Strange/Have I Told You Lately That I Love You?/It Is No Secret/Blueberry Hill/Mean Woman Blues/Peace In The Valley/That's When Your Heartaches Begin/I Believe/Tell Me Why/All Shook Up/Take My Hand, Precious Lord

    9589-1-R   CD: PD 90250   **

All further listings are of compact discs.

79 1990
THE MILLION DOLLAR QUARTET
You Belong To My Hear/When God Dips His Love In My Heart/Just A Little Talk With Jesus/Jesus Walked That Lonesome Valley/I Shall Not Be Moved/Peace In The Valley/Down By The Riverside/I'm With A Crowd But So Alone/Farther Along/Blessed Jesus/As We Travel Along The Jericho Road/I Just Can't Make It By Myself/Little Cabin Home On The Hill/Summertime Is Past And Gone/I Hear A Sweet Voice Calling/Sweetheart You Done Me Wrong/Keeper Of The Key/Crazy Arms/Don't Forbid Me/Too Much Monkey Business/Brown Eyed Handsome Man/Out Of Sight, Out Of Mind/Don't Be Cruel/Paralyzed/There's No Place Like Home/When The Saints Go Marching In/Softly And Tenderly/Is It So Strange/Rip It Up/I'm Gonna Bid My Blues Goodbye/That's My Desire/End Of The Road/Black Bottom Stomp/You're The Only Star In My Blue Heaven

    2023-1-R 74321 138402   ***

80 1991
THE LOST ALBUM/FOR THE ASKING
Long Lonely Highway/Western Union/Love Me Tonight/What Now, What Next,

230

Where To?/Please Don't Drag That String Around/Blue River/Never Ending/Devil In Disguise/Finders Keepers, Losers Weepers/Echoes Of Love/Slowly But Surely/It Hurts Me/Memphis, Tennessee/Ask Me
    61024-2 ND 90513   **

81 1991
COLLECTORS GOLD
Three-album box set: Vol 1 – *Hollywood*: 18 songs from the movies, Vol 2 – *Nashville*: 15 songs, Vol 3 – *Live In Las Vegas*: 18 songs [including alternate takes]
    3114-2-R PD 90574   **

82 1991
ELVIS PRESLEY NBC TV SPECIAL
This CD contains eight more tracks than was issued on the original vinyl release; the recording quality has not been significantly improved
    61021-2   *(*)

83 1992
THE KING OF ROCK 'N' ROLL – THE COMPLETE 50s MASTERS
140 songs, some with alternate versions; digitally remastered
    66050-2 PD 90698   ***

84 1993
FROM NASHVILLE TO MEMPHIS – THE ESSENTIAL 60s MASTERS I
130 songs, some with alternate versions; digitally remastered
    74321 15430   ***

Miscellaneous albums
The following albums are listed for those who may be interested.

1 ELVIS SAILS
Press Interviews With Presley/Newsreel Interview/Interview On Board USS *General Randall* By Pat Hernon
    45 rpm RCX 131   (7 inch)

2 HAVING FUN ON STAGE WITH ELVIS
Various spoken comments by Elvis Presley on stage, introducing songs and linking narratives
    APM 1 0818 APM 10818   (12 inch – 30 cm – 33^1/₃ rpm)

3 ELVIS TAPES
Press conference 1957
    Ace – not RCA/BMG – RED 1   (12 inch – 30 cm – 33^1/₃ rpm)

III

A chronology

The following chronology lists the important events in Presley's personal and professional life insofar as they relate to the subjects covered in this book. It should be remembered that the purpose of this chronology is merely to provide a quick and easy reference guide to these main events. It makes no claim to completeness and does not, for example, list every live appearance or series of engagements. Recording sessions are shown here, but for a complete list of the titles recorded at each session, readers are referred to the relevant entry in Part II of this book.

Occasionally, however, important songs (especially in the early part of Presley's recording career) are shown, and also – where it is considered important – the number of songs recorded during a session, which could of course be spread over a number of days.

Perhaps the most interesting observations one can make with regard to the recording sessions is the change in making records then compared with today. In this field, the most significant recent development has to be the rise of the producer. In Presley's heyday, the producer of a recording quite simply did not exist. He was not credited on the album cover, and his tasks were confined (if indeed he was considered as 'producer' at all) to ensuring that the sessions ran with as little fuss, and in as artistically a conducive environment, as possible, and keeping a watchful eye on the recording engineer (again, a title which was virtually unknown in those days: 'recording engineer' effectively meant the person who operated the tape machine and noted the takes on the tape box and pad). The 'producer' in the 1950s and 1960s would hardly ever suggest a creative addition to the performance being recorded.

233

In addition, artists – especially Presley – would come to the studio with a very clear idea of what it was they wanted to record, and perform in front of the microphones (more often than not, without headphones). In this way the song would probably be recorded in several complete takes, with the absolute minimum of editing, and the best take would be released. Through this simple manner a great deal of recording could be accomplished within a short space of time, certainly by today's standards.

Towards the end of his life, of course, Presley would avail himself of the greater creative freedom brought about by recent technological advances, and overdub to previously laid-down tracks. But there are those who feel today that the role of the producer of a pop or rock album – as in the opera house – has got too much in the way of the music he is there to ensure is realised in the best possible way with the least amount of fuss.

Another observation is the absence of international travelling. Although Presley had an early fear of flying (when one considers the aircraft of the early 1950s, that is not altogether surprising), later in life he thought nothing of travelling anywhere by plane. But it is an unusual facet of his life that he could remain the giant world figure he was without travelling, or appearing on transcontinental television music or chat shows. Perhaps in these two areas – that of the record producer and international communication – younger hopefuls can take comfort from the undoubted fact that it is not necessary to indulge in either of these things in order to be a success.

The reader should bear in mind, in scanning this chronology, that the more salacious details of Presley's life are not to be found. In the first place, they do him – and those involved – no good; nor do I think we are enhanced by having them listed as if in some kind of directory. More importantly, they add noting to our appreciation of his unique musical genius.

Finally, the reader should not use this chronology as a substitute for the short biographical chapters in Part I. In the introduction, I stated my belief that it is only when the broad biographical details of an artist's life have been grasped can the artistic side of his work be more properly put into perspective. This chronology lists the barest of bare bones, and is therefore a quick reminder of events, rather than detailing the background and substance of those events already been covered in the opening chapters.

The figures in brackets after the year indicates Elvis Presley's age at the time.

1933

17 June: Vernon Presley (17) marries Gladys Smith (21), Pontotoc, Mississippi. They move back to East Tupelo, where they met.

1935

8 January: Birth of Elvis Aron Presley and Jesse Garon Presley, twin boys to Gladys and Vernon, at East Tupelo. Jesse Garon does not survive and is buried the following day.

1937 (2)

November: Vernon Presley charged with forgery with two other men.

1938 (3)

May: Vernon Presley pleads guilty; sentenced to three year's imprisonment.

1939 (4)

3 September: Outbreak of World War II in Europe.

1940 (5)

Elvis and mother now regular church-goers.

1941 (6)

4 June: Vernon Presley released from prison.

7 December: Japan attacks Pearl Harbor, Hawaii. USA enters World War II, subsequently introduces compulsory military service. Vernon Presley, otherwise liable, is exempted owing to his prison record.

1945 (10)

Birth of Priscilla Wagner, later adopted as Priscilla Beaulieu following her mother's remarriage after death of husband (Priscilla's father).

1946 (11)

Presley family moves to Tupelo.

1948 (13)

Presley family moves to Memphis, Tennessee, the city of their permanent residence thereafter. Elvis sees the television for the first time. He enrols in L.C. Humes High School.

1949 (14)

Summer: Presley family moves into federal-funded apartment on Lauderdale Courts, Memphis.

1950 (15)

Early: Elvis makes first public appearance as singer, Memphis Veterans' Hospital.

November: Elvis obtains job at Loew's State Theater, Memphis; leaves after few weeks.

1951 (16)

Early: Elvis returns to Loew's; leaves again shortly afterwards following a fight. Becomes night-shift worker at Marl Metal Products Company; leaves as irregular sleeping hours have deleterious affect on schooling.

1952 (17)

Christmas: Elvis appears in school variety concert to remarkable ovation from fellow pupils.

1953 (18)

Summer: Graduates from L.C. Humes High School. Elvis obtains first job with Precision Tool Company; soon replaced by second job as truck driver with Crown Electric Company. Secretly makes first recording (for a few dollars, paid by himself) at Sun Studios, Memphis as present for his mother's birthday. Voice impresses Sun secretary Marion Keisker.

1954 (19)

4 January: Records two more songs (also self-financed) at Sun, probably as birthday present for himself (8 January). Sam Phillips, owner of Sun Records, recognises Elvis's talent, begins to seek suitable material for him to record commercially.

6 July: First commercial recording sessions – Sun Studios, Memphis.

8 July: First broadcast of a Presley recording (acetate cut of 'That's All Right, Mama') by Dewey Phillips on station WHBQ, Memphis. Astonishing public reaction to broadcast: station is swamped by calls; Elvis is fetched from cinema to broadcast live interview that evening.

18 July: First Elvis Presley record goes on sale.

31 July: Record reaches number three in Memphis Country Music Chart.

**August/
September:** Live appearances in Nashville and Shreveport; first live broadcasts.

September: Second 'Sun' sessions.

December: Third 'Sun' sessions.

1955 (20)

January: Second single issued, also reaches number three in Memphis Charts.

**January/
February:** Fourth 'Sun' sessions.

1 May: Begins first tour, 'Hank Snow Jamboree', promoted by Col Tom Parker. On seeing public reaction to Presley during tour, Col Parker soon becomes Presley's manager exclusively thereafter.

3 July: Fifth (and final) 'Sun' sessions. Signs exclusive recording contract with RCA, who also purchase all 'Sun' tapes.

1956 (21)

10/11 January: First RCA recording sessions, Nashville, Tennessee. Includes 'Heartbreak Hotel'.

End January: Release of first RCA Presley single ('Heartbreak Hotel'); becomes biggest-selling record in USA within weeks.

**30/31 January;
1 February:** Recording sessions, RCA studios, New York City. Includes 'Blue Suede Shoes'. Appears on 'Tommy and Jimmy Dorsey Stage Show' – first networked TV appearance.

11 April: Recording sessions, RCA studios, Nashville.

May/June: Screen tests, Hollywood.

6 June: Appears on Milton Berle's TV show: seen by over 40 million viewers.

2 July: Recording sessions, RCA studio, New York City. Includes 'Hound Dog'.

July: Appears for the first time on *Ed Sullivan Show*, CBS TV, New

York City (following appearance on *Steve Allen Show*, and after Sullivan declares Prelsey would never appear on his programmes); attracts 54 million viewers (highest viewing audience for any TV programme up to that time, not exceeded for eight years).

August/
September: Makes first feature film, *Love Me Tender*', Hollywood. Records songs for film.

1–3
September: Recording sessions, Radio Recorders Studios, Hollywood. Thirteen songs recorded. Buys ranch south of Memphis, and three cars.

October: Reappears on *Ed Sullivan Show*.

15 November: 'Love Me Tender' simultaneously released at 550 cinemas in USA.

December: Makes second film, *Loving You*'.

1957 (22)

6 January: Appears on *Ed Sullivan Show*.

12/13 January; 19 January; 23/24
February: Recording sessions, Radio Recorders Studios, Hollywood.

February/
March: Begins recording songs for second film, *Loving You*, Radio Recorders Studios, Hollywood.

March: Completes recording songs for second film, MGM Studios, Hollywood.

May: Makes third film, *Jailhouse Rock*.

9 July: Second film, *Loving You,* is released.

239

Summer: Buys large house, Graceland, in Whitehaven, a Memphis suburb.

5–7 September: Recording sessions, Radio Recorders Studios, Hollywood. First album of Christmas songs.

September: Returns to Tupelo for charity concert. Flies to Hawaii for concerts – first trip outside mainland America.

21 October: Third film, *Jailhouse Rock,* released. Received Draft papers for compulsory Army two-year service.

1958 (23)

January: Recording sessions, Radio Recorders Studios, Hollywood: songs for fourth film, *King Creole*.

20 January: Scheduled to appear before Memphis Draft Board, but granted deferment until 24 March in order to complete *King Creole* filming.

1 February: Recording sessions, Radio Recorders Studios, Hollywood. Last sessions prior to Army enlistment.

24 March: Inducted into US Army as Private Presley 53310761; begins basic training at Fort Chaffee, Arkansas. RCA splits with EMI (His Master's Voice) in UK, after association of over fifty years and sets up own label for first time in Britain and other European countries, initially under aegis of Decca Records.

May: Transfer to Fort Hood; family joins him after renting bungalow at nearly Killean.

4 June: Fourth film, *King Creole*, is released.

10/11 June: Recording sessions, RCA Studios, Nashville, on weekend leave from Army. (Elvis's only recordings during his Army service.)

July: Gladys Presley unwell, subsequently admitted to Methodist

Hospital, Memphis, suffering from suspected hepatitis.

11 August: Gladys's condition deteriorates; Elvis flies to Memphis.
14 August: Gladys Presley (46) dies of heart attack. Elvis is distraught.

September: Transfers to 3rd Armoured Division, prior to posting in West Germany.

26 September: Embarks Brooklyn Naval Yard, New York, USS *General Randall*. Sails to Bremerhaven, West Germany and is stationed at Freiburg.

October: Vernon, with his mother Minnie and two close friends of Elvis, travels to Germany. They rent house, living with Elvis near Army camp for duration of posting.

1959 (24)

January/
February: Vernon meets Mrs Dee Stanley.

Spring: Elvis takes karate lessons.

August: Elvis meets Capt Joseph Beaulieu and his fourteen year old adopted daughter Priscilla.

1960 (25)

1 March: Farewell party in Freiburg as Elvis prepares for discharge, organised by Capt Marion Keisker ('Sun' Studios Secretary in 1953/4, now in US Army).

2 March: Flight home from Germany refuels in Prestwick, Scotland. Elvis disembarks for one hour – his only time on British soil.

5 March: Discharged from US Army at Fort Dix, New Jersey. Train home to Memphis from New Jersey mobbed en route.

20/21 March: Recording sessions, RCA Studios, Nashville. First sessions for twenty-one months, six songs recorded.

3/4 April: Recording sessions, RCA Studios, Nashville. Twelve songs recorded.

April: Appears with Frank Sinatra on his TV show and sings duet with him; first appearance since Army discharge.

27/28 April: Recording sessions, RCA Studios, Hollywood.

6 May: Recording sessions, Radio Recorders Studios, Hollywood; songs for fifth film, *G.I. Blues*. This first post-Army film based on Elvis's Army service.

3 June: Vernon Presley and Dee Stanley married. Elvis does not attend ceremony.

July/August: Makes sixth film, *Flaming Star*.

8 August: Records songs for *Flaming Star*, Twentieth-Century Fox Studios, Hollywood.

October: Begins seventh film, *Wild In The Country*. Records songs for same, Twentieth-Century Fox Studios, Hollywood.

20 October: Fifth film, *G.I. Blues,* released. Great success world-wide.

20 December: Sixth film, *Flaming Star,* released; only two songs used (within first five minutes of start of film). Lack of singing, together with the film's dramatic story and treatment (in complete contrast to *G.I. Blues*, then still doing big business), leads to comparative commercial failure, and abandonment of further dramatic roles.

1961 ₍₂₆₎

Spring: Makes eighth film, *Blue Hawaii*.

12/13 March: Recording sessions, RCA Studios, Nashville. Twelve songs recorded.

21–23 March: Recording sessions, Radio Recorders Studios, Hollywood: songs for *Blue Hawaii* recorded.

March: Dee Presley suffers miscarriage. Has no further children.

15 June: Seventh film, *Wild In The Country*, released.

25/26 June: Recording sessions, RCA Studios, Nashville. Five songs
recorded.

Summer: Makes ninth film, *Follow That Dream*.

5 July: Recording sessions, RCA Studios, Nashville. Records songs for
Follow That Dream.

Summer: Refuses invitation to appear at Royal Command Variety
Performance in London later in year before Queen Elizabeth II.
Makes tenth film, *Kid Galahad*.

**15/16
October:**   Recording sessions, RCA Studios, Nashville.

**October/
November:**   Recording sessions, Radio Recorders Studios, Hollywood: songs
for *Kid Galahad*.

14 November: Eighth film, *Blue Hawaii*, released. Priscilla Beaulieu spends
Christmas at Graceland.

1962 (27)

January: Priscilla Beaulieu (16) moves permanently at Graceland.

March: Makes eleventh film, *Girls! Girls! Girls!* and records songs for
same at Radio Recorders Studios, Hollywood.

9 March: Ninth film, *Follow That Dream*, released.

June/July: Makes twelfth film, *It Happened At The World's Fair*.

25 July: Tenth film, *Kid Galahad,* released.

Autumn: Records songs for *It Happened At The World's Fair*, Hollywood.
Makes thirteenth film, *Fun In Acapulco*.

2 November: Eleventh film, *Girls! Girls! Girls!*, released.

1963 (28)

22/23 January: Recording sessions, Radio Recorders Studios, Hollywood: songs for *Fun In Acapulco*.

26/27 March: Recording sessions, RCA Studios, Nashville.

July: Makes fourteenth film, *Viva Las Vegas* and records songs for same, Hollywood.

October: Makes fifteenth film, *Kissin' Cousins* and records songs for same at RCA Studios, Nashville.

21 November: Thirteenth film, *Fun In Acapulco*, released.

22 November: President John F. Kennedy assassinated in Dallas, Texas.

1964 (29)

12 January: Recording sessions, RCA Studios, Nashville.

Spring: Makes sixteenth film, *Roustabout*.

24, 28 February;
2, 6 March: Records songs for *Roustabout*, Radio Recorders Studios, Hollywood.

6 March: Fourteenth film, *Kissin' Cousins*, released.

20 April: Fifteenth film, *Viva Las Vegas*, released.

Summer: Makes seventeenth film, *Girl Happy* and records songs for same in July at Hollywood.

12 November: Sixteenth film, *Roustabout*, released.

1965 (30)

22 January: Seventeenth film, *Girl Happy*, released.

Winter 1964–
Spring 1965:   Makes eighteenth, nineteenth and twentieth films: *Tickle Me*, *Harum Scarum*, *Frankie And Johnny* respectively.

February: Records songs for *Harum Scarum*, RCA Studios, Nashville.

May: Records songs for *Frankie And Johnny*, Hollywood.

15 June: Eighteenth film, *Tickle Me*, released.

Summer: Makes twenty-first film *Paradise Hawaiian Style*. Records songs for same at Radio Recorders Studios, Hollywood on 14 and 26 July, and 2 and 4 August.

27 August: Hosts party for visiting Beatles at his Hollywood home. All five sing together. Makes twenty-second film, *Spinout* (US title). Film released as *California Holiday* in UK.

15 December: Nineteenth film, *Harum Scarum*, released.

1966 (31)

February: Records songs for *Spinout* (venue unconfirmed).

Spring: Begins twenty-third and twenty-fourth films: *Double Trouble* and (into summer) *Easy Come, Easy Go*.

25, 28 May;
10 June: Recording sessions, RCA Studios, Nashville (twenty songs recorded).

June: Records songs for *Double Trouble* and another song not used in film.

20 July: Twentieth film, *Frankie And Johnny* released.

6 August: Twenty-first film, *Paradise Hawaiian Style*, released.

Autumn: Makes twenty-fifth film, *Clambake*.

**28/29
September:**   Records songs for *Easy Come, Easy Go*, Radio Recorders Studios, Hollywood.

14 December: Twenty-second film *Spinout* released.

1967 (32)

February: Buys 160-acre ranch in DeSoto County, Mississippi, named Circle G. Records songs for *Clambake* (and other titles) RCA Studios, Nashville.

Spring: Makes twenty-sixth film, *Speedway*.

1 May: Marries Priscilla Beaulieu at Las Vegas Aladdin Hotel, at 9.41 am. Very few friends and family attend. Completes *Double Trouble* in Hollywood (remaking two scenes).

24 May: Twenty-third film, *Double Trouble*, released.

June: Records songs for *Speedway* and others in Hollywood.

14 June: Twenty-fourth film, *Easy Come, Easy Go*, released. Buys Hollywood mansion, for residence there while filming/recording. Makes twenty-seventh film, *Stay Away, Joe*.

**10–12
September:**   Recording sessions, RCA Studios, Nashville.

4 December: Twenty-fifth film, *Clambake*, released.

1968 (33)

15, 17 January: Recording sessions, RCA Studios, Nashville.

1 February: Birth of only child, daughter Lisa Marie.

246

Spring: Makes twenty-eighth film, *Live A Little, Love A Little* and records songs for same in Hollywood in March.

14 March: Twenty–sixth film, *Stay Away, Joe*, released.

4 April: Dr Martin Luther King, black civil rights leader, assassinated in Memphis.

June: Robert F. Kennedy, brother of President John F. Kennedy and candidate for that year's presidential election, assassinated in Los Angeles.

13 June: Twenty-seventh film, *Speedway*, released.

27–29 June: Makes KBC TV special (first ever such programme for him), Burbank, Los Angeles.

July: Makes twenty-ninth film, *Charro* and records songs for same, Hollywood.

September/ October: Makes thirtieth film, *The Trouble With Girls* and records songs for same, Hollywood.

9 October: Twenty-eighth film, *Live A Little, Love A Little*, released.

November: Richard M. Nixon elected president of USA.

1969 (34)

13–23 January: Recording sessions, American Studios, Memphis, his first in that city for fifteen years; twenty-one songs recorded, including 'Hey Jude', Presley's first Lennon/McCartney recording.

17–22 February: Recording sessions, American Studios, Memphis; fourteen songs recorded.

March: Makes thirty-first film, *Change Of Habit* (his final feature film) and records songs for same, 5/6 March at Universal Studios, Hollywood.

22/23 July: Neil Armstrong becomes first man to walk on moon. Presley buys refractor telescope but interest in astronomy soon wanes.

22–25 August: Short season at International Hotel, Las Vegas, inaugurates career move: such appearances become main performing outlet, recorded live by RCA to issue in album form in succession to 'sound-track' albums from films (now no longer to be made, although whether this is realised at the time is uncertain). Filming for major feature-length documentary film on Presley commenced.

3 September: Twenty-ninth film, *Charro*, released.

10 December: Thirtieth film, *The Trouble With Girls* released.

1970 (35)

21 January: Thirty-first (and final – although not, of course, so announced) film, *Change Of Habit*, released.

16–19 February: International Hotel, Las Vegas: live recordings.

4–8 June: Recording sessions, RCA Studios, Nashville: thirty-five titles recorded.

13–15 August: International Hotel, Las Vegas: live recordings.

22 September: Recording sessions, RCA Studios, Nashville.

15 December: First documentary film, *Elvis – That's The Way It Is*, released.

1971 (36)

15 March: Recording sessions, RCA Studios, Nashville. Sessions cancelled after only four songs recorded, owing to Elvis contracting an eye infection.

15–21 May: Recording sessions, RCA Studios, Nashville. Thirty songs recorded.

11 December: Audience with President Nixon in the Oval Office of the White House, Washington DC. Nixon makes Elvis a member of the Special Drug Enforcement Bureau of Narcotics and Dangerous Drugs.

1972 (37)

18 January: Ten miles of US Highway 51 (which runs outside Graceland) renamed 'Elvis Presley Boulevard'.

January: Meets Mike Stone, bodyguard at Las Vegas Hilton.

February: Encourages Priscilla to take karate lessons from Stone.

23 February: Priscilla leaves Presley home in Los Angeles, rents two-bedroomed apartment.

27–29 March: Recording sessions, RCA Studios, Nashville.

31 March: Mrs Stone brings divorce petition against her husband.

Late spring: Elvis meets Linda Thompson, 'Miss Tennessee 1972'.

5 June: Stones divorce.

10 June: Elvis appears at Madison Square Garden, NYC; recorded live.

Late summer: Elvis dates other girls.

Autumn: Elvis and Priscilla officially separate.

1973 (38)

4 January: Appears Honolulu International Center Arena, Hawaii; records *Aloha From Hawaii*. Resultant quadraphonic double album becomes first such recording to sell 1,000,000 copies.

19 February: Elvis rushed by four men on stage while appearing live at Las

Vegas Hilton; he fights off one man and his bodyguards deal with the other assailants. Continues with performance in front of 1,700 people.

6 June: Second (and final, but not known at the time) documentary film, *Elvis On Tour* released.

21–25 July: Recording sessions, Stax Studio, Memphis (first studio recording for ten months).

24 September: Recording sessions, Presley home, Palm Springs, Los Angeles.

9 October: Elvis and Priscilla divorced, Santa Monica Courthouse. Subsequent to divorce, Priscilla leaves Mike Stone and takes up with her hairdresser.

10–16 December: Recording session, Stax Studios, Memphis. Eighteen songs are recorded.

1974 (39)

20 March: Appears Midsouth Coliseum, Memphis. Recorded live (unsatisfactory, but released nonetheless).

Spring/ summer: Refuses to appear on televised gospel show.

Summer: Vernon and Dee Presley separate over Vernon's association with a Mrs Sandy Miller.

Late: Elvis collapses. Taken to Baptist Hospital, Memphis.

1975 (40)

8 January: Fortieth birthday celebrations world-wide.

29 January: Enters Baptist Hospital Memphis for two weeks of tests and treatment.

9–12 March: Recording sessions, RCA Studios, Hollywood (first studio recordings for fifteen months).

Summer: Vernon has heart attack.

August: Breaks off two week engagement at Las Vegas Hilton. Readmitted to Baptist Hospital, Memphis.

1976 (41)

1 January: Appears live before 60,000 people at Pontiac, Michigan. Biggest crowd of his career.

2–8 February: Recording sessions, Graceland. First sessions at Presley's home.

Spring: Donates 12,530 square feet of land directly outside Graceland to City of Memphis to create a parking lot for sightseers.

July: Mayor of Memphis presents Vernon with plaque honouring Elvis at Presley Convention.

29–31 October: Recording sessions, Graceland.

Late: Elvis takes up with Ginger Alden (20).

1977 (42)

21 March: Cancels performance at Baton Rouge, Louisiana; returns to Baptist hospital, Memphis. During hospitalisation, ex-President Nixon telephones personally to offer Elvis best wishes. Possible glaucoma diagnosed, along with other ailments.

25 April: Appears at Civic Center, Saignaw. Recorded live.

May: Vernon files for divorce from Dee in Memphis, citing irreconcilable differences.

19–21 June: Appears Rapid City, Omaha. Recorded live, for planned CBS TV spectacular.

26 June: Final appearance, Indianapolis.

16 August: Found by Joe Esposito on floor of combination bathroom-dressing room about 2.30pm. Unsuccessful attempts to revive him at home and in ambulance en route to Baptist Hospital, Memphis. Pronounced 'Dead On Arrival' 3.30pm.